ALL THINGS BEING EQUAL

ALL THINGS BEING EQUAL

INSTIGATING OPPORTUNITY

IN AN INEQUITABLE TIME

Edited by Brian D. Smedley

and Alan Jenkins

THE NEW PRESS

NEW YORK
LONDON

Published in conjunction with
The Opportunity Agenda

Requests for permission to reproduce selections
from this book should be mailed to:
Permissions Department, The New Press, 38 Greene Street,
New York, NY 10013.

Published in the United States by The New Press, New York, 2007
Distributed by W. W. Norton & Company, Inc., New York

LIBRARY OF CONGRESS CATALOGING-IN-PUBLICATION DATA

All things being equal : instigating opportunity in an inequitable time /
edited by Brian D. Smedley and Alan Jenkins.
p.   cm.
Includes bibliographical references.
ISBN: 978-1-59558-210-2 (hc.)
1. United States—Economic conditions—2001–. 2. United States—Social
conditions—1980–. 3. Educational equalization—United States.
4. Minorities—United States—Economic conditions. 5. Immigrants—
United States—Economic conditions. 6. Equality—United States.
I. Smedley, Brian D.   II. Jenkins, Alan.
HC106.83.A44   2007
330.973—dc22   2007027728

The New Press was established in 1990 as a not-for-profit alternative to the large,
commercial publishing houses currently dominating the book publishing industry. The New Press operates in the public interest rather than for private gain, and
is committed to publishing, in innovative ways, works of educational, cultural, and
community value that are often deemed insufficiently profitable.

www.thenewpress.com

Composition by dix!
This book was set in Walbaum MT

Printed in the United States of America

2   4   6   8   10   9   7   5   3   1

CONTENTS

ACKNOWLEDGMENTS

Many individuals and organizations contributed directly and indirectly to this book, and we wish to thank them for their assistance. First, we wish to thank the authors who contributed chapters to this volume. They took a chance to help a new organization gain footing by preparing papers that challenged them and us to think about the implications of their work for opportunity in America. Their contributions shaped our thinking and, we hope, will shape the work of other scholars and activists. These authors—Jared Bernstein, Linda Darling-Hammond, Carla Herbig, Marc Mauer, Vilma Ortiz, Philip Tegeler, Edward Telles, and Margery Austin Turner—also worked hard to meet our production deadlines and accommodate our frequent requests for information. We owe a great debt to them for their tireless work.

We also wish to thank the staff of the Opportunity Agenda. They, too, took a chance to join a nascent organization with a purposefully ambitious mission—to build the national will to expand opportunity—and have helped the organization grow in fruitful and sometimes unexpected ways. They include Beatrice Alvarez, Sabrineh Ardalan, Michael Connery, Lauren Cotton, Jason Drucker, Nicole Goldkranz, Kisha Parks, Deborah Rodriquez Samuelson, and

Julie Rowe. We are especially grateful for the support and encouragement of our founding partners, Phoebe Eng and Bill Lann Lee, who shared our vision of a just, equitable America that extends full opportunity to all, and who decided to act upon this vision by creating the Opportunity Agenda. In addition, numerous interns, consultants, and advisers also supported our work and helped to develop the organization's programs and ideas, some of which are reflected in this book.

The Opportunity Agenda's founding advisory board was also a tremendous source of inspiration, ideas, and encouragement for the organization and for this book. They include Bill Lann Lee, the board's chair; Jared Bernstein; Tessie Guillermo; Monique Harden; Margaret Hempel; Olati Johnson; Ichiro Kawachi; Amber Khan; Kit Laybourne; Gay McDougall; Marc Mauer; Steve Montiel; Michael Omi; Tom Perez; Steve Phillips; john powell; Susan Sandler; Edward Telles; Emily Tynes; and Robert West. Not surprisingly, some of the chapter contributions in this book are from members of this distinguished group, who shaped the organization in innumerable ways.

We extend special thanks to Diane Wachtell, Melissa Leviste, and Sarah Fan of The New Press, who saw the potential of this book to move scholarship from a recitation of problems to a more hopeful, forward-thinking, solution-oriented agenda. We deeply appreciate their support and encouragement.

The work of the Opportunity Agenda, including this book, would not be possible without the generous support of (in alphabetical order) the Aetna Foundation; the Carnegie Corporation of New York; the Marguerite Casey Foundation; Equal Justice America; the Ford Foundation; the William and Flora Hewlett Foundation; the Libra Foundation; the Josiah Macy, Jr. Foundation; the Mertz Gilmore Foundation; the Ms. Foundation for Women; the Open Society Institute; the Overbrook

Foundation; the Reed Foundation; the Starry Night Fund of the Tides Foundation; the Tides Foundation; the Twenty-first Century Foundation; and the U.S. Human Rights Fund.

Finally, and most importantly, we would like to thank our families—particularly our spouses, Evita and Kirsten, and our children—for their love and support throughout our work. Building the national will to expand opportunity can be exhausting and consuming work, but they have cheered us on every step of the way.

B.D.S.
Washington, D.C.

A.J.
New York, NY

Introduction

Instigating Opportunity
in an Inequitable Time

Alan Jenkins, Brian D. Smedley, and Bill Lann Lee

Opportunity is one of our country's most deeply held ideals
and one of our most valuable national assets. Bridging lines of
race, class, gender, nationality, and politics, the promise of opportunity inspires each generation of Americans to improve
their lot while moving our country forward.

While the pursuit of opportunity is not uniquely American, it is profoundly American. From the challenge of the
frontier to the Civil War and Reconstruction, from the Statue
of Liberty's call to the New Deal's promise, from the Universal Declaration of Human Rights to the dynamic equality
movements of the twentieth century and beyond, opportunity has been a focal point for the hopes and dreams of our
country and its people.

And when our country has invested in keeping the ladder
of opportunity sturdy and accessible to all, our entire country
has benefited—in economic prosperity and productivity, in
democratic participation and accountability, in innovation
and creativity, and in the strength that flows from a diverse
but united people. National investments like universal public
education, fair labor standards, and antidiscrimination laws
have unleashed the potential of millions of Americans and
moved our country closer to the ideal of opportunity for all.

But despite that progress, most Americans believe that we still have a long way to go in realizing full opportunity. And those concerns are echoed in emerging national trends. Wage and wealth gaps are increasing, making it harder for low-income people to escape difficult economic conditions. Our educational system is failing to keep up with other developed nations and is particularly inadequate for low-income and minority children. Record numbers of Americans lack health insurance, placing them at risk for poor health and significant debt. Enduring racial and gender inequity pose steep challenges to the opportunity ideal. And despite historically low levels of crime and violence, record levels of incarceration are decimating families and communities, draining resources, and failing to rehabilitate people who will one day be released. Opportunity now appears at a crossroads.

Observing these trends, we set out to analyze more thoroughly and empirically the status of opportunity in our country. Just as we regularly measure the strength of our economy, our military preparedness, and other bellwethers of our nation's health, we saw it as crucial to measure how opportunity is faring.

What Is Opportunity?

We began our inquiry with this simple question, posed to scholars, community leaders, advocates, service providers, and thousands of everyday Americans from different walks of life. Those conversations complemented our review of public-opinion research, cultural and religious narratives, and our society's seminal texts, including the Declaration of Independence, the Constitution and the Bill of Rights, and the Universal Declaration of Human Rights.

What we learned profoundly shaped our research. Opportunity, our inquiry showed, is the idea that everyone deserves a fair chance to achieve his or her full potential. Realizing opportunity, moreover, is not merely a matter of national conditions but also of national commitment to a core set of values: equality, mobility, voice, redemption, community, and security. These values, described in greater detail below, play an important role in the American consciousness.

Equality.   True opportunity requires that we all have equal access to the benefits, burdens, and responsibilities of our society regardless of race, gender, class, religion, sexual orientation, or other aspects of our appearance or our origin. Ensuring equal opportunity does not mean treating people identically but, rather, treating everyone as an equal. When Americans who have different needs and circumstances have access only to systems and services that ignore those differences, equality is not served. Equality, therefore, requires proactive efforts to remake our institutions in ways that ensure fairness and inclusion.

Mobility.   Where we start out in life should not preordain where we end up. Everyone should have a fair chance to advance and participate fully in the economic, political, and cultural life of the nation; any child in the United States should be able to fulfill his or her full potential through effort and perseverance, and status at birth should not determine ultimate achievements.

Voice.   Americans embrace democracy as a system that depends on the ability of all of us to participate in the public dialogue. This democratic value demands the right to vote and freedom from censorship, as well as affirmative opportunities to participate in the decisions that affect us and to be part of the nation's social and cultural fabric. The importance of voice spans the town hall, newspaper, and the voting booth, as well as electronic and interactive media, arts, and culture. It is the fundamental right to seek, receive, and share information and ideas.

Redemption.   Americans believe strongly in the value of a chance to start over after misfortune or missteps. Redemption as an element of opportunity relates not only to personal forgiveness and contrition, but also to societal conditions and systems that allow people to develop, rebuild, and reclaim full responsibility for their lives.

Community.   As Americans, we are all in it together and see a shared sense of responsibility for each other as crucial to opportunity. While Americans have long adhered to a strong belief in individualism and self-reliance, this ethic is accompanied by a conviction that we are part of a common national enterprise, linked in our successes and challenges, and responsible to each other as well as to ourselves. We recognize that the strength of our people and our nation depends on the vibrancy and cohesiveness of our diverse communities, as we strive to evolve with our changing population.

Security.   Americans believe that we are all entitled to a basic level of education, economic well-being, health care, and other protections necessary to human dignity. Without this security, it is impossible to access society's other rights and responsibilities or to enjoy full opportunity. In the context of opportunity, security relates to basic protection from physical and economic harm, as well as access to the tools to meet our basic needs and those of our families.

For opportunity to flourish, these values must coexist. An economically mobile society that lacks equal treatment or access fails to embody the American ideal of opportunity, as does a society in which people enjoy equal opportunity but lack basic security or a chance to start over after misfortune.

Measuring Opportunity

In 2006, we worked with an esteemed group of scholars and national experts in economics, education, housing, health care, criminal justice, immigration, and other fields to produce *The State of Opportunity in America* (available online at www.opportunityagenda.org/report), the first major national assessment of opportunity in our country. In 2007, we updated that assessment based on newly available government data (www.opportunityagenda.org/update).

Primarily using census data and other government sources, our analysis used the definition and values of opportunity to develop measures and indicators of how opportunity is faring in the United States. The research, which in some cases reviewed trends over a thirty-year period, showed some areas of great progress, such as increases in college attendance—especially for women of color—and historically low rates of violent crime in most communities.

But the broader and more recent trends were troubling. They showed that, at the start of our new century, many of the stepping-stones to opportunity—a decent job at a living wage, affordable housing and health care, quality schools and a college education—were moving farther and farther out of reach for everyday Americans. They also showed that unequal opportunity based on race, gender, socioeconomic status, and immigration status remain major obstacles, despite significant progress in decades past.

In this book, we asked prominent thinkers and researchers, some of whom contributed to *The State of Opportunity in America*, to deepen this analysis, discussing in greater depth our progress toward full opportunity, the challenges that remain, and the most promising strategies for reigniting the ideal and reality of opportunity for all. It is our hope that this work will not only spur a new conversation about opportunity but also lead to a new set of pragmatic and effective policy solutions that meet the challenges of the new century.

The Essays in This Volume

The scholars and thinkers invited to contribute to this volume were asked to explore how the issues that they study relate to American opportunity, and to provide a guiding framework that places opportunity at the forefront of the nation's social and economic policies. Collectively, these essays connect the concerns and experiences of different segments of the United States and link a range of social justice issues under the broad frame of opportunity. They provide an affirmative vision for societal progress, one that draws upon the core values of an opportunity society, while at the same time emphasizing the role of rigorous social science research to provide an empirical foundation for policy recommendations.

American folklore often suggests that everyone in our country has a fair chance to overcome difficult economic circumstances at birth solely through hard work and determination. But many Americans believe that the rags-to-riches narrative is less and less reflective of reality in our country. In an innovative set of analyses, economist Jared Bernstein of the Economic Policy Institute explores actual intergenerational economic mobility by tracking the income progress of the same persons and families over time. This analysis differs from prior research that tracks the income of family cohorts over time—essentially, a snapshot of the economy at different points in time. Bernstein finds income mobility is restricted, as a generation's position in the income scale is partially dependent on its parents' position. One way to view the significance of this finding is to note that it would take a poor family of four with two children approximately nine to ten generations—over two hundred years—to achieve the income of the middle-income four-person family. In other words, the extent of income mobility across generations plays a determinant role in the living standards of American families. It is a key determinant of how many generations a family is likely to be stuck at the low end of the income scale, or snuggly ensconced at the high end.

Access to high-quality education is clearly important as one measure of opportunity. One of the nation's foremost educational equity scholars, Linda Darling-Hammond of Stanford University, reviews national trends in educational equity and identifies policies and practices that may reduce educational inequality. In particular, she reviews trends in segregation (and resegregation) of K–12 schools along racial and ethnic, socioeconomic, and immigration status dimensions, and shows how segregation is correlated with disparities in educational resources (for example, teacher training, instructional quality, per-pupil expenditures) across school districts. Drawing on her own scholarship and promising practices across the country, she identifies policies that promote educational equity for students from a range of marginalized groups.

In recent years, the criminal justice system has emerged as one of the most significant barriers to opportunity for millions of people who live in the United States. Marc Mauer of the Sentencing Project explores how a century-long national emphasis on rehabilitation as a guiding philosophy in corrections has been replaced by a crime policy that places a priority on retribution as a means of social control. Rather than investing in programs and policies designed to strengthen families and communities, Mauer argues, the guiding framework has relied upon an expanded criminal justice system, and particularly an unprecedented use of incarceration, as a primary means of addressing social problems. This trend, combined with the rise of policies that attach lasting disabilities to past criminal convictions, has had profound consequences for opportunity prospects for the millions of Americans with a felony conviction or a history of incarceration. In addition to the harmful experiences that are commonplace in prison, individuals released from prison continue to suffer from the stigma of incarceration in access to employment, social services, and electoral participation. Growing numbers of children are now living with the experience of having a parent behind bars, and the ripple effects of high rates of incarceration on low-income communities can be seen in measures of family stability, health indicators, and informal social control. Mauer also explores how the nation can achieve a better balance between rehabilitation and social control in its criminal justice policies.

The ideal of opportunity in the United States is undermined when people experience discrimination based on their race, ethnicity, disability, or other fundamental attributes. By limiting access to housing, neighborhoods, jobs, and capital, discrimination can help sustain—or even exacerbate—inequality of income, wealth, and educational achievement. Some have argued that little discrimination exists in the United States today—that unequal outcomes are attributable instead to differences in people's qualifications or their behavior and effort. But a large body of rigorous empirical research demonstrates that discrimination persists, often in ways that have profound implications for opportunity. Margery Austin Turner and Carla Herbig of the Urban Institute—two of the nation's leading social scientists exploring discrimination—summarize compelling evidence from paired-testing research that discrimination remains a serious problem in housing, employment, lending, and other critical economic sectors. Drawing upon their own research and that of others, they also suggest a number of strategies for combating discrimination and enforcing the nation's civil rights laws.

Policymakers are increasingly aware of inequality among different segments of the American population in health status and in access to, and quality of, health care. A large body of research demonstrates that many communities of color experience shorter life spans and a higher incidence of health problems than white Americans. To compound this disparity in health status, these populations often have less access to health care and experience a poorer quality of care than white Americans, even when their economic backgrounds are equal. The Opportunity Agenda's research director, Brian Smedley, draws upon a large body of research to show how inequality in health status and health care present significant barriers to opportunity in our country. He also discusses how a human rights–based approach can create an equitable and effective national health-care system, one that expands access to comprehensive health care and addresses the needs of an increasingly diverse nation, thereby addressing a cornerstone of an opportunity society.

Opportunity is often inequitably distributed on the basis of geography and place: *where one lives* is a powerful predictor of opportunity. Philip Tegeler of the Poverty and Race Research Action Council reviews national trends in patterns of residential housing segregation and discrimination faced by communities of color, women, immigrants, and low-income Americans, with a particular focus on effective practices at the state and federal level to promote residential desegregation. In particular, Tegeler discusses implications of housing segregation for broader opportunity (including mobility, equality, health and income security, community, redemption, and voice), reviews the effectiveness of federal housing programs such as the Section 8 and low-income housing tax-credit programs, and points to effective policy solutions.

Immigration has emerged as one of the most contentious

domestic policy issues in the United States. The issue has also helped to spark a major social movement that is redefining what opportunity means. UCLA sociologists Edward Telles and Vilma Ortiz, two of the nation's leading authorities on Latino immigration, review opportunity trends among Mexican Americans, with a focus on some of the pathways and challenges for successfully incorporating the descendants of Mexican immigrants into American society. In particular, the authors address two questions: What has opportunity meant to Mexican Americans of different generations? And how have perceptions of opportunity changed over time? This paper will help to fill an important data void, in that most federal data on health, housing, employment and wages, and education lack important information regarding the nation's largest immigrant population.

Collectively, these rigorous, thought-provoking essays provide a framework for understanding our national progress, the challenges that remain, and an affirmative vision for the United States as a true land of opportunity. They point to a broad framework of policies to instigate opportunity in America.

Instigating Opportunity in America

Fulfilling the promise of opportunity for all will be one of the great challenges of the twenty-first century. It will require bold leadership from our government, civic, and business leaders; creative and effective solutions; and the sustained political will of the American people. Fortunately, however, a significant body of pragmatic policies has proven effective in expanding opportunity in concrete and measurable ways.

This book, accordingly, moves beyond announcing problems and sets out new solutions. Our guiding framework is a positive vision: What would it take to create an equal opportunity society? How can America do better in its approach to housing, education, employment, criminal justice, and health care? And how can we ensure that opportunity values guide future policies? Our discussions, and the chapters in this volume, make clear that expanding opportunity for everyone in our country is within our grasp. Based on the research and analysis set out in this book, we recommend six types of policy approaches.

Planning for Opportunity

Experience shows that it is important to consider all aspects of opportunity when fashioning new policies and programs that will affect Americans' life chances. With these principles in mind, we recommend that:

- Governments use a new policy tool—an opportunity impact statement—as a requirement for publicly funded or authorized projects like school, hospital, or highway construction, or the expansion of the telecommunications infrastructure. The statements would explain, based on available data, how a given effort would expand or contract opportunity in terms of equitable treatment, economic security and mobility, and shared responsibility. The statements would also require public input and participation.
- Government leaders take up the challenge of measuring our progress in providing opportunity to all Americans. This includes gathering the demographic data and other information necessary to determine how different groups of Americans are faring.
- Land use, zoning, and transportation policies actively promote opportunity by encouraging the development

of mixed-income communities; reversing the isolation of highly segregated racial, ethnic, and high-poverty communities; supporting public transportation that helps people commute from areas of high unemployment to areas of high job growth; and planning regionally to address inequality among urban, suburban, and rural communities.

- Government make expanding opportunity a condition of its partnerships with private industry by requiring, for example, public contractors to pay a living wage tied to families' actual cost of living, insisting on employment practices that promote diversity and inclusion, and ensuring that new technologies using the public electromagnetic spectrum include public interest obligations and extend service to all communities.

Mending the Safety Net

Well-crafted programs that enable people to meet the basic needs of their families have lifted millions of Americans out of poverty and sustained millions more in times of crisis or transition. Despite the popularity and proven success of Social Security, the federal and state Child Health Insurance Program, and food assistance for low-income families, these programs are increasingly underfunded and reach fewer and fewer Americans in need. We recommend modernizing the traditional safety net by focusing on moving Americans from poverty and crisis to economic security and mobility. These recommendations include:

- Rapidly moving toward a system of high-quality, equitable, and comprehensive health care that covers all Americans' basic health needs.

- Expanding state and federal food assistance programs such as food stamps and school lunches to serve all children and adults in need, and providing incentives for grocery stores to stock affordable, nutritious foods in low-income urban and rural communities.
- Scaling up successful pilot programs that help lower-income families to save, build assets, and acquire financial skills.

Updating Skills in a Changing America

Americans are in the midst of monumental changes fueled by a global economy, rapidly evolving technology, and an increasingly diverse population. The new American reality demands new skills and knowledge. We must ensure that all Americans have access to the education, training, and information needed to embrace the opportunities of the new century. Our recommendations include:

- Expanding job-training programs focused on quality jobs in the new economy and tailored to the differing skills and needs of different workers.
- Reducing financial barriers to college by increasing the share of need-based grants over student loans and improving private-sector participation through scholarship aid. For example, funding for federal Pell grants should be doubled and state, federal, and private financial aid should be better integrated, in order to create a complementary system that allocates resources more efficiently.
- Creating effective and inclusive immigrant integration policies that educate new Americans about their rights and responsibilities in the workplace, political participation, and the naturalization process, while better equip-

ping our institutions and communities to incorporate diverse new members. An important element of these policies is helping new Americans to learn English and providing multilingual access to necessities like health care and basic rights like voting.

Renewing America's Commitment to Human Rights

Some of the greatest strides in advancing American opportunity emerged from the twentieth-century movements for racial equality, women's rights, and workers' rights. The essays in this volume show that this work is not yet complete and that what is needed is both vigorous enforcement of existing antidiscrimination protections and a new generation of human rights laws that address evolving forms of bias and exclusion. Our recommendations include:

- Increasing the staffing and resources that federal, state, and local agencies devote to enforcing antidiscrimination laws in voting, employment, housing, education, lending, criminal justice, and other spheres. This includes using data more effectively to better detect potential bias, for instance, by comparing workplace diversity with the composition of an area's qualified workforce.
- Assisting employers and other institutions committed to providing a fair and diverse environment, for example, by promoting model performance evaluation practices, greater cultural fluency, and other tools to counter bias and exclusion.
- Crafting new human rights laws that complement existing civil rights protections by addressing subconscious and institutional biases more effectively, protecting economic and social rights like the right to education,

and correcting exclusion based on socioeconomic status and other characteristics not fully covered by current laws.

Prioritizing Prevention, Rehabilitation, and Reentry

The last two decades have seen significant progress in reducing violent crime but also a leap in the number of nonviolent and drug-addicted women and men in jails and prisons, major racial disparities among the incarcerated, and new barriers to the reentry of people with criminal records into productive society. We recommend a set of policies that build on successful crime prevention strategies while fostering rehabilitation and productive reentry, including:

- Expanding community policing—a crime prevention strategy that emphasizes community input, collaboration, and tailored responses to crime and disorder. These approaches have a demonstrated track record of improving police-community relations and community satisfaction.
- Increasing the availability of substance abuse treatment, including using it as an alternative to incarceration. Emerging research suggests that drug courts—specialized judicial proceedings that provide substance abuse treatment, testing, supervision, and a range of other coordinated services for people addicted to drugs who might otherwise face incarceration—are effective in reducing recidivism, increasing retention of addicted people in treatment, and saving taxpayer money. Where possible, these programs should allow successful participants to avoid a criminal record that will hamper their future progress.

- Basing criminal sentencing on individualized culpability, control, and circumstances. Mandatory minimum-sentencing policies have exacerbated racial and ethnic inequality in incarceration rates, significantly increased the number of women behind bars, and led to many unjust sentences, while doing little to deter crime. Replacing these policies with sentencing based on the circumstances of each case will reduce racial inequality and adverse impacts on women while better promoting the interests of justice.
- Reviewing criminal justice practices to identify and address the junctures at which stereotypes and discrimination currently influence the outcome.
- Restoring voting rights and removing other barriers to the reentry into society of people who have been incarcerated.

Strengthening Our Democracy
Through Stepped-Up Leadership

National leadership is necessary to protect democratic participation and promote diverse involvement in the American political process. Voting and political participation are among our most cherished federal rights; the federal government has the greatest authority and responsibility to protect them. Our recommendations include:

- Establishing minimum federal standards for voting equipment and procedures, including straightforward voter registration requirements, nationwide voting hours, and federal guidelines to verify voter identity. Meeting those standards will require federal support to help local authorities improve training, machinery, and polling stations.

- Vigorously enforcing the Voting Rights Act and fully implementing the Help America Vote Act, while providing greater assistance to new Americans and others in obtaining and exercising the right to vote.

Going Forward from Here

The American ideal of opportunity is deeply embedded in our national consciousness. It embodies our highest aspirations as a people and, though we've never fully achieved it, opportunity represents much of what we seek to accomplish in our personal, professional, and civic lives.

At their best, our nation's public policies have sought to protect and expand opportunity by opening avenues for education, home ownership, entrepreneurship, wealth creation, and health, while ensuring that access to those opportunities was widely and equally shared. When our national policies have focused on strengthening opportunity through measures like Social Security, Pell grants, fair labor standards, and federally guaranteed home loans, we have made great strides in improving our nation's strength and prosperity. And when the human rights movements and policies of the late twentieth century extended those opportunities to large numbers of people of color, women, people with disabilities, and other historically excluded Americans, we moved closer still to fully realizing our national values and potential. Conversely, when we have neglected our shared responsibility to uphold opportunity—due to discrimination and bias, corporate greed, or a failure to invest in effective government systems—we have compromised our national values, as well as our national promise.

Mounting evidence and the experience of millions of Americans show that we are again at a crossroads when it comes to opportunity. This book is an effort to understand where our country is headed, to offer an affirmative vision of the land of opportunity that we can and should be, and to provide concrete guidance on the steps that are needed to get us there. We hope that it will prove useful to policymakers, advocates, scholars, and others who seek to expand opportunity for everyone in our country.

1

You *Can* Take It with You
Income and Wealth Across Generations

Jared Bernstein

Any serious examination of opportunity in the United States needs to consider economic mobility. In fact, mobility across the life cycle—the question of how a family progresses through the income scale over time or how one generation does relative to prior cohorts—is arguably a telling indicator of how opportunity is distributed.

Surprisingly, many of our measures of economic progress fail to capture such dynamics. Most often, our comparisons essentially take a snapshot of the economy at one point in time and compare it to the same snapshot at a later date. By examining, for example, the inflation-adjusted level of the median income at two points in time, we can learn about changes in the living standards of families in and around the median. These are clearly not, however, the same families. That is, the family in the middle of the income scale in 1997 may be at the 70th percentile ten years later.

In this chapter we track the economic progress of the same persons and families over time, examining income, wealth, and other aspects of living standards through a lens of mobility. A closely related part of the analysis examines the extent to which children's fortunes differ from that of their parents. A central dimension of this analysis is the role of *intergenera-*

tional mobility: the degree to which a child's position in the economy is determined by that of his or her parents. Surely, if class barriers are such that children's economic fate is largely determined by their family's position in the income scale, then the likelihood that, for example, a middle-class child will be a rich adult is diminished.

In fact, we report significant correlations between parents and their children, implying that income mobility is at least somewhat restricted as one generation's position in the income scale is partially dependent on its parents' position. For example, one recent study finds the correlation between parents and children to be 0.6.[1] We provide a detailed analysis of the implications of this correlation below, but one way to view the significance of this finding is to note that it implies that it would take a poor family of four with two children approximately nine to ten generations—over two hundred years—to achieve the income of the middle-income four-person family. Were the correlation only half that size, meaning income differences were half as persistent across generations, it would take four to five generations for the poor family to catch up.

In other words, the extent of income mobility across generations plays a determinant role in the living standards of American families. It is, for example, a key determinant of how many generations a family will be stuck at the low end of the income scale, or snuggly ensconced at the high end. Our folklore often emphasizes the rags-to-riches, Horatio Alger stories which suggest that anyone with the gumption and smarts to prevail can lift themselves up by their bootstraps and transverse the income scale in a generation. Our reality, however, shows much less mobility. Surprisingly, international comparisons reveal less mobility in the United States than other countries with comparably advanced economies, such as Germany, Canada, and the Scandinavian countries.

Note that these are countries that U.S. economists often criticize for their extensive social protections—each one has universal health coverage, for example. Yet their citizens experience greater mobility than do our own.

What explains the lack of mobility here? Certainly unequal education opportunities and historical discrimination play a role. In fact, the transmission of these variables appears to be correlated as well, such that opportunities for advancement are limited for those with fewer economic resources. For example, we show that children from wealthy families have much greater access to top-tier universities than kids from low-income families, even once we control for innate skills. Though the data on the persistence of wealth across generations are less rich, such data also suggest that this is an important channel through which mobility of the have-nots is dampened.

Policy solutions need to be crafted with that reality in mind, designed to clear the historical brush that blocks those with a disadvantaged start from the pathways of opportunity. The conclusion to the chapter offers some ideas in this spirit.

Intergenerational Mobility

The extent of intergenerational mobility is one measure of the prevalence of economic opportunity in a society. If one's position in the earnings, income, or wealth distribution is largely a function of birth, we are left with a more rigid society where even those with prodigious talents will be held back by entrenched class barriers. Conversely, a society with a high level of intergenerational mobility, implying little correlation between parents' position and that of their children, is one with more fluidity between classes.

Economists measure the extent of intergenerational mobility by measuring the correlation in income or earnings be-

tween parents and children. These analyses reveal that about
half of the variation in the incomes of children is explained
by their parents' position in the income scale.[2]

Is this a high, medium, or low level of income persistence?
Certainly, a correlation of about half belies any notion of a to-
tally fluid society with no class barriers. Yet without various
benchmarks against which to judge these correlations, it is
difficult to know what to make of their magnitude. In what
follows, we try to present such benchmarks.

Figure 1-1, based on earnings correlations from mobility
expert Gary Solon, shows where sons of low-income fathers
(10th percentile) would be expected to end up in the earnings
scale, based on their fathers' position.[3]

The figure shows that while income mobility certainly exists, the apple does not end up too far from the tree. Sons of
low-earning fathers have slightly less than a 60 percent
chance of reaching above the 20th percentile by adulthood,
about a 20 percent chance of surpassing the median, and a
very slight chance—4.5 percent—of ending up above the
80th percentile. Using earnings levels from today's families, a

FIG. 1-1
Likelihood that low-income son ends up above various percentiles

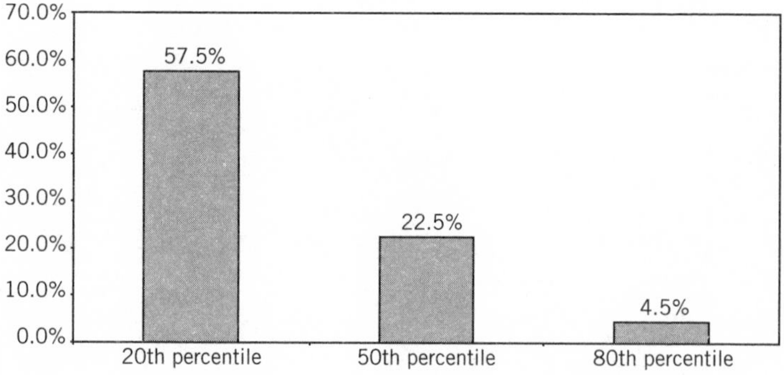

Source: Gary Solon, undated.

son whose father earns about $16,000 a year has a 5 percent chance of earning over $55,000 per year.

While the discussion so far has focused on the degree of mobility between generations, another question is, how stable are these values over time? That is, has the degree of mobility between generations increased or fallen in recent years?

Given the rise in point-in-time inequality over the past few decades,[4] this is a particularly important question. Some analysts have argued that because our economy is so dynamic and mobile, we needn't worry about bigger gaps between income classes at any given point in time. That is, they claim that mobility over time offsets the rise in cross-sectional inequality.

Sure, these critics concede, the distance from the basement to the penthouse has grown over time as inequality has increased. But if a family that starts out in the basement has a better chance these days of making it to the top floor than it used to, then we needn't be so concerned about cross-sectional inequality.

In fact, those who make this mobility argument fail to either articulate or substantiate this claim. Instead, they simply show evidence of economic mobility and leave it at that, as if mobility in and of itself should lessen the concern about increased inequality. But unless the rate of mobility is increasing relative to that of earlier decades, families are no more likely today to span the now-wider income gap. As shown below, there has been no such increase, implying that cross-sectional inequality corresponds to widening income inequality over a lifetime.

Aaronson and Mazumder have tracked the extent of intergenerational mobility since 1940, finding that, in fact, the rate of mobility has declined significantly in recent decades.[5] As shown in Figure 1-2, the correlation between the earnings of sons and the income of their families was flat or falling

FIG. 1-2
Intergenerational mobility, 1950–2000

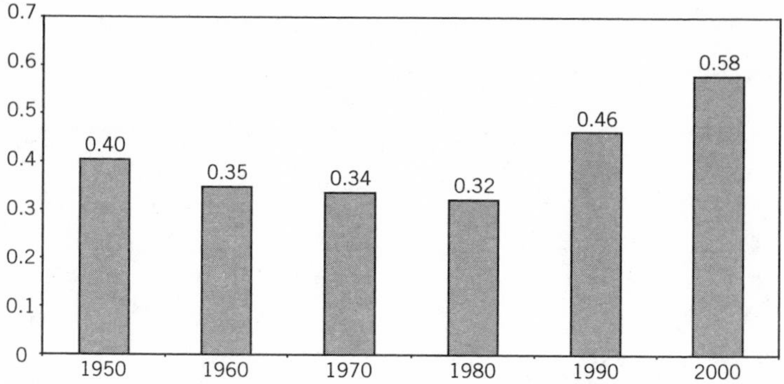

Source: D. Aaronson and B. Mazumder, "International Economic Mobility in the U.S., 1940 to 2000," Federal Reserve Bank of Chicago WP 2005-12, Chicago, 2005.

from 1950 to 1980; it then climbed through 2000, implying a trend toward diminished mobility. (The relationship between mobility and the intergenerational correlation is inverse: higher correlations mean greater income persistence across generations and thus less mobility.) Note that this trend occurred over the very post-1970s period when cross-sectional inequality was increasing. Thus, instead of faster mobility, which might have offset the rise in inequality, the opposite trend occurred.

How do these correlations translate into actual income trends? In 2000, according to income data from the Congressional Budget Office, the average income of the top fifth was 3.9 times that of the bottom fifth (twenty years earlier, that ratio was 2.6). Applying the lower correlation from 1980 (0.32), it would have taken about six generations to close an income gap of that magnitude. But with the diminished mobility implied by the higher correlation—0.58—it would take almost twice as many years, eleven generations, to close that income gap.

There is disagreement, however, among mobility experts regarding Aaronson and Mazumder's conclusion. Gary Solon, a premier expert in this field, has not found evidence of any trend in intergenerational mobility in his work.[6] Even so, this finding simply confirms that there has been no increase in mobility that might have offset the clear increases in inequality.

The Roles of Wealth and Education

Mobility experts have investigated the mechanisms that influence the degree of mobility across generations. Two such mechanisms are education and wealth. Since education is correlated with income, if children of highly educated parents have a better chance of achieving high levels of education themselves, this will lead to greater persistence of income positions across generations. Similarly, we might expect wealth to be a particularly correlated variable across generations, as wealthy parents make bequests to their children. Both factors arguably play a role in the income persistence discussed thus far.

An obvious way to track wealth persistence is to track where children of parents of different wealth levels ended up when they themselves grew up. Charles and Hurst provide such analysis.[7] Table 1-1 shows the extent of wealth mobility between children and their parents over the past few decades. The analysis shows the percent of children who had reached a particular wealth level by their midthirties.

For example, 36 percent of those with parents in the bottom wealth quintile ended up there as adults; only 7 percent ended up in the top quintile. Two-thirds of children with parents in the bottom quintile ended in the bottom 40 percent. Moving to the middle, 25 percent of the children of quintile 3 parents stayed in the middle; 24 percent moved up one-fifth

TABLE 1-1
Shifts in intergenerational wealth

Wealth Level of Child by Age Midthirties*

Parent Level	Quintile 1	Quintile 2	Quintile 3	Quintile 4	Quintile 5
Quintile 1	36	29	16	12	7
Quintile 2	26	24	24	15	12
Quintile 3	16	21	25	24	15
Quintile 4	15	13	20	26	26
Quintile 5	11	16	14	24	36

* Quintile 1 = lowest wealth level.
Source: Based on K.K. Charles and E. Hurst, "The Correlation of Wealth Across Generations," Journal of Political Economy 111, no. 6 (December 2003).

and 21 percent moved down one-fifth. At the top of the wealth scale, 36 percent of the children of the wealthiest parents were themselves in the top fifth, and 60 percent stayed in the top two-fifths.

Turning to education, researchers have found that about 40 percent of the extent of a person's educational attainment is determined by that of their parents. An interesting corollary to the role of education is the increase in education returns (the wage advantage of more highly educated workers over those with less education) over the last few decades. That is, a child of a parent who went to college has a greater chance of also attending college. Therefore, that child also has a greater chance of benefiting from the higher relative wages earned by college-educated workers today relative to decades earlier.

Blandon shows the significant role played by the large wage advantage of more highly educated workers in the United States relative to other countries (her work again focuses on the correlation between fathers' income and sons' earnings).[8] Compared to other countries, U.S. college graduates earn a lot more than our high school graduates. The higher returns to education in the United States lead to significantly higher levels of earnings immobility here relative to the United Kingdom and West Germany. In fact, if the U.S. educational returns were more like those in Germany and the UK, our mobility correlation would be 24 percent lower. (Remember, lower correlations imply more mobility.)

Another relevant issue regarding mobility and education is in regard to the quality of education accessible to children from families in different positions in the income scale. If we compare the family income of children in the entering classes at top-tier universities and at community colleges, we find a strong positive correlation between family income and attendance at top-tier schools.* Over 70 percent of those in the top tier come from families with the highest incomes, while 3 percent and 6 percent of the entering class come from the lowest and second-lowest income groups, respectively—that is, the bottom half of families.

Still, one might argue that these findings simply represent a meritocracy at work, as those from high-income families have, perhaps through their privileged positions, acquired the intellectual tools to succeed at the top schools. Figure 1-3 belies this argument: even when we control for academic ability, higher-income children are still more likely to complete college.[9] Each set of bars shows the probability of completing college for children based on income and math test scores in grade 8. For example, the first set of bars, for the students with the lowest test scores, shows that 3 percent of students with both low scores and low incomes completed college, while 30 percent of low-scoring children from high-income families managed to complete college.

---

* "Top tier" is defined by (1) the grades of entering students (grade point average of B or better and at least 1240 on the SAT) and (2) colleges that accept less than half of their applicants. See A.P. Carnevale and S.J. Rose, "Socioeconomic Status, Race/Ethnicity, and Selective College Admissions," 2003. Available at http://www.tcf.org/publications/education/carnevale_rose.pdf.

FIGURE 1-3
College completion by income status and test scores

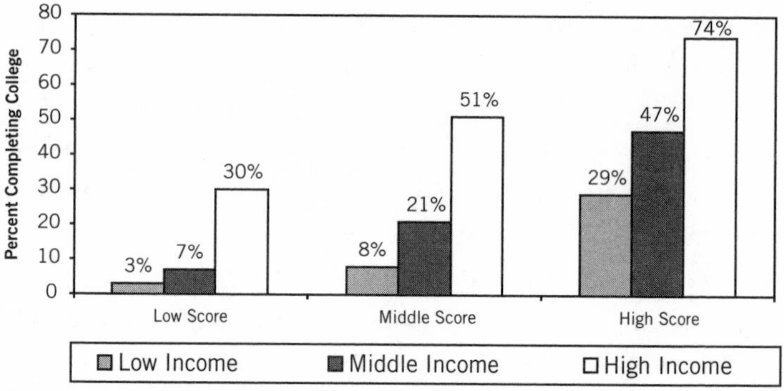

Source: M.A. Fox, B.A. Connolly, and T.D. Snyder, *Youth Indicators 2005: Trends in the Well-Being of American Youth*, U.S. Department of Education, National Center for Education Statistics, 2005.

The fact that each set of bars has an upward gradient is evidence against a completely meritocratic system. The pattern implies that at every level of test scores, higher income led to higher completion rates. The third set of bars, for example, shows that even among the highest-scoring students in grade 8, only 29 percent of those from low-income families finished college, compared with 74 percent of the students from the most wealthy families.

Mobility from an International Perspective

A deeply embedded piece of U.S. social mythology is the Horatio Alger story: the notion that anyone who is willing and able can "pull himself up by his bootstraps" and can achieve significant upward mobility. What's more, conventional wisdom holds that there are many more Horatio Algers in the United States than in Europe. The idea behind such thinking is that there is a trade-off between unregulated markets and mobility. Since our economic model hews much more closely to the fundamentals of market capitalism—

lower tax base, fewer regulations, less union coverage, no universal health care, and a much less comprehensive social contract—there should be greater mobility here.

However, this is not the case. Figure 1-4 shows that the correlation between fathers' and sons' earnings is lower in all the comparison countries except the UK.[10] Finland, Canada, and Sweden have significantly lower correlations (and therefore higher rates of mobility) than the United States.

These differences mean that poor families in the United States, for example, have a lesser chance of exiting their low-income status than similarly placed families in other countries. A study by Jäntti et al. shows that in several Scandinavian countries and in the UK, the chance of sons having the same low earnings as their fathers is at or below 30 percent; in the United States, the sons face a 42 percent chance of remaining low earners. Daughters have greater earnings mobility, though here too the United States is the least mobile country.

Note also that these figures are derived before taxes and transfers and thus reflect greater mobility generated by market outcomes in these other countries. That is, they do not *directly* reflect the more extensive social safety nets in countries other than the United States. However, it may well be the case that these safety nets serve to diminish class barriers that loom large in this country. For example, among the advanced economies, countries with more economic mobility also have universal health care and greater child-care subsidies for working parents. This may free up some of the less advantaged members in these societies to better reach their economic potential.

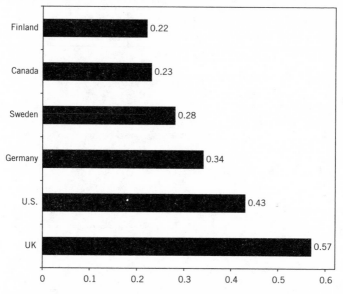

FIGURE 1-4
Correlation between fathers' and sons' earnings in six countries
(lower numbers equal higher mobility)

Source: Gary Solon, "Cross-Country Differences in Intergenerational Earnings Mobility," *Journal of Economic Perspectives* 16, no. 3 (December 2003).

Family Income Mobility

Intergenerational Mobility

Another way of viewing the extent of income mobility is to follow persons or families over time; this is called "cohort analysis." If we control for the expected growth of income as families age, most families end up in or near the income position in which they started out.

Table 1-2 shows the likelihood that low-income teenagers will become low-, middle-, or high-income adults, comparing a 1950s cohort with a 1960s cohort, by race.[11] Two important findings can be seen in these data. First, about half of white

TABLE 1-2

Earnings outcome for low-income teenagers, by cohort and race

Cohort Income Levels at Ages 24–26* (%)

Cohorts, ages 15–17	Quintile 1	Quintile 2	Quintile 3	Quintile 4	Quintile 5
Whites					
Born 1952–1959	22.0	26.1	21.1	17.5	13.2
Born 1962–1969	26.7	27.6	18.4	19.3	8.0
Blacks					
Born 1952–1959	55.4	22.1	8.3	10.0	4.2
Born 1962–1969	61.2	12.2	19.6	4.7	2.3

* Quintile 1 = lowest income level.
Source: Mary Corcoran and Jordan Matsudaira, "Is It Getting Harder to Get Ahead? Economic Attainment in Early Adulthood for Two Cohorts," in Richard A. Settersten Jr., Frank F. Furstenberg, and Rueben G. Rumbaut, eds., *On the Frontier of Adulthood: Theory, Research, and Public Policy*, 2006.

young adults and three-quarters of African American young adults ended up at or near where they started—in the bottom two income tiers (quintiles 1 and 2). Compared to white children, more than twice as many poor black children remained in the bottom fifth (quintile 1). On the other end of the income scale, only a small share of poor teenagers made it to the top fifth (2.3 percent), compared to 8 percent for whites.

Second, the later cohort was less likely to experience upward mobility; this was especially true for African Americans. Whereas 55.4 percent of black teenagers from the first cohort remained in quintile 1, the share was 61.2 percent for the later cohort. For white cohorts, the increase was smaller: from 22 percent to 26.7 percent. In other words, we again see the conspicuous absence of evidence that increased mobility offset growing inequality.

Intragenerational Mobility

The analysis so far has examined mobility between generations and absolute gains for a given cohort over different time
periods. Here we turn to mobility within a particular generation as they age—how families progress through the income
distribution over time. This research seeks to understand
whether families are more or less likely to end up in a higher
or lower quintile as they age.

For this research, each person is assigned to an income fifth
at the beginning and end of the relevant periods of observa-
tion based on his or her family's income. Since most families'
incomes grow as they age, different income cutoffs are used
for each period: quintile 5, the upper limit in 1979, for example, will be different than that of 1989. This approach to income mobility examines whether a family becomes better or
worse off relative to other families, as opposed to better or
worse off in terms of its actual incomes.

In particular, the analysis tracks how families are doing
relative to others they started with at the beginning of the periods in the same age cohort and income class. If each family's
income grew by the same amount (in percentage terms),
there would be no change in mobility: that is, no changes in
the relative positions of families in the income distribution.
If, however, a family that starts out in the bottom fifth experiences faster income growth than other low-income families,
it may move into a higher fifth: that is, this family will experience upward mobility.

Absolute gains—the increase in real incomes as families
move through the life cycle—are of course important, since
higher real incomes enable families to raise their living standards. But inequality researchers have also found that relative
positions mean a lot to people. Our well-being, along with our

sense of accomplishment, is apparently not simply a matter of what we can afford to buy given our income levels. It is also a matter of how we are faring relative to others from our own generation. Research shows that if they pass us by—if we are downwardly mobile relative to others in our cohort—we experience economic stress, even if our buying power is up.

Table 1-3 presents three transition matrixes for three time periods, the 1970s, the 1980s, and the 1990s.[12] Going across each row in the table, the numbers reveal the percent of persons who either stayed in the same quintile or moved to a higher or lower one. For example, the first entry in the top panel shows that just under half (49.4 percent) of families in the bottom fifth in 1969 were also in the bottom fifth in 1979 (the family income data are adjusted for family size). About the same share (49.4 percent) started and ended the 1970s in the richest fifth. The percent of "stayers" (those who did not move out of the fifth they started out in) is shown in bold.

Note that large transitions are uncommon. In each of the periods covered, the share of families moving from the poorest to the richest fifth never exceeds 4.3 percent. Conversely, the share moving from the top fifth to the bottom fifth never exceeds 5 percent. Those transitions that do occur are most likely to be a move up or down by one quintile. For example, in both the 1970s and 1980s, about a quarter of the families began and remained in the middle fifth. But close to half of those who started in the middle ended up in either the second or the fourth quintile. For example, of those in quintile 3 in 1979, a total of 47.9 percent moved up (24.6 percent) or down (23.3 percent) one quintile.

From the perspective of the inequality debate the critical point comes from comparing the differences in these mobility matrixes over time. Recall that the argument against the evidence presented using the cross-sectional data above de-

TABLE 1-3
Family income mobility over three decades

Quintile in 1969	Quintile in 1979*				
	1	2	3	4	5
1	**49.4**	24.5	13.8	9.1	3.3
2	23.2	**27.8**	25.2	16.2	7.7
3	10.2	23.4	**24.8**	23.0	18.7
4	9.9	15.0	24.1	**27.4**	23.7
5	5.0	9.0	13.2	23.7	**49.1**

Quintile in 1979	Quintile in 1989				
	1	2	3	4	5
1	**50.4**	24.1	15.0	7.4	3.2
2	21.3	**31.5**	23.8	15.8	7.6
3	12.1	23.3	**25.0**	24.6	15.0
4	6.8	16.1	24.3	**27.6**	25.3
5	4.2	5.4	13.4	26.1	**50.9**

Quintile 1988	Quintile in 1998				
	1	2	3	4	5
1	**53.3**	23.6	12.4	6.4	4.3
2	25.7	**36.3**	22.6	11.0	4.3
3	10.9	20.7	**28.3**	27.5	12.6
4	6.5	12.9	23.7	**31.1**	25.8
5	3.0	5.7	14.9	23.2	**53.2**

* Quintile 1 = lowest income level.
Source: Katherine Bradbury and Jane Katz, "Women's Labor Market Involvement and Family Income Mobility When Marriages End," *New England Economic Review* Q4 (2002).

pends upon an increase in the rate of transitions, particularly from low quintiles to high ones. If anything, the panels in Table 1-2 and Figure 1-3 show the opposite.

In the 1990s, the entries in boldface, that is, the "stayers," are larger than in either of the other two decades. For example, 36.3 percent started and ended in the second fifth in the 1990s, compared to 31.5 percent in the 1980s and 27.8 percent in the 1970s. In terms of upward mobility, whereas 12.4 per-

cent moved from the poorest fifth to the fourth and fifth
highest in the 1970s, in the 1980s and 1990s that share was
10.6 percent and 10.7 percent, respectively. Finally, the share
of families staying in the top fifth grew consistently over the
decades, implying diminished mobility over time.

Combining all family types masks important differences
in mobility by race. Analysis by economist Tom Hertz examines the extent of upward and downward mobility across
race.[15] The data presented in Table 1-4 give the percent of
families by race who moved between the bottom and top
quarter of the income scale between 1968 and 1998 (income
data are adjusted for family size). The total share of upwardly
mobile families—those moving from the bottom quartile to
the top—was slightly lower than the share moving from top
to bottom. But this overall measure is quite different by race.
White families were almost two and a half times more upwardly mobile than black families, a statistically significant
difference. And black families were twice as likely as whites
to fall from the top to the bottom quartile, though given the
small sample size of black families in the top quartile, the difference does not reach statistical significance.

These mobility studies show that while some degree of

TABLE 1-4
Income mobility for white and black families

	Bottom to Top Quartile (%)	Top to Bottom Quartile (%)
All	7.3	9.2
White	10.2	9.0
African-American	4.2	18.5

Source: From Tom Hertz, "Rags, Riches and Race: The Intergenerational Eco-
nomic Mobility of Black and White Families in the United States," in Samuel
Bowles, Herbert Gintis, and Melissa Osborne, eds., *Unequal Chances: Family
Background and Economic Success* (New York and Princeton: Russell Sage and
Princeton University Press, 2005), Table 9.

family income mobility certainly exists in the United States, it has not accelerated in such a way as to offset the increase in income inequality discussed in the previous section. To the contrary, it appears to have diminished somewhat over the 1990s. In addition, what upward mobility does exist varies significantly by race; white families are more than twice as likely as black families to be upwardly mobile.

Conclusion

Research findings show that here in the United States, income, wealth, and opportunity are significantly correlated across generations. A child of a low-income father has only a small chance of achieving very high earnings in adulthood. Almost two-thirds of children of low-income parents (those in the lowest quintile) will themselves have wealth levels that place them in the bottom two quintiles. And while there is some disagreement in the literature, some of the research shows that we have become considerably less mobile over time. This finding is important, because it means there has been no increase in mobility that might serve to offset the higher levels of cross-sectional inequality.

One of the most surprising findings of this research is that the United States has less mobility than other advanced economies, even including those of Scandinavia. Certainly these results belie a simplistic story of a favorable trade-off between less regulation and social protection and greater mobility. These other countries manage to provide far more extensive safety nets and families there appear to face fewer class barriers. An important question for future research is whether these two features are causally linked: do more elaborate social protections clear mobility pathways that are blocked in economies that operate in a freer market framework?

What should we do to diminish these correlations and boost mobility, especially among those who are disadvantaged at the starting line? It's an important question, because equal opportunity at the start is a core American value. We generally reject notions that support equality of outcomes; ours will always be an economy and a society with some degree of inequality. But if this inequality results not from a meritocracy wherein the most able "win the race," but from a rigged race where too many contestants are running with weights strapped on their backs, we sense that economic injustice is in play.

Thus, a primary concern of public policy in this area is to remove the weights—that is, lower the barriers created by economic, racial, or political differences that stand between people and their ultimate potential.

The findings from this chapter suggest a few good leverage points. Obviously, education is key, and the fact that "smart" poor children access college at the same rate as lower-performing rich children suggests an economic barrier. Programs that identify high-performing students in low-income settings could help in this area, but thinking more broadly, perhaps any student who has the ability should be able to go to college. In other words, would it not make sense to promote full access to higher education for anyone who is interested and able? Costing out such a program is beyond the scope of this chapter, and, of course, budgetary trade-offs need to be considered. But given the role of college education in boosting economic mobility, this is worth considering.*

Better social safety nets and greater work supports—any

---

* Of course, educational disadvantages start way before college. State-based programs that provide access to college for disadvantaged but high-performing students have found that remediation is an important part of the process, because some of these students need extra services to help them adapt to college.

work-related subsidy provided to low-income workers—are
also part of the solution to raising mobility. Especially in the
low-wage U.S. labor market, there is a significant gap between what low-income workers earn and what they need to
make ends meet. While such supports are associated with current consumption, and thus may sound less relevant regarding mobility, it is difficult for such persons to get ahead
without these supports. Child care is a good example. Research has shown that the absence of affordable child care has
led to either interruption in labor market participation, inferior child-care provision, or both. Clearly, this dynamic works
against building mobility-enhancing experience in the labor
market and a head start for children.

Finally, the data shown above suggest that the persistence
of wealth across generations gives a leg up to the haves relative to the have-nots. Offsetting this mobility blocker is at the
heart of the asset-building movement, a broad set of programs designed to increase wealth among the poor.* Often,
these programs have operated at too small a scale to make
much of a dent in the historical persistence of wealth accumulation. But larger initiatives, such as sizable demo grants
for all children, have also been proposed. In fact, the "college
for all who are able" idea can be viewed in this light as well,
as an ambitious investment in building human capital assets
for the disadvantaged.

---

* See, for example, the program on asset development for the poor listed at
www.newamerica.net/programs/asset_building.

2

Educational Quality and Equality
What It Will Take to Leave No Child Behind

Linda Darling-Hammond

Of all the civil rights for which the world has struggled and fought for 5,000 years, the right to learn is undoubtedly the most fundamental. . . . The freedom to learn . . . has been bought by bitter sacrifice. And whatever we may think of the curtailment of other civil rights, we should fight to the last ditch to keep open the right to learn, the right to have examined in our schools not only what we believe but what we do not believe; not only what our leaders say, but what the leaders of other groups and nations, and the leaders of other centuries have said. We must insist upon this to give our children the fairness of a start which will equip them with such an array of facts and such an attitude toward truth that they can have a real chance to judge what the world is, and what its greater minds have thought it might be.

—W.E.B. DuBois, *The Freedom to Learn*

Universal access to high-quality, intellectually empowering education for all citizens has long been a struggle. Fifty years after *Brown v. Board of Education*, the gaps in educational achievement between white and non-Asian minority students remain large, and the differences in access to educational opportunities are growing. Many students in the **United States, especially low-income students and students of** color, do not receive even the minimum education needed to become literate and join the labor market. This is increasingly problematic, as the knowledge economy we now face demands higher levels of education from all citizens: about 70 percent of current U.S. jobs require specialized skill and training beyond high school, yet only about 75 to 80 percent of high school students graduate and only about 25 percent complete college. Those who are undereducated can no longer access the labor market. While the United States must fill many of its high-tech jobs with individuals educated overseas, a growing share of its own citizens are unemployable and relegated to the welfare or prison systems. The nation can ill afford to maintain the structural inequalities in access to knowledge and resources that produce persistent and profound barriers to educational opportunity for large numbers of its students.

International studies continue to confirm that the U.S. educational system not only lags behind most other industrialized countries in mathematics and science achievement by high school but also allocates more unequal inputs and produces more unequal outcomes than its peer nations. In contrast to European and Asian nations, which fund schools centrally and equally, the wealthiest 10 percent of U.S. school districts spend nearly ten times more than the poorest 10 percent, and spending ratios of three to one are common within states.[1] These disparities reinforce the wide inequalities in income among families, with the most resources being spent on children from the wealthiest communities and the fewest on the children of the poor, especially in high-minority communities. This reality creates the disparities in educational outcomes that plague the United States and ultimately weaken the nation.

The Current Legacy of Inequality in U.S. Education

From the time southern states made it illegal to teach an enslaved person to read, throughout the nineteenth century and into the twentieth, African Americans, Native Americans, and, frequently, Mexican Americans faced de facto and de jure exclusion from public schools throughout the nation and experienced much lower quality education.[2] These disparities have continued. In 1991, Jonathan Kozol's *Savage Inequalities* described the stark differences between segregated urban schools and their suburban counterparts, which generally spent twice as much: places like Goudy Elementary School, which served an African American student population in Chicago, using "15-year-old textbooks in which Richard Nixon is still president" and "no science labs, no art or music teachers. . . . [and] two working bathrooms for some 700 children," in contrast with schools in the neighboring town of New Trier (more than 98 percent white), where students had access to "superior labs . . . up-to-date technology . . . seven gyms [and] an Olympic pool."[3] More than a decade later, school spending in New Trier, at nearly $15,000 per student, still far exceeded the $8,500 per student available in Chicago for a population with many more special needs. Nationwide, many cities spend only half of what their wealthier suburbs can spend.[4]

Recent analyses of data prepared for school finance cases in Alabama, California, Massachusetts, New Jersey, New York, Louisiana, South Carolina, and Texas have found that on every tangible measure—from qualified teachers and class sizes to textbooks, computers, facilities, and curriculum offerings—schools serving large numbers of students of color have significantly fewer resources than schools serving mostly white students. This description of one San Francisco school serving African American and Latino students was typical of others in the California complaint.

> At Luther Burbank, students cannot take textbooks home for homework in any core subject because their teachers have enough textbooks for use in class only. . . . For homework, students must take home photocopied pages, with no accompanying text for guidance or reference, when and if their teachers have enough paper to use to make homework copies. . . . Luther Burbank is infested with vermin and roaches and students routinely see mice in their classrooms. One dead rodent has remained, decomposing, in a corner in the gymnasium since the beginning of the school year. The school library is rarely open, has no librarian, and has not recently been updated. The latest version of the encyclopedia in the library was published in approximately 1988. Luther Burbank classrooms do not have computers. Computer instruction and research skills are not, therefore, part of Luther Burbank students' regular instruction. The school no longer offers any art classes for budgetary reasons. . . . Two of the three bathrooms at Luther Burbank are locked all day, every day. . . . Students have urinated or defecated on themselves at school because they could not get into an unlocked bathroom. . . . When the bathrooms are not locked, they often lack toilet paper, soap, and paper towels, and the toilets frequently are clogged and overflowing. . . . Ceiling tiles are missing and cracked in the school gym, and school children are afraid to play basketball and other games in the gym because they worry that more ceiling tiles will fall on them during their games. . . . The school has no air conditioning. On hot days classroom temperatures climb into the 90s. The school heating sys-

tem does not work well. In winter, children often wear coats, hats, and gloves during class to keep warm. . . . Eleven of the 35 teachers at Luther Burbank have not yet obtained regular, nonemergency teaching credentials, and 17 of the 35 teachers only began teaching at Luther Burbank this school year.[5]

Luther Burbank, like the schools described by Kozol, represents a growing number of "apartheid" schools that serve low-income racial-and-ethnic-minority students exclusively in settings that are extraordinarily impoverished. In California, for example, many such schools are so severely overcrowded that they run a multitrack schedule offering a shortened school day and school year, lack basic textbooks and materials, do not offer the courses students would need to be eligible for college, and are staffed by a parade of untrained, inexperienced, and temporary teachers.[6]

Such profound inequalities in resource allocations are supported by the increasing resegregation of schools over the decades of the 1980s and 1990s. In 2000, 72 percent of the nation's black students attended predominantly minority schools, up significantly from the low point of 63 percent in 1980. The proportion of students of color in intensely segregated schools also increased. More than a third of African American and Latino students (37 percent and 38 percent, respectively) attended schools with a minority enrollment of 90 to 100 percent. (See Table 2-1.) Furthermore, for all groups except whites, racially segregated schools are almost always schools with high concentrations of poverty.[7] Nearly two-thirds of African American and Latino students attend schools where most students are eligible for free or reduced-price lunch. (See Table 2-2.)

African American and Hispanic students continue to be concentrated in central-city public schools, many of which

TABLE 2-1
Distribution of students in public elementary and high schools
by race and ethnicity, fall 2000

Race/Ethnicity	Total	Less than 10%	10–24%	25–49%	50–74%	75–89%	90% or more
Total	100	28	19	19	13	8	14
White, non-Hispanic	100	43	26	20	8	2	1
Black, non-Hispanic	100	2	7	19	21	13	37
Hispanic	100	2	7	15	20	19	38
Asian/Pacific Islander	100	7	15	23	22	18	15
American Indian/ Alaska Native	100	9	19	27	17	8	20

Note: Percentages may not add to 100 due to rounding.
Source: U.S. Department of Education, National Center for Education Statistics, unpublished data from Common Core of Data, 2000–2001.

have become "majority minority" over the past decade even as their funding has fallen further behind that of schools in the suburbs. As of 2003, students of color comprised 69 percent of those served by the one hundred largest school districts.[8] The continuing segregation of neighborhoods and communities intersects with funding formulas and school administration practices that create substantial differences in the educational resources made available in communities serving white children and children of color.

Such disparities in resources are largely a function of how public education in the United States is funded. In most cases, education costs are supported by a system of general taxes— primarily local property taxes and state grants-in-aid. Because these funds are typically raised and spent locally, districts with higher property values have greater resources with which to fund their schools, even when poorer districts tax themselves at proportionally higher rates.

These disparities translate into real differences in the ser-

TABLE 2-2
Distribution of public school grade 4 students eligible for
free/reduced-price lunch by race and ethnicity, 2000

Race/Ethnicity	Total	0%	1–5%	6–10%	11–25%	26–50%	51–75%	76–99%	100%
Total	100	6	11	11	14	20	20	11	6
White, non-Hispanic	100	7	14	15	18	23	17	5	1
Black, non-Hispanic	100	2	2	2	7	14	28	32	13
Hispanic	100	4	4	7	9	16	26	16	17
Asian/Pacific Islander	100	7	27	16	9	13	10	17	2
American Indian/ Alaska Native	100	3	2	1	9	25	32	16	12

Note: Percentages may not add to 100 due to rounding.
Source: U.S. Department of Education, National Center for Education Statistics, National Assessment of Educational Progress, 2000 Reading Assessment.

vices provided in schools: higher-spending districts have smaller classes, higher-paid and more experienced teachers, and greater instructional resources, as well as better facilities, more up-to-date equipment, and a wider range of course offerings. Districts serving large proportions of poor children generally have the fewest resources. Thus, those students least likely to encounter a wide array of educational resources at home are also least likely to encounter them at school.[9] As Taylor and Piche note:

Inequitable systems of school finance inflict disproportionate harm on minority and economically disadvantaged students. On an *inter*-state basis, such students are concentrated in states, primarily in the South, that have the lowest capacities to finance public education. On an *intra*-state basis, many of the states with the widest disparities in educational expenditures are large industrial states. In these states, many minorities and economically disadvantaged students are located in property-poor urban districts which fare the worst in educational expenditures. In addition, in several states economically disadvantaged students, White and Black, are concentrated in rural districts which suffer from fiscal inequity.[10]

Not only do funding systems and other policies create a situation in which urban districts receive fewer resources than their suburban neighbors, but schools with high concentrations of students of color receive fewer resources than other schools within these districts. And tracking systems exacerbate these inequalities by segregating many students of color within schools, allocating still fewer educational opportunities to them at the classroom level. As I describe below, these compounded inequalities explain much of the achievement gap that has often been attributed to genetic differences in intelligence or child-rearing practices or a "culture of poverty," rather than to the distribution of opportunity itself.

The Achievement Gap

During the years following *Brown v. Board of Education*, when desegregation and early efforts at school finance reform were launched and the Great Society's War on Poverty increased investments in urban and poor rural schools, substantial gains were made in equalizing both educational inputs and outcomes. Gaps in school spending, access to qualified teachers, and access to higher education were smaller in the mid- to late 1970s than they had been before and, in many states, than they have been since. In the mid-1970s college attendance rates were actually equivalent for a short period of time for white, black, and Hispanic students. (See Fig. 2-1.)

FIGURE 2-1
College enrollment rates.
Actual and trend rates of immediate enrollment in
postsecondary education, by race/ethnicity, October 1972–2003

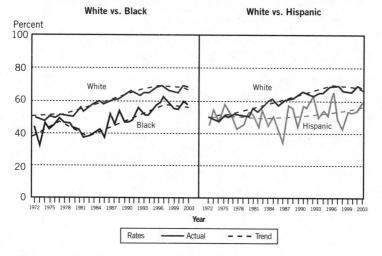

Source: National Center for Education Statistics, *The Condition of Education* (Washington, DC: U.S. Department of Education).

The gains from the Great Society programs were later pushed back. Most targeted federal programs supporting investments in college access and K–12 schools in urban and poor rural areas were reduced or eliminated in the 1980s. Meanwhile, childhood poverty rates, homelessness, and lack of access to health care also grew. Thus, it is no surprise that gaps in achievement began to widen again after the mid-1980s and have, in many areas, continued to grow in the decades since.

On national assessments in reading, writing, mathematics, and science, black students' performance continues to lag behind that of white students, with uneven progress in closing the gap. In reading, large gains in black students' performance during the 1970s and 1980s were reversed in 1988, with scores registering declines for 13- and 17-year-olds since then. In 2002, the average black or hispanic student in grade 12 was reading at the level of the average white eighth-grader. (See Fig. 2-2.) Scores in writing have also declined for grade 8 and grade 11 black students since 1988. Although there have been some improvements in mathematics and science for grade 4 and grade 8 students, the achievement gap has stayed constant or widened since 1990.[11] The lack of progress in closing the gap during the 1990s is not entirely surprising, as the situation in many urban schools deteriorated over the decade. Drops in real per-pupil expenditures accompanied tax cuts and growing enrollments. Meanwhile, student needs grew with immigration, concentrated poverty

FIGURE 2-2
Achievement trends in reading

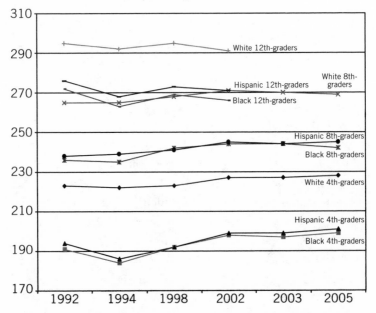

Source: National Assessment of Educational Progress, data compiled from http://nces.ed.gov./nationsreportcard/reading.

and homelessness, and increased numbers of students requiring second-language instruction and special educational
services.

Progress in educational attainment, which was substantial
after 1950, has also slowed. While white graduation rates
were stable at about 80 percent between 1969 and 2004, graduation rates for blacks age 18 to 24 increased rapidly from
under 50 percent to just over 75 percent between the 1950s
and the early 1980s. However, these rates have been stagnant
for the two decades since 1985. In recent years, dropout rates
for African Americans have increased from about 13 percent
to 15 percent.[12] Meanwhile, graduation rates in a number of
states have declined as high-stakes testing policies have been
implemented, with the strongest decreases for black and
Latino students. Data from the National Center for Education
Statistics (NCES) indicate that four-year graduation rates decreased between 1995 and 2001 in Florida, New York, North
Carolina, and South Carolina where new high-stakes testing
policies were introduced.* (See Fig. 2-3.) In all of these cases,
four-year graduation rates for African American and Latino
students have dropped below 50 percent, having decreased
even more precipitously than graduation rates for whites.

With a more educationally demanding economy, the effects of dropping out are more negative than they have ever
before been, and are much worse for young people of color
than for whites. In 1996, a recent school dropout who was
black had only a 1-in-5 chance of being employed, whereas
the odds for his white counterpart were about 50 percent.[13]
Even recent high school graduates struggle to find jobs.
Among African American high school graduates not enrolled
in college, only 42 percent were employed in 1996, as com-

---

* Graduation rates are calculated as the number of students in a graduating class
divided by the number of students in grade 9 three and a half years earlier.

FIGURE 2-3
State graduation rates, 1995–2001

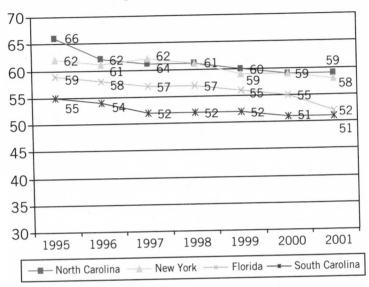

Source: National Center for Education Statistics, Common Core of Data, 2003.

pared to 69 percent of white graduates.[14] Those who do not succeed in school are becoming part of a growing underclass, cut off from productive engagement in society.

Because the economy can no longer absorb many unskilled workers at decent wages, lack of education is increasingly linked to crime and welfare dependency. Women who have not finished high school are much more likely than others to be on welfare, while men are much more likely to be in prison. National investments in the last two decades have tipped heavily toward incarceration rather education. Nationwide, during the 1980s, federal, state, and local expenditures for corrections grew by over 900 percent, and for prosecution and legal services by over 1,000 percent, while prison populations more than doubled.[15] During the same decade, per-pupil expenditures for schools grew by only about

26 percent in real dollar terms, and much less in cities.[16] Between 1980 and 2000, three times as many African American men were added to the nation's prison system as were added to colleges. In 2000, there were an estimated 791,600 African American men in prison or jail, and 603,000 in higher education.[17]

Increased incarceration—and its disproportionate effects upon the African American community—is a function not only of criminal justice policies,[18] but also of the lack of access to education that could lead to literacy, needed skills, and employment. More than half the adult prison population has literacy skills below those required by the labor market, and nearly 40 percent of adjudicated juvenile delinquents have treatable learning disabilities that were undiagnosed and untreated in the schools.[19] This is substantially an educational problem associated with inadequate access to the kinds of teachers and other resources that could enable young people to gain the skills that would enable them to become gainfully employed.

The failure of many states to invest adequately in the education of children in central cities, to provide them with qualified teachers and the necessary curriculum and learning materials, results in many leaving school without the skills needed to become a part of the economy. These social choices increasingly undermine the United States' competitive standing. While the highest achieving nations are making steep investments in education, especially their higher-education systems, the United States is trading off resources for education with spending on prisons. By 2001, state correctional expenditures had grown to $38.2 billion (up from $15.6 billion in 1986), a rate of increase nearly double that of higher-education spending. By 2005, two states—California and Massachusetts—spent as much on prisons as they spent on higher education. Ultimately, the price of educational inequality is the loss of opportunity and progress both for individuals and for the society as a whole.

Structuring Inequality

A number of studies have documented how instructional disparities influence learning and achievement for students of color. For example, when Robert Dreeben studied reading instruction and outcomes for 300 black and white first-graders across seven schools in the Chicago area, he found that differences in reading outcomes among students were almost entirely explained not by socioeconomic status or race, but by the quality of instruction the students received:

> Our evidence shows that the level of learning responds strongly to the quality of instruction: having and using enough time, covering a substantial amount of rich curricular material, and matching instruction appropriately to the ability levels of groups. . . . When Black and White children of comparable ability experience the same instruction, they do about equally well, and this is true when the instruction is excellent in quality and when it is inadequate.[20]

However, the study also found that the quality of instruction received by African American students was, on average, much lower than that received by white students, thus creating a racial gap in aggregate achievement at the end of grade 1. In fact, the highest-ability group in Dreeben's sample at the start of the study was in a school in a low-income African American neighborhood. These students, though, learned less during first grade than their white counterparts because their teacher was unable to provide the quality of instruction this talented group deserved.

In addition to factors like class size and school size, which influence the personal attention students receive, the combined effects of teacher quality and curriculum quality account for much of the school-related contribution to achievement. The combination of these resources can strongly influence school outcomes. For example, a study of African American high school youth randomly placed in public housing in the Chicago suburbs rather than in the city found that, compared to their comparable city-placed peers, who were of equivalent income and initial academic attainment, the students who were enabled to attend better-funded, largely white suburban schools had better educational outcomes across many dimensions. They were substantially more likely to have the opportunity to take challenging courses, receive additional academic help, graduate on time, attend college, and secure good jobs.[21]

As I describe below, much of the difference in school achievement between "minority" students and others is due to the effects of substantially different school opportunities, and in particular greatly disparate access to high-quality teachers and teaching.[22]

Unequal Access to Qualified Teachers

In many cities, increasing numbers of unqualified teachers have been hired since the late 1980s, when teacher demand began to increase while resources were declining. In 1990, for example, the Los Angeles City School District was sued by students in predominantly minority schools because their schools were not only overcrowded and less well funded than other schools; they were also disproportionately staffed by inexperienced and unprepared teachers hired on emergency credentials. Unequal assignment of teachers creates ongoing **differentials in expenditures and access to educational re-**

sources, including curriculum offerings requiring specialized expertise and the knowledge well-prepared teachers rely on in offering high-quality instruction.[23]

The disparities in access to well-qualified teachers are large and growing worse. In 2001, for example, students in California's most segregated minority schools were more than five times as likely to have uncertified teachers than those in predominantly white schools.[24] (See Fig. 2-4.) Similar inequalities have been documented in lawsuits challenging school funding in Massachusetts, South Carolina, New York, and Texas, among other states. By every measure of qualifications—state certification, content background for

FIGURE 2-4
Distribution of unqualified teachers in California, 2001

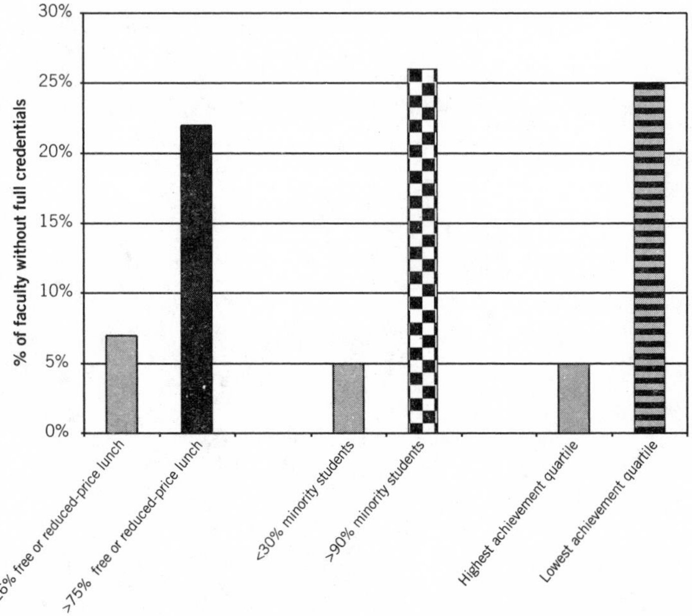

Source: Patrick M. Shields et al., *The Status of the Teaching Profession 2001* (Santa Cruz, CA: The Center for the Future of Teaching and Learning, 2001).

teaching, pedagogical training, selectivity of college attended, test scores, or experience—less qualified teachers are found disproportionately in schools serving greater numbers of low-income or minority students.[25]

Jeannie Oakes's nationwide study of the distribution of mathematics and science opportunities confirmed these pervasive patterns. Based on teacher experience, certification status, preparation in the discipline, degrees, self-confidence, and teacher and principal perceptions of competence, low-income and minority students had less contact with the best-qualified science and mathematics teachers. Students in high-minority schools had less than a 50 percent chance of being taught by math or science teachers who hold degrees and licenses in the field they teach. Oakes concluded:

> Our evidence lends considerable support to the argument that low-income, minority, and inner-city students have fewer opportunities. . . . They have considerably less access to science and mathematics knowledge at school, fewer material resources, less-engaging learning activities in their classrooms, and less-qualified teachers. . . . The differences we have observed are likely to reflect more general patterns of educational inequality.[26]

These disparities are most troubling given recent evidence about the influence of teacher quality on student achievement. In an analysis of nine hundred Texas school districts, Ronald Ferguson found that the single most important measurable cause of increased student learning was teacher expertise, measured by teacher performance on a state certification exam, along with teacher experience and master's degrees.[27] Together these variables accounted for about 40 percent of the measured variance in student test scores. Holding socioeconomic status (SES) constant, the wide variation in teachers' qualifications in Texas accounted for almost all of the variation in black and white students' test scores. That is, after controlling for SES, black students' achievement would have been closely comparable to that of whites if they had been assigned equally qualified teachers.

Ferguson also found that class size, at the critical point of an 18-to-1 student-teacher ratio, was a statistically significant determinant of student outcomes,[28] as was small school size. Other data indicate that black students are more likely to attend large schools than white students with much larger than average class sizes.[29] This is troubling given the evidence that smaller schools and classes can make a difference for student achievement.[30]

A number of other studies have found that teacher quality affects student achievement. Those who lack preparation in either subject matter or teaching methods are significantly less effective in producing student learning gains than those who have a full program of teacher education and who are fully certified.[31]

Whether students have access to well-qualified teachers can be a critical determinant of whether they succeed on the state tests often required for promotion from grade to grade, for placement into more academically challenging classes, and for graduation from high school. Researchers have also found that the proportion of teachers in a school who are fully certified influences the likelihood that students will do well on required state tests, after controlling for student characteristics like poverty.[32]

Strauss and Sawyer found that North Carolina's teachers' average scores on the National Teacher Examination (a licensing test that measures basic skills and teaching knowledge) had a strikingly large effect on students' failure rates on the state competency examinations. A 1 percent increase in teacher quality (as measured by NTE scores) was associated with a 3 to 5 percent decline in the percentage of students failing the exam.[33] This influence remained after taking into account per capita income, student race, district capital assets, student plans to attend college, and pupil-teacher ratios. The authors' conclusion was similar to Ferguson's:

> Of the inputs which are potentially policy-controllable (teacher quality, pupil-teacher ratio and capital stock), our analysis indicates quite clearly that improving the quality of teachers in the classroom will do more for students who are most educationally at risk, those prone to fail, than reducing the class size or improving the capital stock by any reasonable margin which would be available to policy makers.[34]

Futhermore, recruits who are not prepared for teaching are much more likely to leave teaching quickly, many staying only a year or two.[35] This adds additional problems of staff instability to the already difficult circumstances in which urban students attend school. Where these hiring practices dominate, many children are taught by a parade of short-term substitute teachers, inexperienced teachers without support, and underqualified teachers who do not know their subject matter or effective teaching methods well. When large numbers of teachers in a school are inexperienced and underprepared, instructional capacity is further undermined by the fact that there are not enough knowledgeable senior teachers to mentor others, guide curriculum decisions, and keep the instructional program afloat. Professional development funds are wasted on a revolving door of newcomers, while the benefits of these investments do not accrue within the school to produce a stronger schoolwide knowledge base.

In addition, when faced with shortages, districts often assign teachers outside their fields of qualification, expand class sizes, or cancel course offerings. These strategies are used most frequently in schools serving large numbers of minority students.[36] No matter what strategies are adopted, the quality of instruction suffers. This sets up the school failure that society predicts for low-income and minority children— a failure that it helps to create for them by its failure to deal effectively with the issues of teacher supply and quality.

Access to High-Quality Curriculum

In addition to being taught by less qualified teachers than their white counterparts, students of color face dramatic differences in courses, curriculum materials, and equipment. Unequal access to high-level courses and challenging curricula explains another substantial component of the difference in achievement between minority and white students. While course-taking is strongly related to achievement, there are dramatic differences among students of various racial and ethnic groups in course-taking in such areas as mathematics, science, and foreign language.[37] For students with similar course-taking records, achievement test-score differences by race or ethnicity narrow substantially.[38] When students of similar backgrounds and initial achievement levels are exposed to more and less challenging curriculum material, those given the richer curriculum opportunities outperform those placed in less challenging classes.[39]

One source of inequality is the fact that high-minority schools are much less likely to offer advanced and college-preparatory courses in mathematics and science than are schools that serve affluent and largely white populations of students.[40] Schools serving predominantly minority and poor populations have traditionally offered fewer advanced and more remedial courses in academic subjects, and they have smaller academic tracks and larger vocational programs.[41] Furthermore, when high-minority, low-income schools offer any advanced or college-preparatory courses, they offer them to only a very tiny fraction of students. Thus, African Americans, Hispanics, and American Indians have traditionally been underrepresented in academic courses, gifted and talented programs, and honors and advanced-placement programs (see Figs. 2-5 and 2-6). They are overrepresented in general education or vocational education programs, where they receive fewer courses in areas such as English, mathematics, and science.[42] Students of color, especially African Americans, are also overrepresented in special-education courses, where the curriculum is the most watered down and, in many states, teachers are least qualified.

These inequalities in access to high-quality curriculum are

FIG. 2-5
Participation in advanced-placement courses, 2003
Percent of AP Test-Takers by Race / Ethnicity

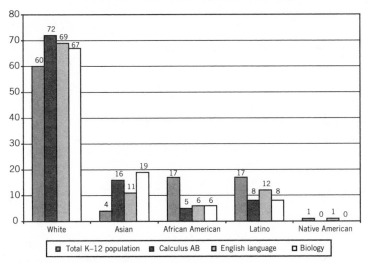

Source: The College Board, AP Summary Reports, 2003.

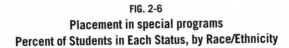

FIG. 2-6
Placement in special programs
Percent of Students in Each Status, by Race/Ethnicity

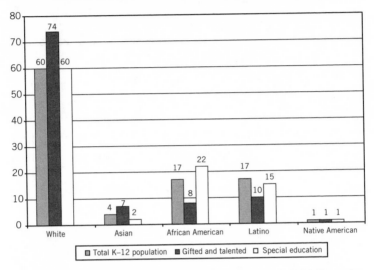

Source: U.S. Department of Education, Office for Civil Rights. 2000 Elementary and Secondary School Civil Rights Compliance Report, 2003. Calculations by the Education Trust (Education Watch).

reinforced by the lack of teachers who can successfully teach heterogeneous groups of students and those who can teach the upper-level courses. Tracking persists in the face of growing evidence that it does not substantially benefit high achievers and tends to put low achievers at a serious disadvantage, in part because good teaching is a scarce resource, and thus must be allocated.[45] Scarce resources tend to get allocated to the students whose parents, advocates, or representatives have the most political clout. This typically results in the most highly qualified teachers offering the most enriched curricula to the most advantaged students. Evidence suggests that teachers themselves are tracked, with those judged to be the most competent and experienced or have the highest sta-

tus assigned to the top tracks, and those with the least experience and training assigned to the lower tracks.[44]

Tracking exacerbates differential access to knowledge. Although test scores and prior educational opportunities may
provide one reason for differential placements, race and socioeconomic status play a distinct role. Even after test scores
are controlled, race and socioeconomic status determine as-
signments to high school honors courses, as well as vocational
and academic programs and more or less challenging courses
within them.[45] Oakes's research in a California urban district
demonstrates vividly how students with the same standardized test scores are tracked "up" and "down" at dramatically
different rates by race.[46] Latino students, for example, who
score near the 60th percentile on standardized tests are less
than half as likely as white and Asian students to be placed in
college preparatory classes. Even those Latino students who
score above the 90th percentile on such tests have only about a
50 percent chance of being placed in a college-preparatory
class, while white and Asian students with similar scores
have more than a 90 percent chance of such placements. (See
Fig. 2-7.)

These patterns are in part a function of prior placements of
students in gifted and talented programs versus remedial
tracks in earlier grades (also associated with race within
equivalent test-score groups), in part due to counselors' views
that they should advise students in ways that are "realistic"
about their futures, and in part because of the greater effectiveness of parent interventions in tracking decisions for
higher-SES students.

Tracking in U.S. schools starts much earlier and is much
more extensive than in most other countries, where sorting
does not occur until high school. Starting in elementary
schools with the designation of instructional groups and pro-

FIG. 2-7
Placement in college-preparatory courses, controlling for standardized grade 9 test scores

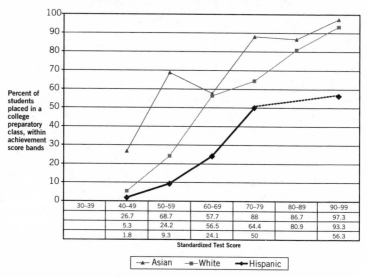

	30–39	40–49	50–59	60–69	70–79	80–89	90–99
		26.7	68.7	57.7	88	86.7	97.3
		5.3	24.2	56.5	64.4	80.9	93.3
		1.8	9.3	24.1	50		56.3

Standardized Test Score

—▲— Asian   —■— White   —◆— Hispanic

Source: Jeannie Oakes, *Ability Grouping, Tracking, and Within-School Segregation in the San Jose Unified School District, Diaz v. San Jose Unified School District,* expert report to the court.

grams based on test scores and recommendations, it becomes highly formalized by junior high school. From gifted and talented programs at the elementary level through advanced courses in secondary schools, the most experienced teachers offer rich, challenging curricula to select groups of students, on the theory that only a few students can benefit from such curricula. Yet the distinguishing feature of such programs, particularly at the elementary level, is not their difficulty but their quality. Students in these programs are given opportunities to integrate ideas across fields of study. They have opportunities to think, write, create, and develop projects. They are challenged to explore. Though virtually all students would benefit from being taught in this way, their opportunities remain acutely restricted. The result of this practice is that challenging curricula are rationed to a very small proportion of students, and far fewer U.S. students ever encounter the kinds of curriculum students in other countries typically experience.[47]

In many instances, the reasons for restricting access to challenging courses is the scarcity of teachers who can teach in the fashion such curricula demand. In addition, schools continue to believe that few students need or will profit from such demanding instruction. Those beliefs are especially strong with respect to students of color. The disproportionately small enrollment of non-Asian minority students in gifted and talented programs is widespread. Meanwhile, students placed in lower tracks are exposed to a limited, rote-oriented curriculum and ultimately achieve less than students of similar aptitude who are placed in academic programs or untracked classes.[48] Teacher interaction with students in lower-track classes is less motivating and less supportive, as well as less demanding of higher-order reasoning and responses.[49] These interactions are also less academically oriented and more likely to focus on behavioral criticisms, especially for minority students.[50]

In addition, many studies have found that students placed in the lowest tracks or in remedial programs are most apt to experience instruction geared only to rote skills, working at a low cognitive level on test-oriented tasks that are profoundly disconnected from the skills they need to learn. Rarely are they given the opportunity to talk about what they know, to read real books, to research and write, to construct and solve problems in mathematics, science, or other subjects.[51] Yet these are the practices essential to the development of higher-order thinking skills and to sustained academic achievement. The most effective teachers provide active learning opportunities involving student collaboration and many uses of oral and written language, help students access prior knowledge that will frame for them the material to be learned, structure learning tasks so that students have a basis for interpreting the new experiences they encounter, provide hands-on learning opportunities, and engage students' higher-order thought processes, including their capacities to hypothesize, predict, evaluate, integrate, and synthesize ideas.[52]

New Standards and Old Inequalities

While these inequalities in educational opportunity continue—and have actually grown worse in many states over the last two decades—the increasing importance of education to individual and societal well-being has spawned an education reform movement in the United States focused on the development of new standards for students. Virtually all states have created new standards for graduation, new curriculum frameworks to guide instruction, and new assessments to test students' knowledge. Many have put in place high-stakes testing systems that attach rewards and sanctions to students' scores on standardized tests. These include grade retention or promotion as well as graduation for students, merit pay awards or threats of dismissal for teachers and administrators, and extra funds or loss of registration, reconstitution, or loss of funds for schools. The recently enacted No Child Left Behind Act reinforces these systems, requiring all schools receiving funding to test students annually and enforcing penalties for those that do not meet specific test-score targets both for students as a whole and for subgroups defined by race and ethnicity, language, socioeconomic status, and disability.

The rhetoric of "standards-based" reforms is appealing. Students cannot succeed in meeting the demands of the new economy if they do not encounter much more challenging work in school, many argue, and schools cannot be stimulated to improve unless the real accomplishments—or deficits—of their students are raised to public attention. There is certainly some merit to these arguments. But standards and tests alone will not improve schools or create educational opportunities where they do not now exist.

The implications of standards-based reform for students who have not received an adequate education are suggested by recent data from Massachusetts, which began to implement high-stakes testing in the late 1990s. As the Massachusetts accountability system was phased in, there was a 300 percent increase in middle-school dropouts between academic 1997–1998 and 1999–2000. When the exit exam took effect in 2003, and school ratings were tied to student pass rates in grade 10, greater proportions of students began disappearing from schools between grades 9 and 10, most of them African American and Latino (see Fig. 2-8). In 2003, graduation rates for the group of ninth-graders who had entered high school four years earlier decreased for all students, but most sharply for students of color. Whereas 71 percent of African American students graduated in the class of 2002, only 59.5 percent graduated among those who began grade 9 with the class of 2003, a proportion that dropped further in the following year.[53] Graduation rates for Latino students went from 54 percent in the class of 2002 to 45 percent in the class of 2003. Meanwhile, many of the steepest increases in test scores occurred in schools with the highest retention and dropout rates. For example, Wheelock found that, in addition to increasing dropout rates, high schools receiving state awards for gains in grade 10 pass rates on the Massachusetts Comprehensive Assessment System test showed substantial increases in prior-year grade 9 retention rates and in the per-

FIGURE 2-8
Ninth-grade students "lost" between grades 9 and 10

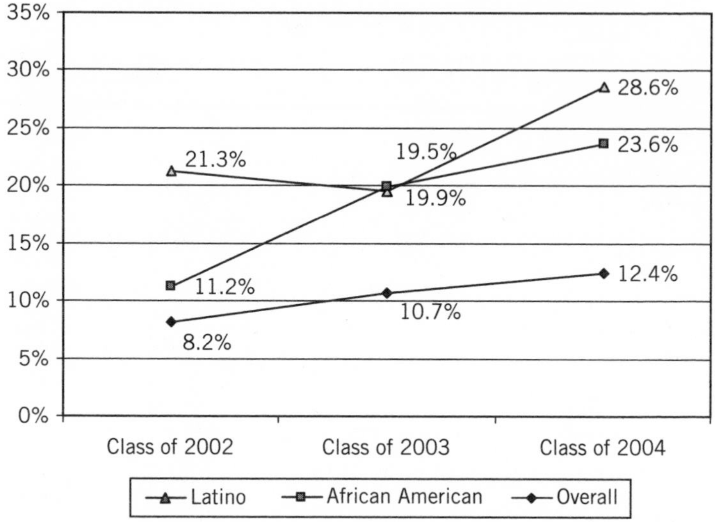

Source: Massachusetts Department of Education, Enrollment Data and Dropout Rates in Massachusetts Public Schools, 1999, 2000, 2001.

centage of "missing" tenth-graders.[54] Thus, schools improved their test scores by keeping low-achieving students out of the testing pool, or out of school entirely.

Studies have linked dropout rates in other states to the effects of grade retention, student discouragement, and school exclusion policies stimulated by high-stakes tests.[55] Researchers have found that systems that reward or sanction schools based on average student scores create incentives for pushing low-scorers into special education so that their scores won't count in school reports,[56] retaining students in grade so that their grade-level scores will look better[57] (a practice that increases later dropout rates), excluding low-scoring students from admissions,[58] and encouraging such students to transfer or drop out.[59]

The advent of high-stakes testing reforms requiring students to achieve specific test-score targets in order to advance in grade or graduate from school has occurred while educational experiences for minority students continue to be substantially separate and unequal. State efforts to set standards for all students for school progression and graduation while failing to offer equal opportunities to learn have stimulated a new spate of equity litigation in nearly twenty states across the country. These lawsuits—which may be said to constitute the next generation of efforts begun by *Brown v. Board of Education*—argue that if states require all students to meet the same educational standards, they must assume a responsibility to provide resources adequate to allow students a reasonable opportunity to achieve those standards, including well-qualified teachers, a curriculum that fully reflects the standards, and the materials, texts, supplies, and equipment needed to teach the curriculum.

Policy for Equality: Toward Genuine School Reform

The common presumption is that unequal educational outcomes are caused by the inadequacies of students who attend schools on a level playing field. In fact, however, U.S. schools are structured such that students routinely receive dramatically unequal learning opportunities based on their race and social status. If the academic outcomes for minority and low-income children are to change, reforms must alter the quality and quantity of learning opportunities they encounter. To improve the achievement of students of color, school reforms must ensure access to high-quality teaching within the context of a rich and challenging curriculum supported by personalized schools and classes. Accomplishing such a goal will require equalization of financial resources, changes in curriculum and testing policies, and improvements in the supply of highly qualified teachers to all students.

Resource Equalization

Progress in equalizing resources to students will require attention to inequalities at all levels—between states; among districts; among schools within districts; and among students differentially placed in classrooms, courses, and tracks that offer substantially disparate opportunities to learn. State funding should be allocated to students based on equal dollars per student adjusted (or weighted) for specific student needs, such as poverty, limited English proficiency, or special-education status. Developing such an equitable, reliable base of funding is critically important so that districts can afford to hire competent teachers and provide reasonable class sizes and pupil loads, which are the foundational components of quality education.

Ferguson's findings about the importance of teacher expertise for student achievement led him to recommend that investments focus on districts' capacity to hire high-quality teachers. Several studies have documented how Connecticut eliminated teacher shortages, improved teacher quality, and raised student achievement by doing just that. When the state raised and equalized teacher salaries under its 1986 Education Enhancement Act, shortages of teachers evaporated, and within three years most teaching fields showed surpluses, even in the urban areas. The state raised standards for teacher education and licensing, initiated scholarships and forgivable loans to recruit high-need teachers into the profession (including teachers in shortage fields, those who would teach in high-need locations, and minority teachers), created a mentoring and assessment program for all beginning teachers, and invested money in high-quality professional development, with special aid to low-achieving districts. By 1998, Connecticut had surpassed all other states in grade 4 reading and mathematics achievement on the NAEP and scored at or near the top of the rankings in grade 8 mathematics, science, and writing.[60]

A systemic strategy like this one is essential if equity and quality are to go hand in hand. The tradition of launching special programs such as compensatory education for low-achieving students will never be effective at remedying underachievement so long as these services are layered on a system that poorly educates such children to begin with. The presumption that "the schools are fine—it's the children who need help" is flawed. The schools serving large concentrations of low-income and minority students are generally not fine, and many of their problems originate with district and state policies and practices that fund them inadequately, send them incompetent staff, require inordinate attention to arcane administrative requirements that fragment educational programs and drain resources from classrooms, and preclude the adoption of more promising curricula and teaching strategies.

Similarly, current initiatives to create special labels and programs for "at-risk" children and youth—including supplemental services, large-scale summer school programs, and mandatory Saturday classes for the thousands of students who are threatened with grade retention under new promotion rules—are unlikely to succeed if they do not attend to the structural conditions of schools that place children at risk in the first place. In the pursuit of equity, useful strategies will improve the core practices of schooling rather than layering additional poorly constructed programs on foundations that are already faulty. The pressures to respond to special circumstances with special categorical programs are great, and the tradition of succumbing to those pressures in an add-on fashion is well established. But add-on programs, with all their accoutrements of new rules and procedures, separate budgets, and fragmented pull-out programs, will be counter-productive as long as the status quo remains unchanged in more significant ways.

As the 1992 interim report of an independent commission on Chapter 1 of the Elementary and Secondary Education Act observed, "Given the inequitable distribution of state and local resources, the current notion that Chapter 1 provides supplemental aid to disadvantaged children added to a level playing field is a fiction." [61] The commission proposed that each state be held accountable for ensuring comparability in "vital services" among all its districts as well as in all schools within each district. Among these vital services, perhaps the most important is highly qualified teachers, not just for specific Chapter 1 services but for all classrooms. This is the genesis of No Child Left Behind's "highly qualified teacher" requirement, which is beginning to make a difference in the availability of better-prepared teachers to students in some states and districts.

The new wave of school finance lawsuits focuses on access to qualified teachers and the availability of curriculum materials (texts, computers, science labs, and so on) adequate to teach the new standards students are expected to achieve. These suits are increasingly able to demonstrate how access to concrete learning opportunities is impaired by differential resources, and how these learning opportunities translate into academic achievement for students. As standards are used to articulate clearer conceptions of what students need to learn to function in today's society and what schools need to do to support these levels of learning, lawsuits like ones recently won in Alabama and New York may be linked to definitions of a quality of education that is "adequate" to meet the state's expectations for student achievement. Such cases require remedies that link levels of funding to minimum standards of learning and teaching. Adequacy cases may establish a principle of "opportunity to learn" that could allow states to define a curriculum entitlement that becomes the basis for both funding and review of school practices.

Opportunity-to-Learn Standards

The idea of opportunity-to-learn standards was first developed by the National Council on Education Standards and Testing (NCEST), which argued for student performance standards but acknowledged they would result in greater inequality if they were not accompanied by policies ensuring access to resources, including appropriate instructional materials and well-prepared teachers.[62] The Council's Assessment Task Force proposed that states collect evidence on the extent to which schools and districts provide opportunity to learn the curricula implied by standards as a prerequisite to using tests for school graduation or other decisions.[63]

Opportunity-to-learn standards would establish, for example, that if a state's curriculum frameworks and assessments outlined standards for science learning that require laboratory work and computers, certain kinds of coursework, and particular knowledge for teaching, resources must be allocated and policies must be fashioned to provide for these entitlements. Such a strategy would leverage both school improvement and school equity reform, providing a basis for state legislation or litigation where opportunities to learn were not adequately funded.

Such standards would define a floor of core resources, coupled with incentives for schools to work toward professional standards of practice that support high-quality learning opportunities. Enacted through a combination of funding commitments, educational indicators, and school review practices, opportunity-to-learn standards would provide a basis for:

- State legislation and, if necessary, litigation that supports greater equity in funding and in the distribution of qualified teachers
- Information about the nature of the teaching and learning opportunities made available to students in different districts and schools across the state
- Incentives for states and school districts to create policies that ensure adequate and equitable resources, curriculum opportunities, and teaching to all schools
- A school review process that helps schools and districts engage in self-assessments and peer reviews of practice in light of standards
- Identification of schools that need additional support or intervention to achieve adequate opportunities to learn for their students[64]

Curriculum and Assessment Reform

The curriculum offered to most African American and other students of color in U.S. schools is geared primarily toward lower-order rote skills—memorizing pieces of information and conducting simple operations based on formulas or rules—that are not sufficient for the demands of modern life or for the new standards being proposed and enacted by states and national associations. These new standards will require students to be able to engage in independent analysis and problem solving, extensive research and writing, use of new technologies, and various strategies for accessing and using resources in new situations. Major changes in curriculum and resources will be needed to ensure that these kinds of activities are commonplace in the classrooms of students of color.

Other important changes concern the types and uses of achievement tests in U.S. schools. As a 1990 study of the implementation of California's then-new mathematics curriculum framework pointed out, when a curriculum reform aimed at problem solving and the development of higher-order thinking skills encounters an already-mandated rote-oriented basic-skills-testing program, the tests win out.[65] As one teacher put it:

> Teaching for understanding is what we are supposed to be doing . . . [but] the bottom line here is that all they really want to know is how are these kids doing on the tests? . . . They want me to teach in a way that they can't test, except that I'm held accountable to the test. It's a catch-22.[66]

Students in schools that organize most of their efforts around the kinds of low-level learning represented by commercially developed multiple-choice tests are profoundly disadvantaged when they encounter more rigorous evaluations requiring more extensive writing, critical thinking, and problem solving like those being developed by states, the College Board, and the federal government. These are also the skills needed to succeed in today's modern economy and in college. Evidence suggests that teaching to lower-level multiple-choice tests undermines the teaching of these more advanced real-world skills, and that such testlike teaching is most pronounced in urban schools serving predominantly low-income students, especially in states emphasizing high-stakes tests.[67]

Initiatives to develop richer curriculum and more performance-oriented assessments that develop higher-order skills have sought to address this problem in states like Connecticut, Vermont, Nebraska, Maine, Oregon, and Kentucky. Their assessments, which use essays and oral exhibitions, as well as samples of student work like research papers and science projects, resemble those used in most countries around the world, including the highest-scoring nations that outrank the

United States. Unfortunately, the administration of the No Child Left Behind Act has tended to discourage the use of performance assessments and has reinforced the reliance on multiple-choice tests, as well as their use for many purposes like grade retention and tracking, for which they were not designed and are not valid.

The issue of how tests are used is as important as the nature of the tests themselves. The standards for test use set by professional organizations—the American Psychological Association, the American Educational Research Association, and the National Council on Measurement in Education—indicate that high-stakes decisions should not be made only on the basis of a test score, and that other indicators of performance, such as class work and teacher observations, should be considered alongside test data. This is because no test is a foolproof predictor of ability or future performance. Most predict a small fraction of the variance in future performance in real-life settings.

Thus, the outcomes of the current wave of curriculum and assessment reforms will depend in large measure on the extent to which developers and users of new standards and tests use them to improve teaching and learning rather than merely reinforcing our tendencies to sort and select those who will get high-quality education from those who will not.[68] Policymakers will also need to pursue broader reforms to improve and equalize access to educational resources and support the professional development of teachers so that new standards and tests are used to inform more skillful and adaptive teaching that enables more successful learning for all students.[69] As a study of state achievement differentials found, the highest-achieving states, after controlling for student poverty and language background, are distinguished by the fact that they have the best-qualified teachers. Most also use thoughtful assessments for instructional improvement, rather than for punishing students and schools.[70]

These efforts to create a "thinking curriculum" for all students are important to individual futures and our national welfare. They are unlikely to pay off, however, unless other critical changes are made in curricula, in the ways students are tracked for instruction, and the ways teachers are prepared and supported. Although mounting evidence indicates that low-tracked students are disadvantaged by current practice and that high-ability students do not necessarily benefit more from homogeneous classrooms than from heterogeneous grouping,[71] the long-established American tracking system will be difficult to reform until there is an adequate supply of well-trained teachers—teachers who are prepared to teach both the more advanced curriculum that U.S. schools now fail to offer most students and the many kinds of students with diverse needs, interests, aptitudes, and learning styles in integrated classroom settings. This, in turn, requires reforms of teacher preparation to enable teachers to become effective in using a wide repertoire of strategies suited to different learning needs.[72]

Investments in Quality Teaching

A key corollary of this analysis is that improved opportunities for students of color will rest substantially on policies that boost attractions to teaching, especially in high-need areas, while increasing teachers' knowledge and skills. This means providing *all* teachers with a stronger understanding of how children learn and develop, how a variety of curricular and instructional strategies can address their needs, and how changes in school and classroom practices can support their growth and achievement.

The students who typically have the poorest opportunities to learn—those attending inner-city schools that are compelled by the current incentive structure to hire disproportionate numbers of substitute teachers, uncertified teachers, and inexperienced teachers—are the students who will benefit most from measures that raise the standards of practice for all teachers. They will also benefit from targeted policies that provide quality preparation programs and financial aid for highly qualified prospective teachers who will teach in central cities and poor rural areas. Providing equity in the distribution of teacher quality requires changing policies and long-standing incentive structures in education so that shortages of trained teachers are overcome and schools serving low-income and minority students are not disadvantaged by lower salaries and poorer working conditions in the bidding war for good teachers.

Building and sustaining a well-prepared teaching force will require local, state, and federal initiatives. To recruit an adequate supply of teachers, states and localities will need to upgrade teachers' salaries to levels competitive with those of college graduates in other occupations, who currently earn 25 to 50 percent more, depending on the field. This should occur as part of a general restructuring effort, which places more resources at the school level and allocates a greater share of education dollars to classrooms rather than to large bureaucracies that oversee them.[73]

Incentive structures must be reshaped to encourage the provision of highly qualified teachers to low-income and minority students. In addition to strategies like Connecticut's, some states have created subsidies to attract individuals into teaching and guide them to fields and areas where they are needed. For example, North Carolina's Teaching Fellows Program has encouraged thousands of high-ability college students—a disproportionate number of them male and minority—to enter teaching by underwriting their entire teacher-preparation program in state universities. After seven years, more than 75 percent had stayed in teaching and many of the remainder had gone on to leadership positions in the public education system.[74]

The federal government can play a leadership role in providing an adequate supply of well-qualified teachers just as it has in providing an adequate supply of well-qualified physicians for the nation. When shortages of physicians were a major problem more than forty years ago, Congress passed the 1963 Health Professions Education Assistance Act to support and improve the caliber of medical training, to create and strengthen teaching hospitals, to provide scholarships and loans to medical students, and to create incentives for physicians to train in shortage specialties and locate in underserved areas. Similarly, federal initiatives in education should seek to:

1. *Recruit new teachers*, through service scholarships and forgivable loans for those who agree to train in shortage fields and practice in high-need locations. As in North Carolina's successful model, scholarships for high-quality teacher education can be linked to minimum service requirements of four years or more—the point at which most teachers who have remained in the classroom have committed to remaining in the profession.

2. *Strengthen and improve teachers' preparation* through improvement incentive grants to schools of education and supports for certification reform focusing on strengthening teachers' abilities to teach a wide range of diverse learners successfully. Policies should support the creation of high-quality programs in the communities where they are most needed. So, for example, just as the federal government has long sponsored efforts to

improve the quality of medical education and the spread of teaching hospitals that are sites for high-quality training, it could sponsor efforts—with strong quality standards—for the development of high-quality teacher education programs, including professional development schools where candidates can learn to teach in settings that are successful with diverse student populations, in urban and poor rural communities that experience teacher shortages.

3. *Improve teacher retention and effectiveness* by improving clinical training and support during the beginning teaching stage when 30 percent of teachers drop out. This would include funding internship programs for new teachers in which they receive structured coaching and mentoring, preferably in urban schools that are supported to provide state-of-the-art practice.[75]

If the interaction between teachers and students is the most important aspect of effective schooling, then reducing inequality in learning has to rely on policies that provide equal access to competent, well-supported teachers. The public education system ought to be able to guarantee that every child who is forced to go to school by public law is taught by someone who is prepared, knowledgeable, competent, and caring. As Carl Grant puts it:

Teachers who perform high-quality work in urban schools know that, despite reform efforts and endless debates, it is meaningful curricula and dedicated and knowledgeable teachers that make the difference in the education of urban students.[76]

Real accountability must start with ensuring all students the right to learn.

3

Connecting Families to Opportunity
The Next Generation of Housing Mobility Policy

Philip Tegeler

Access to opportunity in employment, education, municipal services, and even personal safety and health is strongly influenced by physical location. A growing body of research has found demonstrable harms and measurable disparities associated with living in high-poverty neighborhoods. Similarly, the available evidence shows that housing mobility provides tangible benefits to many families who move to less poor and less segregated neighborhoods.[1]

Recognizing that much of the underlying inequity in our society is engineered in spatial terms is crucial to designing a full and honest range of policy and family alternatives. It is important, of course, to continue to target resources to improve poor, racially isolated communities. But this cannot be

I am grateful for the research assistance of Alanna Buchanan, a law and policy intern at the Poverty and Race Research Action Council (PRRAC) in 2006, and for the ideas and collaboration of my colleagues in the Baltimore Regional Housing Campaign and others working through the *Thompson v. HUD* desegregation case to improve housing mobility options for Baltimore families. Special thanks to Patrick Maier, Barbara Samuels, Gene Rizor, Margy Waller, and Betsy Julian. I am also indebted to Xavier de Souza Briggs and Margery Austin Turner, members of PRRAC's Social Science Advisory Board, whose recent article, "Assisted Housing Mobility and the Success of Low-Income Minority Families: Lessons for Policy, Practice, and Future Research," is a basic point of departure for this chapter.

our only policy alternative; housing choice and mobility must be part of the solution too. For example, families who face challenges relating to health, education, employment, or criminal justice can sometimes be helped by a change in location: a child with serious asthma may benefit more from a move to a neighborhood with cleaner air than from additional drugs and treatment; a child whose academic potential is being squandered or who may have unaddressed learning needs may benefit from a move to a well-resourced and high-performing school district; difficulties in finding and holding on to full-time employment at a living wage may be remedied by a move to a job-rich community; and a young teenage boy who is beginning to experience run-ins with the police might be less likely to end up in prison as a young adult if his family moves to a low-crime community. To achieve these types of outcomes, however, it may not be enough to simply move a family; services must follow. This perspective will be the focus of much of the discussion below.

It is axiomatic that housing, education, employment, and health are interdependent systems. The challenge for housing mobility policy is to recognize the mechanisms of this interdependence and to plan accordingly. The housing-health nexus provides one important example of these dynamics: a family's overall health can be positively affected by moving from a high-poverty neighborhood to a lower-poverty one. However, poor health can constitute a barrier to a successful move, and remaining tethered to city-based health care can sometimes hold families back from a commitment to their new community. Linking families with suburban health providers can both encourage successful long-term relationships with the new community and lead to improved health care. Similarly, the full health benefits of moving to a healthier environment do not suddenly appear after a move is complete. Helping a family to more effectively access both the health-care systems and the environmental benefits of a "healthier" community are crucial steps in the process.

Housing mobility is not the answer for every family—and obviously should not replace economic and social interventions in poor neighborhoods—but it would be wrong not to include mobility as an option to a family seeking assistance, or as a serious policy alternative in response to some of the underlying social problems that are reinforced by geographic location.

Ultimately, federal and state policy in health, education, employment, and criminal justice must incorporate these concepts of place and geographic mobility in a programmatic way. At present, however, the only vehicle we have for housing mobility is the HUD-administered Section 8 Housing Choice Voucher Program. Virtually alone among federal housing programs, the Section 8 program has provided an option to families who choose to move to less segregated areas. Unfortunately, this benefit of the voucher program is not automatic, and is highly dependent on program features that include how higher-rent areas are treated, how public housing agencies (PHAs) receive their funding, how PHAs interact with families and with each other when a voucher crosses jurisdictional lines ("portability"), and the extent to which families receive housing search assistance.[2] Each of these program features is subject to competing political, administrative, and policy demands, and since the voucher program has no significant constituency outside of the housing industry, housing mobility becomes simply one goal among many.[3]

This chapter will not dwell on the failures of the HUD voucher program to promote mobility—that has been briefed elsewhere.[4] Rather, we will look to the future of housing mobility policy, and to the possible outlines of a new national mobility program, based on what we have learned. We will also explore the way that these interconnections with other policy sectors—education, employment, public health, and criminal justice—might lead to a broader constituency for expanding housing choice. As one public health expert recently observed, "[t]his nation's housing voucher program has a natural constituency among public health practitioners and researchers committed to social justice."[5] The same should also be true for advocates working to address the minority achievement gap and the harsh racial impacts of our country's mass incarceration policies. Housing mobility is too important to remain just a housing issue.

The New Focus on Post-Move Counseling: Connecting Families to Opportunity

Recent research on housing mobility programs suggests that—in addition to reinstating the types of front-end interventions used by HUD in the 1990s to expand the range of neighborhoods accessible to voucher families—a more sophisticated effort to assist families *after* they move will be the key to success in future mobility programs. In the Moving to Opportunity (MTO) mobility experiment, low-income families were placed in lower-poverty neighborhoods in five different metropolitan areas, but with little or no assistance in accessing the opportunities available to them in the new neighborhoods. The mixed interim results of the MTO program, one might argue, are related to the absence of policies to actually connect MTO families with opportunity in their new communities. Indeed, after dozens of studies, it seems increasingly obvious that if the goal is to connect low-income families to opportunities in new communities, families may need some initial assistance in *accessing* those benefits. As Briggs and Turner conclude in their recent review of MTO research:

Future policy should be "mobility plus." . . . [W]e can and should link rental housing subsidies and counseling to workforce development, reliable transportation (e.g., through "car voucher" programs . . .) health care, informed school choice, and other family-strengthening supports. These tools would respond to families' varied needs and help families take full advantage of new and better locations.[6]

What might some of these interventions look like? Recent research on the Moving to Opportunity program offers some suggestions. We have also been fortunate to have been looking at these questions in the context of one of the strongest remaining mobility programs in the United States, operating under court order in the *Thompson v. HUD* case in Baltimore, and working with our colleagues and participants in the program there to improve post-move services and outcomes for families.[7] We have also drawn some insights from a similar program in Dallas, which provides post-move counseling services for families in a mobility program originally established under the *Walker v. HUD* desegregation case.[8] The discussion that follows will look to these examples and to recent social science literature in setting out an agenda for better connecting families to opportunities in their new communities.

Housing Mobility and Employment

The continuing "spatial mismatch" between African Americans and job-rich areas is greatest in highly segregated metropolitan areas, which also, not coincidentally, experience high rates of "job sprawl" to outer suburban areas. Latino families are also geographically cut off from employment opportunities, but the geographic distance between African Americans and job-rich areas is greater than for any other racial minority and is an important contributing factor in disproportionate black poverty.[9]

But instead of moving families closer to areas of high job growth, the more recent emphasis seems to have been to leave low-income minority families where they are, while simultaneously trying to improve access to jobs. One of these recent experiments, the Bridges to Work demonstration, sought to bus inner-city public housing residents out to far-flung suburban jobs in a reverse-commute van program. This program appears to have been a failure (although this may be largely a result of flawed implementation and changes in program design).[10] A more ambitious program, Jobs Plus, directed intensive job counseling, job training and placement, child-care assistance, and an earned-income rent incentive to encourage public housing tenants to work without increasing their "tenants' share" of the rent. Jobs Plus had some initial success, increasing employment rates and income for public housing residents in several but not all of the pilot sites.[11]

Oddly, no similar job counseling and placement program has been directed to voucher families who moved to lower-poverty neighborhoods in the parallel Moving to Opportunity housing mobility demonstration. These families were left to fend for themselves, even though the Jobs Plus results suggest that intensive one-on-one job counseling and placement efforts, combined with rent incentives, would improve employment outcomes for voucher families. In the relatively job-rich environment of low-poverty suburbs, one might expect the results of such a program to be dramatic. But such a combined housing-jobs connection has not yet been attempted. Congress did express a desire to make this connection with the 1999 Welfare-to-Work voucher program, which in the end generated many new vouchers but little in the way of intentional job connections.[12]

The first step in bringing employment services into a housing mobility program is to address the employment obstacles
families face in higher-opportunity, often suburban areas.
Reed et al. observe that "[m]oving alone simply cannot alle-
viate many of the obstacles that . . . voucher holders, who are
mostly low-income, single mothers, face when finding and
keeping jobs." [13] These barriers include imperfect information, inadequate transportation, health issues, lack of affordable child care, and financial disincentives. Research also
suggests that many mobility clients face discrimination—or,
to put it more benignly, they may be near the bottom of the
"suburban jobs queue." [14]

Only by addressing these barriers can we expect improved
employment outcomes. In Baltimore, the Regional Housing
Campaign, along with the Greater Baltimore Urban League,
is working to expand a successful city-based job-counseling
program to include suburban employers, and to assist a selected group of families who have moved to the suburbs
through the *Thompson* mobility program. Ultimately, the
goal is to apply the lessons and techniques of Jobs Plus and
other successful workforce development programs in the suburban context. As Greg Duncan and Anita Zuberi recently
observed:

> Perhaps mobility programs need to go beyond merely
> placing families in better neighborhoods and provide
> them with needed family and personal services and sup-
> ports. . . . An example of such a broader program is
> a Milwaukee-based work support program called New
> Hope, which helps families making the transition from
> welfare to work. Workers who documented thirty or
> more hours of work were provided with a package of
> benefits that included an income supplement that
> brought family income above the poverty line, a child-

care subsidy, health insurance, and a temporary community service job if people needed it to make their thirty hours. New Hope provided a package of supports that made it possible for families, through full time work, to balance the kind of work and family demands that all families face. The New Hope package of supports would undoubtedly have helped many Gautreaux and MTO families, as well as many other low-income families.[15]

In order to enhance mobility clients' chances of obtaining employment in suburban markets, another element of the program may include initial placement of workers on a temporary or probationary status, an approach that has already been used successfully by the Urban League in Baltimore and by the Transitional Work Corporation in Philadelphia.[16] Also, it may be advisable to prioritize mobility resources to families who have already found employment in high-opportunity areas but who are still living in the inner city. Helping these families move closer to their jobs has numerous economic and family benefits and will also tend to promote longer-term job stability. There is also a political benefit: focus group research in the Baltimore suburbs has revealed positive attitudes to creating affordable housing options for low-wage workers *already working in the area*, even though general attitudes toward affordable housing development are still problematic.

Transportation

The physical distance from job-rich areas is exacerbated by the lack of flexible transportation. For example, one estimate found that inner-city residents had access to fifty-nine times as many jobs as their neighbors without cars.[17] Another study—in metropolitan Atlanta—found that African Americans overall were far less likely to participate in suburban job markets than their white counterparts.[18] It is not surprising that another recent study found that residential relocation and car ownership are the key factors in predicting the likelihood that welfare recipients will become employed.[19]

To address this problem, foundation- and church-supported low-income car ownership programs have sprung up in a number of cities.[20] Most of these existing subsidized automobile programs are not associated with housing mobility programs, but car transportation is even more important for families seeking to move around *within* suburban areas to obtain and retain jobs. The Baltimore program, Vehicles for Change, has been funded by the Abell Foundation and the Baltimore Housing Authority to provide cars to *Thompson* housing mobility clients who are working in suburban counties. The program provides low-cost financing for used cars, with monthly payments in the range of $70 to $98 for a fifteen-month loan.[21] There is a possibility of adding related supports to this program, including driver-education classes and transportation for clients in the process of seeking employment near their new apartments.

Child Care

Given the demographics of the Housing Choice Voucher program, housing mobility must be viewed, in part, as a gender issue.[22] As one group of researchers observed in its study of "Gautreaux 2" families in Chicago,

> The obstacles these voucher holders face are different from the employment obstacles reported for men in the literature about inner-city joblessness. Our respondents are often the only caregivers for their children, and

sometimes grandchildren, and shoulder all aspects of their care and well-being with few material resources.[23]

Quality child care should be built in to combined housing and job mobility programs. The Jobs Plus program showed that dependable child care was a key factor in job retention for public housing residents.[24] The same result will obviously hold true for voucher holders living outside of public housing. Their children will also benefit from attending racially and economically integrated preschool programs.

Housing Mobility and Health

Interim results from the MTO program suggest that many participating families experience improved physical and mental health outcomes when they move to substantially lower-poverty communities.[25] In particular, adult obesity is "significantly lower among those who moved," and participants experienced marked declines in psychological distress and depression.[26]

The potential of housing mobility has begun to be noticed by public health advocates working to address minority health disparities. For example, Gail Christopher of the Joint Center for Political and Economic Studies recently observed,

> As the links between low socioeconomic status, concentrated poverty, and poor health outcomes become more widely understood, proponents for eliminating health disparities through public health interventions will see housing mobility as an important contextually based intervention strategy. . . . By enabling families to move from concentrated-poverty to low-poverty neighborhoods, many "mechanisms" of the socioeconomic status–disease correlation are addressed.[27]

Other scholars, working in the environmental justice movement, have also begun to see that painstakingly cleaning up the polluted neighborhoods where poor people have been forced to live is not the only solution for all low-income families:

> We must at least acknowledge that, in some instances, exit and integration may be the best option for residents of particularly environmentally beleaguered, racially segregated communities. This contention differs from much of my previous work. I, like many who have been working as environmental justice advocates, have been animated by a vision of community empowerment for residents of poor communities of color. This vision tends to translate into the espousal of remedies aimed at preserving existing communities—"community preservationist" remedies. But I am concerned that I may have been reifying "the community" at the expense of the individuals and families who may have distinct needs and aspirations. These needs and aspirations may in fact be better met by finding ways for people to leave their current communities than by seeking to overcome decades of pollution and neglect.[28]

Like other mobility-related outcomes, the positive health results experienced by MTO families are not related to any specific health "interventions." MTO families received no pre-move health assessment, no health counseling, and no assistance in accessing health resources in their new communities. We can only imagine how much stronger the health outcomes could be for these families if some basic health interventions—to augment the benefits of the move itself—had been taken.

It may also be possible to target housing mobility to those

families and children that need it the most. If it is possible to identify children who are particularly sensitive to asthma triggers in the neighborhood, for example, or adults suffering from stress-related hypertension or depression, a voluntary move may be a cost-effective supplement to other forms of treatment and intervention. A similar analysis may be possible for children with lead-paint poisoning or obesity. Some obvious applications of this principle would include the voluntary transfer of women facing repeat domestic violence, children who have been traumatized by witnessing violent assaults, or teenage girls who may be the targets of repeated sexual harassment.[29]

As noted earlier, for some families, personal health and health system needs present barriers to successful mobility. Some families are reluctant to leave the medical providers they are used to, and some suburban medical providers are unwilling to serve families on Medicaid. Physical disabilities and depression can present obstacles to employment, although perhaps to a smaller number of potential movers. In a recent survey of families in the Gautreaux 2 group in Chicago, researchers found that personal "health concerns were the primary barrier to mobility for less than 10 percent" of families surveyed.[30]

The Baltimore Regional Housing Coalition has proposed several health-based enhancements to the successful regional mobility program there—to help maximize the potential health benefits of mobility for participating families. The initial plan will be to train counseling staff to conduct simple family health and nutrition assessments, which will provide a baseline to assess each family's progress, and also help to develop a plan for health improvement. A second phase of the program will seek to recruit health providers to connect each family with local doctors and dentists in the family's new community.

Housing Mobility and Education

There is a large body of social science evidence on the benefits of school integration for low-income children of color. Attending lower-poverty, racially integrated schools will tend to improve critical thinking skills and academic achievement; promote cross-racial understanding and reduce prejudice; prepare students for an integrated workforce; lead to more integrated residential choices later in life; and lead to higher graduation rates and better access to employment networks after graduation.[31]

At the same time, there is strong evidence that excessive school mobility—moving from school to school—will have detrimental educational impacts for children.[32] The goal for successful educational outcomes for mobility families should be to get children into low-poverty, higher-functioning schools, and to help them stay there—by making sure each family's housing placement is as stable as possible.

One of the limitations of the Moving to Opportunity experiment was its inability to move most participants into significantly higher performing schools.[33] Partly because program placement was defined only in terms of neighborhood poverty rate, in most cases, MTO students moved to schools in other neighborhoods within their original school district. Future housing mobility programs should be careful to avoid this outcome. In most metropolitan areas, differences in academic resources, achievement, and school poverty rates in city versus suburban schools are significant, and in some cases they are extreme. Families need to be given the choice of moving to a higher-performing school district. For example, the Inclusive Communities Project in Dallas is directly linking its landlord recruitment efforts to Texas school accountability standards.[34] A similar approach, using state-by-state school rankings under No Child Left Behind, should be incorporated into future national housing mobility policy. Section 8 programs should be required to offer families the option of placing their children in high-performing schools, and one measurement of Section 8 program performance should include family placement rates in high-performing versus low-performing school zones.

For families that have successfully moved to a high-performing school district, school-focused counseling can help children more quickly and successfully access the benefits of the schools they are now attending, and can help encourage children and families to stay in their new school placements. There are interesting models for this type of support system from long-running city-suburban school transfer programs in Boston, St. Louis, and Hartford, where support services for inner-city children in suburban schools have sometimes proved crucial to their success. For example, the housing mobility program may elect to add specialized educational and social work staff to serve as a resource for families and children, and to work with receiving school districts to ensure appropriate placements for participating children. Other supports might include after-school transportation, assistance with pay-to-play costs for school and town sports leagues, extracurricular activities, driver-education classes, and so on. Some students may also benefit academically from summer camp activities and summer academic enrichment programs.

The housing mobility program in Dallas has recognized the dynamic relationship between housing mobility and education and is focusing its post-move counseling efforts in the schools. As the program's director, Betsy Julian, has observed, "the schools are the best initial point of contact with the community for our families." For mothers who have decided to move, largely for the benefit of their children, involvement in the schools is a natural step, helps them connect socially with other families, and leads easily to other community connections.

Easing the Transition to New Communities for Teenage Boys

One of the most surprising outcomes of the Interim Report on the Moving to Opportunity program was the difference in outcomes for teenage boys and girls.[35] While girls in families moving to lower-poverty neighborhoods had lower rates of delinquency and "risky behavior,"[36] boys did not enjoy the same benefits and had a "higher risk of smoking marijuana and cigarettes, drinking alcohol, problem behavior, and risk behavior" than girls.[37]

Some of the initial explanations for these gender differences point the way to possible interventions:

One possible explanation is that black and Hispanic boys moving to integrated or predominantly white neighborhoods are not engaging in any more criminal behavior but are being arrested more due to racial profiling or higher rates of detecting crime in low-poverty areas.[38]

We speculate that [failure to avoid trouble] is partly responsible for the fact that that experimental group boys are far more likely to forge ties with delinquent peers than control boys.[39]

Another possibility is that some boys respond differently to the loneliness, fears, or boredom associated with relocation: new peers and expectations, a loss of familiar activities, the felt need to act tough to gain respect, and more.[40]

[T]hough we found no differences in contact with bio-
logical fathers across program groups, experimental
group boys are far less likely to have strong connections
to nonbiological father figures.[41]

These gender differences will likely generate important
new research in the coming years, but for mobility practitioners the difficulty faced by some teenage boys is another reason to follow up with families after they move. But no one is
providing the resources to do this. Teenage boys are in a sense
being left stranded in their new neighborhoods.

In Baltimore, our initial response has been to propose programs of connection for teenage boys. It is especially important to ensure that each boy has access to employment, sports,
and social and extracurricular activities through their schools
(including assistance with school uniforms, pay-to-play fees,
and after-school transportation). An active teen employment
program is also part of the solution: after-school connections
for boys in local supermarkets, fast-food restaurants, and institutional employers, and a summer jobs program. We hope
to provide support for after-school programs at selected rental
complexes, to encourage teenage boys to avoid the kind of
innocuous behavior likely to attract suburban police officers.
Outreach to suburban police forces is also part of the
solution.

While teenage girls, in general, seem to be adjusting well
to the transition to new communities, they also have needs
which the next generation of mobility programs will need to
address. Women's rights advocates have recognized the important benefits of housing mobility for increasing access
to economic opportunity, improving women's health, and,
most importantly, protecting women and girls from physical
harm.[42]

Conclusion

In the twenty years since the first studies of the Gautreaux mobility program began to be published, our understanding of housing mobility has become increasingly sophisticated. These programs are not the ultimate solution for low-opportunity communities, but they are crucially important for the families who choose to participate, and they are an important step toward more equitable and integrated metropolitan regions. There will surely be a need for further research, but we have learned enough about the dynamics of housing mobility and its relation to health, education, transportation, child development, and employment to begin to design the next generation of housing mobility programs.

4

Reducing Incarceration
to Expand Opportunity

Marc Mauer

In 2004 the nation celebrated the fiftieth anniversary of the historic *Brown v. Board of Education* decision. In the half century following that decision, major changes occurred in American society to open up social and economic opportunity for many people who had previously been denied full participation in society. Within the criminal justice system, greater diversity of leadership emerged, and the once all-white courtrooms in many parts of the country gradually began to become more representative of their communities.

Despite these constructive changes in society, developments regarding imprisonment have become dramatically worse over this period of time for African Americans, and increasingly for other communities of color. On the day of the *Brown* decision, nearly 100,000 African Americans were in prison or jail in the United States. Today, that figure is 900,000 and we have entered an era in which the criminal justice system has come to play a major role in the life course of many residents of low-income African American communities.

The contours of these developments illustrate the profound shift in public policy in regard to preventing and responding to social disorder. A century-long emphasis on rehabilitation (no matter how imperfectly practiced) as a guiding philosophy in corrections has been replaced by a crime policy that places a priority on "getting tough" as a means of social control. Rather than investing in programs and policies designed to strengthen families and communities, the guiding framework has relied upon an expanded criminal justice system, and particularly an unprecedented use of incarceration, as a primary means of addressing social problems.

These developments have had profound consequences for opportunity prospects for the millions of Americans with a felony conviction or a history of incarceration. In addition to the harmful experiences that are commonplace within prison, individuals released from prison continue to suffer from the stigma of incarceration in access to employment, public benefits, and electoral participation. Growing numbers of children are now living with the experience of having a parent behind bars, and the ripple effects of high rates of incarceration on low-income communities can be seen in measures of family stability, health indicators, and informal social control.

Access to opportunity is also affected through victimization, in particular, the financial or physical harm suffered by victims of crime. Although victimization rates have declined in recent years, one of every forty-seven adults is a victim of a violent crime each year, and one of every six households is victimized by property crime. These rates are significantly affected by considerations of race and class. The violent-crime victimization rate in households with an annual income of $15,000 to $24,999 is nearly double that of households with incomes of $75,000 or more, while African Americans are about a third more likely than whites to be victims of violent crime.[1]

Examining the effects of incarceration and its collateral consequences on access to opportunity in no way suggests that crime is not an issue of concern for all Americans, particularly in the low-income communities that often suffer higher rates of victimization. Nor does it suggest that individuals, regardless of their social or economic circumstances, have no responsibility for their actions. But from the point of view of policymakers and the public, who seek both to address problems of disorder and to increase access to opportunity for all Americans, current policies have had many detrimental effects. This analysis will trace the causes of these policy shifts and their impact on the most affected communities.

The Scale and Impact of Incarceration

For much of the twentieth century, the scale of imprisonment in the United States was relatively stable. For a period of nearly fifty years after 1925, the number of people in federal and state prisons hovered around 200,000, or a rate of incarceration of about 110 per 100,000 population. But beginning in 1972, the prison population began a dramatic rise, one that has been unprecedented in the history of any democratic society. (See Fig. 4-1.)

FIGURE 4-1
State and federal prisoners, 1925–2005

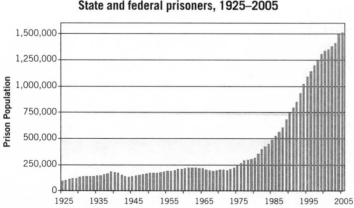

Beginning with about 200,000 prisoners, we have since seen a 500 percent increase over more than thirty years, to a level of 1.44 million.[2] Adding the number of persons incarcerated in local jails, 747,000, produces a total of 2.2 million Americans behind bars. To place this figure in perspective, the United States has now become the world leader in its use of imprisonment (see Fig. 4-2). With a rate of incarceration of 737 per 100,000, the United States is now moving well ahead of second-place Russia in this regard, as Russian authorities have begun implementing a large-scale amnesty program designed to reduce an overcrowded prison system rife with health problems. The United States incarcerates its citizens at a rate five to eight times that of Canada and most nations in western Europe.[3]

During this period of time, incarceration has come to be used much more widely for juveniles as well. From a base of 59,000 detained juveniles in 1980, there are now more than 100,000 youth behind bars. In addition to the growth in sheer numbers, policies and practices have shifted considerably. Since its founding one hundred years ago, the juvenile justice system had historically operated under a different philosophical framework than the adult justice system. Initially established by "child savers," the juvenile court had served as a mechanism for responding to social breakdown in society that manifested itself as juvenile delinquency. In contrast to the adult system, the court was more individualistic and rehabilitative in its approach to juvenile crime. Since the early 1990s, though, legislative bodies have enacted a series of policies designed to blur the boundaries between youth and adults. Most prominently, these have included laws that require more youth to be waived into adult court. Almost every state has passed some type of legislation that either lowers the age of jurisdiction for adult charges, automatically transfers certain cases to adult court, or shifts the discretion for try-

FIGURE 4-2
Rate of incarceration in selected nations

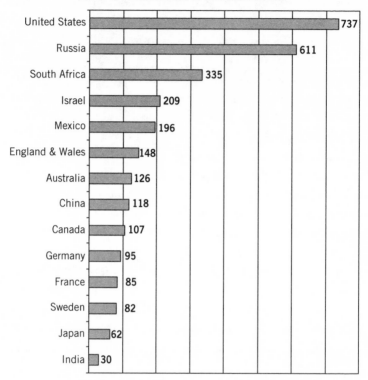

Incarceration rate per 100,000 population

Source: Rate for the United States from *Prisoners in 2005*; for all other nations, International Centre for Prison Studies available online at www.prisonstudies .org. Incarceration data were collected on varying dates and are the most current data available as of 2006.

ing children as adults from judges to prosecutors. At the extreme, youth as young as 13 in some states are now eligible to receive a life sentence. In states such as Michigan, for example, there are now more than three hundred youth who are serving life terms for offenses committed as juveniles.

The explosion in the use of incarceration has affected public policy in regard to immigration violations as well.

Whereas for many years immigration violations were primarily treated as civil offenses, since the 1980s incarceration has become far more widely used in such cases. This is largely a product of legislation that criminalizes these offenses and imposes far harsher penalties than in previous years. These laws also mandate detention and eventual deportation for noncitizens even with minor criminal convictions.[4] Prior to legislation enacted in 1996, there were a limited number of felonies that would subject immigrants to detention and deportation, but the category of "aggravated felony" now includes such offenses as perjury and forgery, and can even include misdemeanor convictions of one year for certain crimes. As a result the immigrant detention population soared from 5,500 in 1994 to 19,500 by 2001.

A Portrait of the Total Prison Population

Looking at the people who populate the nation's prisons, we find that as a group they do *not* look like America. Rather, they are disproportionately low-income and people of color. As of 2005, three-fifths of the prison population were people of color: 40 percent African American and 20 percent Latino (compared to their overall composition of 12 percent and 14 percent, respectively, in the total population). (Note that for most national criminal justice data there are no separate breakdowns for Native Americans, Asian Americans, or other racial groups.) As seen in Table 4-1, the characteristics of this population demonstrate that they suffer disproportionately from a broad range of social and economic disadvantages, including low income and educational attainment and high rates of substance abuse, HIV infection, and mental illness. Of the women who are imprisoned, more than half have been victims of physical or sexual abuse.

The composition of the prison population has changed sig-

TABLE 4-1

Demographics of state prison inmates, 1997*

	Male	Female
Race/ethnicity		
White	33	33
Black	46	48
Hispanic	17	15
Education		
Less than grade 8	14	13
Some high school	25	28
GED	29	22
High school graduate	19	19
Some college	13	17
Monthly income before arrest		
Below $1,199	62	75
$1,200–$1,999	16	11
Above $2,000	22	15
Marital status		
Married	17	17
Widowed	2	6
Separated	19	20
Divorced	6	10
Never married	58	47
History of abuse		
Physical abuse	10	18
Sexual abuse	3	11
Both	3	28
History of drug use		
At time of offense	32	40
In the month prior	56	62
Ever in the past	83	84
Mental illness		
Identified as mentally ill	16	24
Medical problems		
HIV positive	2	4

*Most recently available figures.

Source: Data from reports by Bureau of Justice Statistics, except *Monthly Income Before Arrest*, calculated from the *Survey of Inmates in State and Federal Correctional Facilities, 1997* datafile.

nificantly over time, particularly in regard to the impact of the war on drugs, which has led to substantial increases in arrests and prosecutions beginning in the mid-1980s. Currently, nearly half the prison population is incarcerated for a nonviolent offense, either drugs, property, or public-order offenses, and half for a violent offense. But while the overall prison population increased by 295 percent from 1980 to 2000, the number of people locked up for a drug offense rose by 1,078 percent during this period.

As a result of the dramatic growth of the criminal justice system, imprisonment has come to be almost a commonplace experience in many communities. Table 4-2 indicates that one of every six African American men and one of every thirteen Latino men have served time in prison as of 2001, a near doubling of the rates since 1974. Perhaps more disturbing is the widespread prospect of incarceration for the generation of children growing up today. If current trends continue, one in three black males and one in six Hispanic males born today can expect to serve time in a state or federal prison in his life-

TABLE 4-2
Likelihood of imprisonment for those born in 2001,
based on actual incarceration rates in 1974 and 2001 (%)

	1974	2001	Born in 2001
Male	2.3	4.9	11.3
White	1.4	2.6	5.9
Black	8.7	16.6	32.2
Hispanic	2.3	7.7	17.2
Female	0.2	0.5	1.8
White	0.1	0.3	0.9
Black	0.6	1.7	5.6
Hispanic	0.2	0.7	2.2

Source: Thomas P. Bonczar, "Prevalence of Imprisonment in the U.S. Population, 1974–2001," Bureau of Justice Statistics, August 2003.

time. The overall figures for women are much lower, but the racial disparities are similar.

Rising Incarceration and Its Causes

The initial rise in the use of imprisonment in the 1970s was a function in part of a rising rate of crime. Crime rates rose from the mid-1960s through the mid-1970s, although the scale is difficult to measure because the quality of crime data from that period is much less sophisticated than it is today. These changes were a result of several factors, including the baby boom—more males ages 15–24 in the population—and increasing urbanization, which is often associated with higher rates of crime. But they also reflect the fact that despite a relatively strong economy during those years, the benefits of employment were not uniformly distributed. Criminologist Elliott Currie documents that rates of unemployment for nonwhite youth ages 18–19 rose from 10 percent in 1952 to 20 percent in 1967, and that the proportion of nonwhite youth either working or looking for work declined from 80 percent to 67 percent during this period.[5] Currie concludes that these labor market changes are sufficient to explain rising crime rates in the 1960s.

How to respond to this rising rate of crime became a matter of political concern, transforming an issue that had previously been addressed primarily as a local issue to one that became commonplace in national electoral campaigns. We can see this beginning in Richard Nixon's 1968 law-and-order presidential campaign and subsequently amplified by both Democratic and Republican leaders. These developments heralded the beginnings of the "get tough" movement, a set of policies and practices that would come to dominate criminal justice for thirty years. The origins of this movement can be traced to a growing conservative political climate of the period, with responsibility for crime being viewed more as a function of individual choices and behavior than environmental influences. In this regard, strong parallels can be seen in the transformation of societal views and policies on such issues as welfare and immigration policy.

Prior to this period, the corrections system had been guided by a philosophy of rehabilitation for most of the twentieth century. This framework could be traced back as far as the birth of the penitentiary—with the terminology being derived from the religious founders' belief in penitence—on through the establishment of the American Correctional Association in 1870 as a professional organization committed to using prison as a means of "correcting" individual behaviors. While rehabilitation was never fully supported or practiced during much of this period, it nonetheless remained as a guiding principle.

The advent of the "get tough" movement in criminal justice coincided with the growing conservative climate, but also reflected growing dissatisfaction with sentencing practice from both liberals and conservatives. Through the 1960s, most states used forms of indeterminate sentencing—for example, five to ten years for a robbery conviction—wherein the maximum sentence to be served (ten years) was set by the legislature, and the minimum (five years) was established by the judge. Depending on the particular state's parole policies, an offender sentenced to such a term might be released as early as half the minimum sentence, but might also need to serve out the full term. In states such as California, the range of the indeterminate sentence, and, hence, the discretion granted to parole boards, could be as broad as one to seventy years.

In the 1960s, liberals increasingly came to view indeterminate sentencing as subject to abuse of discretion by justice officials, often based on race, age, gender, or the particular decision maker involved. At the same time, conservatives became dissatisfied with sentencing practices, believing that judges and parole officials were abusing their discretion by handing out short sentences or releasing offenders too early from prison.

Both political camps became increasingly disillusioned with the theory and practice of rehabilitation in prison as well. Particularly influential in this regard was an article by Robert Martinson that appeared in *The Public Interest* in 1974.[6] Martinson's basic question—what works?—was drawn from a larger study he had conducted with two colleagues in which they had analyzed 231 evaluations of juvenile and adult corrections programs and concluded that "nothing works." Martinson contended that, with few and isolated exceptions, "the rehabilitative efforts that have been reported so far have had no appreciable effect on rehabilitation."[7]

Martinson's conclusions were swiftly challenged by many in the field for painting too broad a picture of failure and not paying sufficient attention to signs of success in specific instances. Martinson himself later reconsidered his broad conclusions in a journal article that received far less attention than the original; he and other researchers came to believe that some programs work for some offenders some of the time.

The original "nothing works" finding, though, was embraced by liberals, who believed that rehabilitation was impossible in a coercive setting, and by conservatives, who thought that programming in prison was a poor use of funds. Thus, along with the critique of indeterminate sentencing, this strengthened the call among both liberals and conservatives for a more determinate, or fixed, system of sentencing. Under the liberal vision, prison would be used sparingly, but there would be transparency to the process and offenders would fully understand the terms of punishment. For conservatives, fixed sentencing meant that control over sentencing would be shifted from judges to prosecutors and legislators and more people would be sent to prison for longer periods of time.

For a variety of reasons, the conservative agenda prevailed and sentencing policy has since been dramatically transformed. Almost every state has since adopted some form of mandatory sentencing, applied most frequently to drug offenses, and half the states have adopted "three strikes and you're out" policies. Of the latter, the California law is the most wide-ranging, wherein a third "strike" need not be a violent offense but simply any felony. Thus, in the 2003 challenge to the state's law in the U.S. Supreme Court, one offender's third strike involved stealing three golf clubs from a sporting goods store and the other's was stealing $153 worth of videotapes from a Kmart store. The golf club thief was sentenced to twenty-five years to life, and the videotape thief to fifty years to life. The Court declined to find that the law represented cruel and unusual punishment, deferring to the judgment of the California legislature in setting sentencing policy.

Other sentencing aspects of the "get tough" movement have contributed significantly to the rising prison population as well. These include such practices as cutbacks in parole release and the increasing imposition of life sentences (one of every eleven inmates is now serving a life sentence).

A sophisticated analysis by leading criminologists examining the 240 percent increase in the incarceration rate for state and federal prisons for the period 1980–2000 concluded that the *entire* increase was explained by policy changes rather than changes in crime rates.[8] Essentially, a series of law and practice changes resulted in more offenders being sentenced to prison and being kept there for longer periods of time.

The War on Drugs

No policy has been more instrumental in contributing to the rising inmate population than the modern-day version of the war on drugs. Initially launched in the early 1980s as a federal initiative of the Reagan administration, a complex set of drug policies and priorities have since been adopted by a broad range of federal, state, and local leaders. The primary contours of this movement can be seen in the dramatic growth of drug cases in the criminal justice system. Since 1980, drug arrests have tripled from 500,000 annually to 1.5 million, and the number of persons in prison or jail for a drug offense has increased from 40,000 to nearly 500,000.

Not only have these policies been a key factor in the escalation of the prison system, but they have also contributed to producing greater racial and ethnic disparities within the system. Government data consistently demonstrate that there are no significant differences in the rate at which different racial and ethnic groups report using drugs. African Americans, for example, represented 12 percent of drug users in 2000, the same as their share of the total population, but were 32 percent of persons arrested for drug possession. (There are no arrest data for Latinos since the FBI does not record arrests by ethnicity.) Even these disparities represent a decline from recent peaks, as the overall black proportion of arrests for drug possession had reached as high as 36 percent, and for juveniles 40 percent, in the early 1990s.

Arrest disparities, along with sentencing policies and practices, translate into disparities in imprisonment as well. Three-quarters of the drug offenders in state prison are African American or Latino. Policy changes in sentencing at both the federal and state level have contributed to these dynamics. The most well known such initiative has been the crack cocaine sentencing disparity enacted through federal legislation in 1986 and 1988. Under these laws, possession or sale of crack cocaine is treated far more harshly than powder cocaine, even though crack cocaine is pharmacologically a derivative of powder cocaine. While a five-year mandatory prison term is triggered through sale of 500 grams (about a pound) of powder cocaine, just 5 grams of crack cocaine results in the same sentence. Currently, about 80 percent of persons prosecuted for crack offenses are African American, while whites are far more likely to be charged with powder cocaine offenses.

In addition, spending priorities in the drug war have overwhelmingly favored the back-end approaches of law enforcement and incarceration over front-end strategies of prevention and treatment. Of the $20 billion in federal spending currently allocated for the drug war, about two-thirds is devoted to law enforcement and incarceration and just one-third to prevention and treatment, a ratio that has held steady through both Democratic and Republican administrations.

Another important effect of drug policies has been the increasing incarceration of women. Since 1980, the rate of increase of women's incarceration has been nearly double that for men, with drug offenses contributing to that even more so than for men. As of 2003, 29 percent of women in prison were incarcerated for a drug offense, compared to 19 percent for men, while women were much less likely than men to be incarcerated for a violent offense, 35 percent to 53 percent.

Analyses of the drug offenders in prison have revealed that most are not the kingpins of the drug trade, but rather lower-level users and sellers. A recent study of the 251,000 drug offenders in state prisons found that more than half (58 percent) had no history of violence or high-level drug activity.[9]

Racial and Ethnic Disparities

While the war on drugs has played a key role in exacerbating racial and ethnic disparities in the justice system, these dynamics are broadly shaped by a range of policies and practices throughout the justice system. These include:

Racial profiling. Increasing documentation in recent years has demonstrated the prevalence of decision making by some law enforcement agencies that relies on racial and ethnic identifiers as primary targeting tools. In Volusia County, Florida, in the late 1980s more than 70 percent of traffic stops made by local police were of African American or Hispanic drivers, although they represented only 5 percent of the drivers on the county's highways.[10]

Indigent defense representation. Defendants of color are disproportionately low-income and therefore generally represented by assigned counsel in court proceedings. While many such lawyers are skilled and dedicated, in far too many cases they are placed in situations where they are subject to unreasonable caseloads and receive inadequate fees. The state of Virginia, for example, provides a maximum of just $1,096 for representation of felony cases that can result in a life sentence.[11]

Prosecutorial bias. Research on prosecutorial decision making is limited, but there is evidence that racial dynamics play a role in how cases are handled by the justice system. A review of research in the area suggests that prosecutors stereotype cases according to case-specific characteristics, by making racially biased assessments of the credibility of the victim and offender as witnesses. Nonwhite victims tend to be considered less credible witnesses, while white victims, especially of nonwhite defendants, are considered highly credible.[12]

Sentencing.   In most parts of the country, the Jim Crow practice of all-white courtrooms convicting and sentencing defendants of color to harsh prison terms is a relic of the past. But considerations of race, whether intended or not, still exert a role in sentencing outcomes. Often this is a complex process, whereby race in combination with other factors such as gender and employment results in black offenders receiving harsher sentences than similarly situated white offenders. A comprehensive review of the literature conducted for the National Institute of Justice concluded that "race and ethnicity do play an important role in contemporary sentencing decisions. Black and Hispanic offenders—and particularly those who are young, male, or unemployed—are more likely than their white counterparts to be sentenced to prison; in some jurisdictions, they also receive longer sentences or differential benefits from guideline departures than do similarly situated white offenders." [13]

Within the juvenile justice system, racial disparities are even more severe than in the adult system. An overview of processing and dynamics conducted by the National Council on Crime and Delinquency documented the "cumulative disadvantage of minority youth across the nation." [14] Comparing African American youth with white youth, the researchers found that African American youth were more likely to be detained after referral to juvenile court, more likely to be waived to adult court, less likely to receive probation, and more likely to be incarcerated in state prisons.

Effects of Incarceration: Individuals in Prison

Regardless of whether or not one believes that current levels of incarceration are appropriate, the community at large has an interest in the experience of people while in prison and after their release. Nearly 700,000 offenders are released from prison each year, of whom two-thirds are rearrested within three years, and half are imprisoned again.[15] So, for reasons of public safety, the community has a stake in the effect of prison on the likelihood that released prisoners will have the resources and skills to become productive members of the community.

People leaving prison carry with them the stigma of incarceration, most notably in terms of the obstacles this brings in the job market. People with felony convictions are also formally denied access to many jobs due to a host of occupational and licensing restrictions. Some of these restrictions are premised on a public safety rationale—for example, policies that restrict convicted child molesters from working in daycare centers. But many others—limitations on barbering or asbestos removal, for example—have no obvious connection to public safety and result merely in overly restrictive access to higher-paying jobs for ex-offenders.

Policies enacted in recent years, along with budgetary priorities, have further reduced the prospects for successful reentry into the community. Examining data from the two most recent inmate surveys conducted by the Department of Justice indicates that prison inmates in 1997 were less likely to have participated in educational or vocational programming than were prisoners in 1991.[16]

New legislation at the federal level, much of it related to the war on drugs, has erected additional barriers to successful reintegration and access to opportunity for people with felony convictions. These include policies that permanently deny access to welfare benefits (although states may opt out of this requirement), exclude people with drug convictions from living in public housing, and deny federal financial aid for higher education. Ironically, these policies apply *only* to persons convicted of drug offenses, and not the many other crimes that most people would classify as more violent or serious.

People with felony convictions are not only restricted from full access to economic and employment benefits, but are closed out of the body politic as well through the loss of voting rights (Table 4-3). In forty-eight states and the District of Columbia, persons in prison are ineligible to vote (Maine and Vermont permit inmates to vote); in thirty-five of these states persons on probation and/or parole are also ineligible to vote; and in eleven states persons with a felony conviction can lose the right to vote even after completing a sentence, and often for life.[17] For example, an 18-year-old in Kentucky or Virginia convicted of a first-time nonviolent drug possession felony will be permanently disenfranchised. The only means for such a person to regain the right to vote is through a gubernatorial restoration of rights, a cumbersome and relatively little used process in most states.

As a result of the dramatic increase in the use of incarceration, an estimated 5 million Americans are ineligible to vote as a result of a current or previous felony conviction.[18] Due to the racial disparities in the criminal justice system, the effect of these policies falls most heavily on people of color. One of every eight African American males is ineligible to vote. While data on Latinos are often incomplete, recent analyses suggest that they experience disproportionate rates of disenfranchisement in many states as well.[19]

In addition to the impact of these policies on democratic participation, there is also evidence that disenfranchisement works counter to the goal of public safety. Using data on reported criminal behavior and voting from a sample of Minnesota youth, researchers Christopher Uggen and Jeff Manza found that among persons who had a previous arrest history, 27 percent of the nonvoters were rearrested over a four-year period, compared to 12 percent of voters.[20] Thus, persons who

TABLE 4-3
Disenfranchisement categories under state law

State	Prison	Probation	Parole	Post-Sentence All	Post-Sentence Partial
Alabama	X	X	X		X[b]
Alaska	X	X	X		
Arizona	X	X	X		X[c]
Arkansas[a]	X	X	X		
California	X		X		
Colorado	X		X		
Connecticut	X		X		
Delaware	X	X	X		X[d]
District of Columbia	X				
Florida	X	X	X		X[b]
Georgia	X	X	X		
Hawaii	X				
Idaho	X	X	X		
Illinois	X				
Indiana	X				
Iowa	X	X	X		
Kansas	X	X	X		
Kentucky	X	X	X	X	
Louisiana	X	X	X		
Maine					
Maryland	X	X	X		
Massachusetts	X				
Michigan	X				
Minnesota	X	X	X		
Mississippi	X	X	X		X[b]
Missouri	X	X	X		
Montana	X				
Nebraska	X	X	X		X[e]
Nevada	X	X	X		X[f]
New Hampshire	X				
New Jersey	X	X	X		
New Mexico	X	X	X		
New York	X		X		

(*continued on facing page*)

State	Prison	Probation	Parole	Post-Sentence All	Post-Sentence Partial
North Carolina	X	X	X		
North Dakota	X				
Ohio	X				
Oklahoma	X	X	X		
Oregon	X				
Pennsylvania	X				
Rhode Island	X				
South Carolina	X	X	X		
South Dakota	X		X		
Tennessee	X	X	X		X[b]
Texas	X	X	X		
Utah	X				
Vermont					
Virginia	X	X	X	X	
Washington[a]	X	X	X		
West Virginia	X	X	X		
Wisconsin	X	X	X		
Wyoming	X	X	X		X[d]
Total U.S.	49	30	35	2	9

[a] Failure to satisfy obligation associated with convictions may result in post-sentence loss of voting rights.
[b] Certain offenses.
[c] Second felony.
[d] Five years.
[e] Two years.
[f] Except first-time nonviolent.

are engaged with the community in positive ways, such as through electoral participation, appear to be less likely to become involved in antisocial activities.

Community Impact of Incarceration

While an expanding criminal justice system clearly affects the life prospects and opportunities available to persons with criminal convictions, growing evidence suggests that high levels of incarceration affect communities as a whole. Most directly affected are the families of prisoners. An estimated 1.5 million children have a parent behind bars, and among black children the figure is one in fourteen.[21] These children are now growing up with the shame and stigma of parental incarceration, along with the loss of financial and psychological support of a parent.

These problems are particularly acute for the growing numbers of women in prison, two-thirds of whom have children under the age of 18. Those who are fortunate will have a relative who can care for the children while the mother is in prison. Those less so will see their children placed in foster care. The numbers of children in this category are likely to expand due to the effects of the Adoption and Safe Families Act of 1997, which authorizes states to initiate the termination of parental rights when a child has been placed in foster care for fifteen of the last twenty-two months. The effects of this legislation will be seen over time, since most prison terms, including those for drug offenses, result in sentences of more than fifteen months.

In low-income neighborhoods incarceration policies increasingly contribute to the development of single-parent families as well. This phenomenon is related to the gender gap that results as a function of high rates of incarceration for young men in particular. In some neighborhoods in Washington, D.C., for example, there are now just sixty-two adult men for every one hundred women.[22] (These rates are also a function of men serving in the military and higher rates of homicide, but incarceration plays a significant role.) Developments such as this should provide pause to those who promote marriage as a key policy to confront poverty and related ills. Many women in low-income communities who might otherwise get married, both to have a partner and to aid in child-rearing, are limited in their ability to do so because there literally are not enough men around to meet these needs.

Emerging research demonstrates that the gender gap may contribute to negative health indicators as well. In Onondaga County, New York, African American women have rates of AIDS infection 12.5 times, and Hispanic women nearly 9 times, those of non-Hispanic white women. Researchers examining these disparities suggest that high rates of incarceration of black males contribute to these health outcomes both by creating a gender gap and due to higher rates of HIV infection in prison. They note that "disproportionate incarceration both limits the number of individuals available as intimate partners and increases the proportion of infected individuals in the community because individuals who unknowingly become infected while in prison return to their home communities and may in turn infect their sexual partners." [23]

Low-income communities are also affected by the diversion of resources, as funding is directed to prisons that could otherwise be used to address deep-seated social and economic problems. An assessment of the fiscal cost of incarceration in densely populated neighborhoods of Brooklyn, New York, finds that there are thirty-five "million-dollar blocks" in the borough, where taxpayers fund $1 million in prison costs each year just for the incarceration costs of people from that block.

The political influence of high-incarceration communities is affected by imprisonment policies through two means. First, high rates of felony disenfranchisement affect not just individuals but the ability of communities to function as a voting bloc. A study of voter registration in Atlanta documented a registration gap of ten percentage points between black males and other groups, but found that two-thirds of this gap was a result of disenfranchisement policies. [24] These communities are further disadvantaged by the counting of prisoners as part of the census. People in prison are counted as residing in the location of the prison, not their home communities, even though they are not functioning in any significant sense as members of the prison community. The effect of this methodology, though, is to artificially increase the population of the often rural prison towns with a population that is largely composed of people of color from urban communities. The population shift then results in greater political clout and resources for rural communities, at the expense of the urban neighborhoods from which many prisoners come. One study estimates that each prisoner brings in between $50 and $250 annually to the local government where he or she is housed.[25] Thus, a new five-hundred-bed prison may yield about $50,000 in annual revenue.

Finally, any crime control impact that incarceration may provide may be muted by the effects of high rates of imprisonment on informal means of social control in a community. Studies in Tallahassee, Florida, by criminologists Dina Rose and Todd Clear find that there may be a "tipping point" in the interaction between incarceration and public safety.[26] At relatively low levels of incarceration, imprisonment can provide some benefits for public safety through incapacitating persons who present a threat to the community. But at high levels, incarceration can destabilize communities as people cycle in and out of prison on a regular basis. This dynamic is particularly significant as increasing numbers of low-level offenders are sent to prison. A low-level drug offender has broken the law, but he or she may also be a parent, a worker, a consumer, or a child-care provider. So, incarcerating that person removes the potential for committing crime, but also disrupts the positive bonds and connections to family and community.

Policies to Create Opportunity

Criminal justice policy of the past three decades has in many respects served to limit access to opportunity for vulnerable populations. While prison is clearly one element of a system of providing public safety, serious questions remain regarding the scale of imprisonment and the balance between the use of prison and other means of crime control, both within and outside the criminal justice system.

There are nonetheless a number of developments in recent years which suggest that a different orientation is possible, one that addresses both crime and the causes of crime and promotes policies to produce fewer victimizations. These changes have come about as a result of several factors. First, the fiscal challenges faced by many states have led to a reconsideration of spending trade-offs between prisons and priorities such as higher education. Whether or not it was ever a good idea to pursue massive prison expansion, it is no longer possible to build both prisons *and* colleges. Second, the declining crime rate since the early 1990s has made discussions of crime and punishment less politicized than was the case a decade ago, and consequently less subject to political demagoguery. Finally, the implementation of a variety of alternative sentencing and treatment programs has provided judges and communities with greater confidence in the viability of nonprison options for many offenders.

In order to realize the potential of this altered climate, we need to build on the models developed in recent years as well as create new policies and structures that can promote the linkage between public safety and increased opportunity. A framework for such an approach should include the following.

Expand Community Policing

Since the mid-1980s many law enforcement agencies have adopted aspects of a community-policing strategy that employs a problem-solving framework for addressing community conflicts. This involves a shift in orientation from measuring success by the number of arrests to one that evaluates the degree to which problems are resolved. Such a model can aid crime control efforts while also minimizing the potential for police-community conflict that has erupted regularly in New York City and other urban areas.

Community policing has also demonstrated its potential to have a sustained effect on crime rates. We can see this most strikingly in a comparison of homicide rates in New York City and San Diego. The substantial decline in murder rates in New York since the early 1990s has been the subject of much popular press attention, encouraged in large part by former mayor Rudolph Giuliani and former police chief William Bratton. While there is still debate regarding the extent to which the city's often heavy-handed policing efforts were responsible for the crime decline, the drop in murder rates—68 percent from 1991 to 2005—is striking. But little noticed is the fact that San Diego—which was one of the first large cities to adopt a community-policing model of crime control that emphasized improving neighborhood environments—achieved an even greater crime reduction, 73 percent, during this period. And in contrast to New York, citizen complaints regarding police conduct declined for much of this period.

Promote Police-Community Partnerships

The community-policing model has also been an element of the Boston model of addressing juvenile violence. In response to a spate of juvenile homicides in the early 1990s, criminal justice practitioners joined with community leaders to develop a multipronged approach to stemming youth violence. Using a mix of enforcement strategies, prevention programs, and interventions with at-risk families, the partnership achieved an 80 percent decline in homicides for individuals under the age of 25 over the course of the 1990s. Unfortunately, these achievements were not sustained over time, a development that many attribute to complacency regarding the success that had been achieved and that speaks to the need for ongoing leadership and support.

Expand the Use of Treatment-Based Alternatives to Incarceration

The drug court movement, initially begun with demonstration projects in 1989 in Miami and Oakland, operates under a premise that the community is often better served when persons with substance abuse problems are placed in treatment programs rather than in prison. Specialized courts with access to treatment resources divert persons charged with drug possession or other offenses with an underlying drug problem into court-supervised treatment programs as an alternative to incarceration. The National Center for Drug Court Professionals estimates that there are now 1,500 such courts in operation or being planned. Despite this, nearly every sentencing judge will acknowledge the gaps in treatment options, in both quantity and variety, for appropriate defendants. Drug treatment is not a panacea for crime, but a substantial body of evidence demonstrates the cost-effectiveness of such programs and their potential for expansion.

Reintroduce the Appropriate Use of Discretion in the Criminal Justice System

One of the hallmarks of the "get tough" movement of recent decades has been the adoption of determinate sentencing policies, such as mandatory sentencing, that eliminate judicial discretion in a range of cases. These policies have been demonstrated to be unfair, ineffective, and overly broad in their application to less serious offenders. There are now encouraging signs of a reconsideration of these policies. In the federal system, the Supreme Court declared the mandatory nature of the federal sentencing guidelines to be unconstitutional in its 2005 *Booker* decision, thus granting judges greater latitude in imposing sentences. And at the state level, states such as Connecticut, Michigan, and Mississippi have scaled back or repealed their mandatory sentencing provisions in favor of enhanced judicial discretion.

Reduce the Length of Prison Terms

The record rate of incarceration in the United States is a function not only of too many people sentenced to prison but of longer prison terms as well. During the period 1990–1999, the average time served in prison for first-time releases rose by 32 percent. Increasing the amount of time served produces no gains in deterrence or recidivism, yet is costly to taxpayers and contributes to financial and emotional hardships for the families of prisoners. Policymakers should establish a goal of reducing the average time served by at least one-third—a conservative goal since that would still mark U.S. sentencing practices as more severe than other industrialized nations. This can be achieved through policy initiatives by legislative bodies and sentencing commissions, as well as by modifying community supervision policies.

Eliminate Barriers to Employment for Ex-offenders

City councils in Minneapolis, Boston, and San Francisco have enacted policies that restrict inappropriate access to criminal records by potential employers. In an effort to address the societal stigma against persons with criminal records, these initiatives generally prohibit city agencies and/or private employers from asking for information about arrest or conviction records on an initial job application. Once an applicant has been deemed to have met the requirements for employment, employers may then request information on criminal records. Exceptions are often made for appropriate job-related conduct, such as a conviction for embezzlement for an accounting position applicant. Limiting the impact of criminal records is particularly significant in light of recent research showing that by seven years after release from prison, the risk of an offender committing a new crime is almost indistinguishable from that of a person with no criminal record.[27]

Enhance Community Participation Through Electoral Participation

Since 1997, sixteen states have enacted provisions designed to expand the electorate by removing various restrictions on voting for people with felony convictions.[28] These have included a 1997 Texas bill signed by then-governor George W. Bush that removed a two-year waiting period after completion of sentence and a complete repeal of the lifetime voting ban for people who have completed sentences in New Mexico. Public support for such reforms has been most evident by a 2006 statewide vote in Rhode Island that endorsed the expansion of voting rights to persons on probation or parole. Guaranteeing the right to vote—and providing information and support in registration—to all citizens regardless of a felony conviction would build a healthier democracy as well as engage formerly incarcerated people in positive community institutions.

Expand Restorative Justice Initiatives

While the U.S. court system functions to make determinations of guilt or innocence, it is not necessarily charged with, or capable of, resolving the underlying relationships and conflicts that lead to crime. Recognizing this problem, many jurisdictions have begun experimenting with various types of problem-solving courts and restorative justice programs. The basic theme underlying these approaches is that the process of understanding the victim-offender relationship is key to resolving crime problems and reducing victimization. Courts and community groups have partnered in increasing numbers of jurisdictions to fashion sentences that provide for both offender accountability and victim compensation. Not only do such initiatives hold the potential for more effective resolution of underlying conflict, but compared to an often bureaucratic court system they provide greater levels of closure for victims.

Address Racial Disparity in the Criminal Justice System Proactively

In various areas of public policy, policymakers employ means of assessing the projected effects of new initiatives. Thus, environmental-impact statements are produced to analyze the effect of housing development on wildlife habitat and fiscal-impact statements provide projections of the long-term costs of various energy policies. Similarly, legislative bodies should enact a requirement that racial-impact statements be prepared for any legislation that would affect the size and racial distribution of a jurisdiction's prison population. In the notorious case of the crack cocaine sentencing disparities, for example, had members of Congress been required to assess the effects of the law prior to its adoption, a public discussion could have focused on whether there were alternative measures of responding to the drug problem that would not exacerbate racial disparities in incarceration.

Enhance Reentry Programming

The growth of incarceration results not only in more people being admitted to prison, but in growing numbers of people being released from prison as well. Nearly 700,000 offenders leave federal and state prisons each year to return to the community. With two-thirds of this group being rearrested within three years, community safety is significantly affected by how prepared prisoners are to reenter the community. This understandably has led to a shift in attention to both programming needs in prison and transition services during the first months that offenders come home. Congress has provided initial planning and implementation grants to the states to develop frameworks for addressing this growing need, but an effective reentry strategy will require reentry planning as a component of sentencing as well as a large-scale shift of resources from institutions to community-based transitional services.

Provide Vouchers for Juvenile Services

Conservative advocates of educational reform have promoted the concept of vouchers to permit families of children in low-performing schools to transfer their children to private schools. Many people view this as a thinly veiled attack on the public school system, but a voucher system might instead work well for young people in trouble with the law. Consider that when teenagers from well-off families are caught for drug or property offenses, they rarely are prosecuted by the justice system, but rather are placed in substance abuse or counseling programs. Why, then, could we not issue vouchers to the families of low-income kids who get in trouble in order to allow them to access similar services?

To implement such a policy, a jurisdiction could set aside the amount of funding that would normally be used to process a case through the juvenile justice system—generally hundreds, if not thousands, of dollars—and issue vouchers for the child's family. These could then be used to purchase services that would not otherwise be available. Thus, a teenager who has a substance abuse problem would not need to get on a waiting list for a publicly supported program, but could enter into a high-quality treatment program. A learning-disabled student might need to engage a private tutor for educational support. Or a family could decide that private counseling would aid in coping with a difficult teenager. By doing so, we could also begin to address the inequities in the two-tiered system of justice that differentiates the societal response to behavioral problems in low-income communities from communities with adequate resources. To the extent that such a model could be developed, the feasibility of extending it to the adult court system could be explored as well.

Promote Justice Reinvestment

As previously described, the concentrated nature of incarceration policy has resulted in enormous amounts of public resources being allocated for incarceration of people from low-income communities. If we think of these funds as investments in public safety, it becomes clear that they are skewed to the back-end institution of prison at the expense of front-end investments in strengthening families and neighborhood networks. In order to address this imbalance we should advocate for policymaking and funding structures that treat these issues not as separate budgets for "corrections" or "prevention," but rather as public safety problems to be addressed through a comprehensive strategy. For example, if we were to reduce prison terms in a million-dollar block by just 10 percent, that would free up $100,000 in funds that could be invested in community policing, drug treatment, job placement, and other services to promote opportunity. Different communities might prefer various allocations of resources to address these problems, but this is precisely the type of discussion that should take place to promote locally based public safety initiatives.

The above programs and approaches are illustrative of ways in which we could reshape our approach to crime and justice. Initiatives such as these hold the promise of both reducing the scale of imprisonment and promoting more effective public safety outcomes. But a true framework for promoting safety needs to incorporate a framework that goes beyond the criminal justice system to recognize that building strong families and communities is also the most effective crime prevention program since it both creates opportunity and increases the efficacy of informal means of social control. Thus, for example, investments in Head Start programs or prenatal care are means of improving the health and welfare of low-income families, but also provide measurable long-term benefits in reduced crime. A national dialogue on the interrelationships among these various programs and policies would provide a healthy beginning for a successful public safety strategy.

5

Why Health-Care Equity Is Essential to Opportunity—and How to Get There

Brian D. Smedley

When it comes to health care, Americans face a profound contradiction between belief and reality. We believe that all are entitled to a basic level of security and other protections necessary to human dignity. Without this security, it is impossible to access society's other rights and responsibilities, or to enjoy full opportunity. Access to high-quality health care is among the most important of these elements of security.

Tens of millions of Americans, however, experience significant problems trying to access health care, and many others receive poor-quality care that doesn't meet their needs. These problems constrict opportunity, most often among groups that have historically lacked opportunity, and carry a heavy human and economic toll. An inability to pay for care—on the rise as the number of people who lack health insurance increases—places millions at risk for poor health and financial ruin. Inadequate health care limits people's ability to take advantage of educational or work opportunities, or to participate in the economic and social life of the nation, particularly among those who face health challenges. Health-care inequality therefore affects all Americans, both directly and indirectly, as it corrosively weakens health care across communities and contributes to higher health-care costs.

This chapter focuses on the causes and consequences of health-care inequality in the United States. It defines and distinguishes between inequality in health status, health-care access, and health-care quality; this distinction is important, because any serious effort to eliminate health status gaps must focus on strategies that are largely outside of the purview of health care. Finally, it draws upon human rights and civil rights standards to point to solutions to equalize health care for all, particularly those who have historically suffered from inadequate care.

Defining Health Status and Health-Care Inequality

Health Status Inequality

The nation's health status is improving overall as life expectancy has increased and overall mortality has declined.[1] But gaps in health status between racial and ethnic groups and socioeconomic groups haven't narrowed significantly in nearly a generation. Some racial and ethnic minorities—specifically, African Americans, American Indians, Alaska Natives, and Pacific Islanders—have dramatically poorer health than the nation as a whole. These groups have higher rates of infant mortality, chronic and infectious diseases, and lower life expectancy than national averages.[2] And while some racial and ethnic minority groups are healthy relative to national averages, data often mask considerable heterogeneity within racial and ethnic groups. For example, Vietnamese American women experience the highest rates of cervical cancer among any U.S. racial, ethnic, or socioeconomic group, and first-generation Hispanic women tend to have better health than similarly situated second- and third-generation Hispanic women, whose health status approaches that of some of the least healthy groups.[3] Whites who live in poverty are also disproportionately burdened with poor health, although the social and economic factors that contribute to these disparities differ from those of racial and ethnic minorities.[4] And while women can expect to live longer than men, their longer life span is offset by higher rates of functional impairment and disability.[5]

These examples of health status inequality—differences in the toll of disease, disability, and mortality among population groups—reflect long-standing patterns of social and economic disadvantage. The causes of health status inequality are complex and multifactorial but are strongly related to opportunity in other dimensions, such as housing, education, discrimination, and economic mobility.[6] For example, a large body of research demonstrates a strong linear relationship between income, education, and health status. This socioeconomic gradient occurs at all levels, as the incidence of disease, disability, and mortality generally declines at each ascending step of the socioeconomic ladder. Job prestige and power are also inversely correlated with health status. The Whitehall study in Britain, for example, which has followed thousands of British civil servants for more than two decades, reveals that mortality among clerical and manual workers was about three and a half times higher than for senior administrators and managers. Recent analysis of Whitehall data shows that employees with little control over their working environment face a significantly higher risk of heart disease than those with authority to influence their job conditions. This remains true even after controlling for differences in known health risks, such as low social support, smoking, inadequate exercise, and poor diet. And this health inequality occurs despite the fact that all residents of the United Kingdom have access to a universal health-care system.[7]

To that end, many of the papers in this volume offer important prescriptions for reducing health status inequality. For example, given the relationship between educational attainment and health status, many in public health are concluding that improving educational opportunities may be the most important public health intervention. Linda Darling-Hammond's essay demonstrates that inequality in the U.S. K–12 public education system replicates existing socioeconomic hierarchies, but that these effects can be ameliorated by a more equitable distribution of educational resources. Racial and ethnic residential segregation is another fundamental cause of health status inequality. Segregated communities often suffer from poorer-quality schools, higher levels of environmental degradation, inadequate food resources (including higher concentrations of fast-food establishments and fewer major grocery stores carrying fresh, low-cost fruits and vegetables), and poorer community resources.[8] Phil Tegeler's essay demonstrates that strategies to address neighborhood segregation can reduce these risks and improve opportunity.

There is strong reason to be concerned that, rather than taking the kinds of steps noted above, the United States is headed in the other direction. Growing wage and wealth inequality, educational inequality, dependence upon incarceration to solve social problems, and other sources of unequal opportunity must be reduced to meaningfully close the health status gap.

While these "upstream" social and economic determinants of health lie largely outside of the health-care arena, high-quality health care can ameliorate some of the effects of inequality in other dimensions of U.S. life. Improving and equalizing the quality of care is therefore a critical component of an overall strategy to expand opportunity for all. Moreover, because health-care inequality problems often mirror prevailing social and economic disadvantage, all stakeholders in the health-care delivery enterprise must work toward solutions to inequality.

Health-Care Access Inequality

Health-care access inequality occurs when racial and ethnic minorities, low-income populations, immigrants, those who aren't proficient in English, and others experience greater barriers to attaining needed health care relative to more advantaged groups. These barriers occur as a result of a lack of health insurance or being underinsured,[9] an inability to meet out-of-pocket costs,[10] geographic barriers,[11] and linguistic or cultural barriers.[12] Evidence demonstrates that these health-care access barriers are increasing, threatening the health and financial well-being of millions of Americans.

The number of uninsured Americans has risen steadily over the past thirty years to unprecedented levels today. Nearly 47 million Americans lack health insurance, and over 87 million Americans were uninsured at some point over the last two years.[13] The consequences of uninsurance—in both human and economic terms—are staggering. Over 18,000 Americans die prematurely each year because they lack health insurance.[14] Sixty million Americans face financial insecurity and a greater risk for poor health due to a lack of health insurance.[15] The Institute of Medicine estimates that the poorer health and shortened life spans attributable to uninsurance costs the nation between $65 billion and $130 billion.[16] And a recent report by Families USA demonstrates that in 2005, average premium costs for family health insurance coverage provided by private employers rose by $922 due to the cost of care for the uninsured, while premiums for individual coverage cost an extra $341.[17]

Racial and ethnic minority and immigrant communities are disproportionately uninsured. For example:

- While about 21 percent of white Americans were uninsured at any point in 2002, communities of color were more likely to be uninsured at any point (including 28 percent of African Americans, 44 percent of Hispanic Americans, 24 percent of Asian Americans and Pacific Islanders, and 33 percent of American Indians and Alaska Natives) and are more likely to be dependent upon public sources of health insurance.[18]
- While Hispanic children constitute less than one-fifth of children in the United States, they represent over one-third of uninsured children.[19] And among children in fair or poor health who lack insurance (nearly 570,000 children in 2002), over two-thirds are Hispanic.[20]
- More than 11 million immigrants were uninsured in 2003, contributing to one-quarter of the U.S. uninsured.[21] Between 1998 and 2003 immigrants accounted for 86 percent of the growth in the uninsured population.[22]
- Foreign-born people are 2.5 times more likely than the native-born to lack health insurance, a gap that remains unchanged since 1993.[23]

Regular Source of Health Care

Having a regular source of health care—a local physician, clinic, or health center that patients can consider their "medical home"—is important, particularly for individuals who face or are at risk for chronic illness. When patients are able to see a health-care provider consistently, they are better able to build trusting relationships, ask questions, and give and receive information. Patients who lack a regular source of health care often report miscommunication, misdiagnoses, and greater frustration about their ability to receive needed care.[24] The uninsured and underinsured, many racial and ethnic minorities, people who are not proficient in English, those who live in rural communities, and those who have low incomes are more likely to report not having a regular source of health care.[25] Yet in this respect, the gap between both racial and ethnic groups and income groups is growing.

- African Americans, Hispanics, and the poor and near poor of all racial and ethnic groups are more likely than white nonpoor groups to face barriers to having a regular source of health care. These gaps have increased since 2000. Over 42 percent of Hispanic poor and 37 percent of Hispanic nonpoor people lacked a regular source of health care in 2001 and 2002, an increase of more than 30 percent and 18 percent, respectively, since 1995 and 1996.[26]

- During this same period, the percentage of poor and near-poor African Americans and whites without a regular source of health care went largely unchanged. But these groups were up to 75 percent more likely than nonpoor African Americans and whites to lack a regular source of health care in 2001 and 2002.[27]

- The percentage of Hispanics from all income groups who lacked a regular source of health care increased between 1993 and 2002, despite a 15 percent decline over the same period in the ranks of white poor individuals who lacked a regular source of health care.[28]

Language Barriers

More than 46 million people in the United States speak a language other than English. Of those, more than 35 million speak English "well" or "very well," but over 10 million speak the language "not well" or "not at all." [29] Individuals with limited English proficiency are less likely than those with strong English-language skills to have a regular source of primary care or to receive preventive care. Moreover, they tend to be less satisfied with the care they receive, are more likely to report overall problems with care, and may be at increased risk of experiencing medical errors.[30] The quality of their health care therefore depends on the ability of medical professionals to effectively communicate. But many health-care organizations do not provide adequate interpretation services.

- Nearly half of Latinos who are primary speakers of Spanish report having difficulty communicating with doctors or other health-care providers because of language barriers.[31]
- Over one in five non-English-speaking patients avoid seeking medical help altogether because of language barriers.[32]

Health-Care Quality Disparities

A substantial body of evidence demonstrates that racial and ethnic minorities receive a lower quality and intensity of health care than white patients, even when they are insured at the same levels and present with the same types of health problems. Below are a few examples from the research literature.

- Insured African American patients are less likely than insured whites to receive many potentially lifesaving or life-extending procedures, particularly high-tech care, such as cardiac catheterization,[33] bypass graft surgery,[34] or kidney transplantation.[35]

- Black cancer patients fail to get the same combinations of surgical and chemotherapy treatments that white patients with the same disease presentation receive.[36]
- African American heart patients are less likely than white patients to receive diagnostic procedures, revascularization procedures, and thrombolytic therapy, even when they have similar patient characteristics.[37]
- Even routine care suffers. Black and Latino patients are less likely than whites to receive aspirin upon discharge following a heart attack, to receive appropriate care for pneumonia, and to have pain—such as the kind resulting from broken bones—appropriately treated.[38]
- Minorities are more likely to receive undesirable treatment than whites, such as limb amputation for diabetes.[39]

The Causes of Health-Care Inequality

Many factors contribute to inequitable health care in the United States. In general, these factors are attributable to the way that health care is financed and structured in the United States and to aspects of the clinical encounter, including cultural and linguistic barriers in health-care systems and the interaction of patients and providers.

Financial and Structural Factors

In its landmark series on the causes and consequences of uninsurance, the Institute of Medicine concluded that the availability and quality of health care in the United States suffer when large segments of the population lack health insurance.[40] Uncompensated health-care costs are shifted to those who have insurance, contributing to rising overall health-care costs. Employers, still the predominant source of private health insurance benefits for Americans, are increasingly unable or unwilling to offer health benefits. Even when health insurance benefits are offered, many employees cannot afford to enroll; over half of workers do not enroll in employer insurance plans because they are too costly.[41] Absent action, these trends are likely only to worsen: insurance premiums have increased at a higher rate than overall inflation and workers' earnings for most of the last fifteen years.[42] And since 2000, premiums for family coverage have increased by 59 percent, compared with a 9.7 percent increase in inflation and 12.3 percent increase in workers' earnings.[43]

The crisis of health insurance disproportionately hurts low-income families and communities of color, in no small part because health insurance in the United States remains linked to employment. Persistent racial and ethnic employment stratification contributes to racial and ethnic gaps in the kind and quality of health insurance coverage. Higher-paying jobs tend to offer more comprehensive health benefit packages, while lower-paying jobs—jobs disproportionately occupied by people of color—tend to offer only limited health benefits, if offered at all, that are often accompanied by high cost-sharing arrangements with employees.

But as the research above demonstrates, health-care inequality persists even among the insured. Insured minority patients tend to be covered by plans that are less comprehensive and more restrictive than those of insured white patients.[44] Minorities are more likely to receive care in emergency rooms and lower-quality health-care facilities—the by-product of residential segregation and economic pressures that reward the concentration of services in outer suburbs and wealthier communities and create disincentives for practice in urban centers. For example, African American and Hispanic patients are nearly twice as likely as whites to report having a "non-mainstream" usual source of care (for example, a hospital-based provider, rather than a private physi-cian).[45] And nearly one in five Latinas (18 percent) and one in ten African American women reported not seeking needed health care in the last year owing to transportation problems, compared to 5 percent of white women.[46]

These economic pressures can sustain a form of "medical apartheid"—that is, separate and unequal care for low-income and minority patients.[47] Evidence suggests that these problems persist. For example, physicians who serve predom-inantly racial and ethnic minority patients are less likely to possess board certification and have greater difficulties ac-cessing high-quality specialists, diagnostic imaging, and non-emergency admission of their patients to the hospital than physicians who serve predominantly nonminority patients.[48] And the geographic segregation of services contributes to the problem. For example, a study of the availability of pain medication revealed that only one in four pharmacies located in predominantly nonwhite neighborhoods carried adequate supplies, compared to 72 percent of pharmacies in pre-dominantly white neighborhoods.[49] This is potentially get-ting worse with the rise of "boutique" health-care clinics in the outer suburbs and other high-profit areas.[50]

The Clinical Encounter

Aspects of the clinical encounter—the interaction between patients, their providers, and the health systems in which care is delivered—can play a powerful role in contributing to health-care inequality. Patients and providers bring a range of expectations, preferences, and biases to the clinical en-counter that can be expressed both directly and indirectly. For example, at least part of the disparity results from biases and stereotypes that health-care providers may carry about racial and ethnic minorities. Experimental studies confirm that physicians can hold a host of negative beliefs about minority patients. They are presumed to be more likely to abuse drugs or alcohol and to be less educated. They aren't expected to comply with physicians' instructions, to want an active lifestyle, or to participate in rehabilitation if prescribed. Doctors are likely to consider white patients more "pleasant" and "rational" than black patients, and to prefer white patients as "the kind of person I could see myself being friends with." These kinds of stereotypes and biases are often unconscious, the Institute of Medicine reported, but nonetheless they can influence physicians' decisions regarding when and what treatments to offer.[51] Minority patients, whose own beliefs and preferences may lead them to refuse certain types of care or fail to follow doctors' instructions, may also share a role.[52]

Eliminating Health-Care Inequality

The United States is the last modern, industrialized nation to adopt a universal health-care program. Health insurance coverage is primarily provided by employers, but as benefit costs rise employers are declining to offer coverage or are purchasing plans that require greater employee cost sharing. Moreover, health insurance coverage is increasingly unequal, disproportionately hurting those who need health care the most—particularly racial and ethnic minorities, children, and lower-income women and their families. For example, less than half of low-wage workers have employer-provided health insurance from their own employer or a family member's employer, and female low-wage workers are half as likely as male low-wage workers to receive health insurance from their employer.[53]

Universal Access to Comprehensive Health Insurance

Health-care access inequality must be tackled by state and federal efforts to develop a universally accessible, comprehensive, and equitable health-care system. The most cost-effective way to achieve this goal is by pooling risk as broadly as possible in a common, comprehensive health insurance system—a national, single-payer health insurance plan. Such an approach allows patients to choose their health-care provider and ensures that the delivery of care remains in public and private systems while more fairly allocating health-care resources. For example, by allowing employers and individuals to buy into Medicare, policymakers can create a "Medicare for all" national single-payer plan. Medicare is more efficient than private plans because of its low administrative costs (less than 5 percent, a figure four to five times lower than most estimates of administrative costs in private health plans). And because Medicare is a federal program, subject to the Civil Rights Act of 1964 (particularly Title VI, which prohibits discrimination on the basis of race, ethnicity, language status, and other factors), it contains mechanisms of accountability that can be expanded and enhanced to ensure that inequitable health care is addressed.

In the United States, however, powerful private-interest groups—specifically, health insurance companies, pharmaceutical companies, and others that derive great profits from the status quo—have successfully fought against efforts to recast health care as a human and civil right available for all, rather than a consumer good—a commodity that is available on the market only for those who can afford it. Nonetheless, because of the United States' strong market orientation, it is often difficult for policymakers and the public to think outside the market framework. It is therefore often more politically pragmatic to focus on piecemeal policy solutions that seek to expand public health insurance programs while at the same time encouraging private-sector reforms to expand coverage for all. From an equity perspective, these efforts should:

- Ensure the fair sharing of costs between patients, employers, and payers so that low-income beneficiaries are not discouraged from accessing care as a result of high deductibles or out-of-pocket costs;
- Encourage all health insurance plans to provide comprehensive benefit packages that include coverage of services that are likely to help address disparities (for example, language-interpretation services, community health workers—more on these below);
- Improve and streamline enrollment in public health insurance programs and consistently evaluate outreach efforts, to ensure that all who are eligible for these programs and need insurance are enrolled.

Several states have successfully adopted elements of these practices, making health care more equitable as they expand access to health insurance. They offer instructive examples of how states have designed and implemented new programs. For example, as of 2005 New Jersey has required that all physicians practicing in the state must attain minimal cultural competency training as a condition of licensure. California's Department of Managed Health Care has implemented new regulations mandating that HMOs in the state collect and report data on measures of health-care access and quality by patient, race, ethnicity, and language. Massachusetts has also mandated data collection in its recently enacted universal health care legislation, and has deepened its commitment to address health-care disparities by coordination and oversight of health equity programs.

Mechanisms for Equity in Health Care

Federal and state governments should ensure that the provision of health care is equitable and meets all patients' needs, regardless of race, ethnicity, gender, residency, or language status. Policies that promote equity in health care should include certain mechanisms to ensure that health-care providers are accountable to the patients they serve. They should:

- Require all public and private health systems to collect data on patients' race, ethnicity, gender, primary language, and educational level and to monitor for inequality in access to needed services and in the quality of care received;
- Publicly report health-care access and quality disparities at the institutional (for example, hospital or health clinic) level, so that the public and policymakers are aware of when and where health-care inequality occurs;
- Aggressively investigate patient complaints about potential discrimination, and investigate instances where significant access and quality disparities occur;
- Use financial incentives to encourage health systems to adhere to evidence-based clinical guidelines, as a means of promoting the highest standards of health care for all patients.

Strengthening the Health-Care Infrastructure

State and federal governments should also assess geographic disparities in the distribution of health-care resources and create incentives to strengthen the health-care infrastructure in medically underserved communities. A single-payer system would greatly reduce financial barriers to ensuring an equitable distribution of health-care resources, as health-care providers and institutions would experience the same financial incentives to establish practices in all communities, regardless of the community's economic resources. In addition, a single-payer system would gradually reduce inequality in the availability of health-care services and technology. High-end technology and state-of-the-art procedures would become more available to a range of communities, as economic incentives for the distribution of these services would equalize. Until a single-payer system is achieved, state and federal governments can take a number of steps to promote a more equitable distribution of health-care resources. They can:

- Resurrect and reinvigorate state "certificate of need" assessments. These were originally intended to help states and communities regulate where health-care facilities and services were located as a means of ensuring that these institutions—which often benefit from taxpayer funds to assist everything from their construction to reimbursement for services—meet community needs.[54]
- Create and/or enhance incentives, such as education loan repayment or debt forgiveness, to encourage health-care professionals to establish practices in underserved communities.

Strengthening the Health-Care Provider Infrastructure

State and federal governments must also take steps to strengthen the health professions' ability to serve the nation's increasingly diverse population. By the middle of this century, nearly half of all who live in the United States will be members of racial or ethnic minority groups, and four states—California, Hawaii, New Mexico, and Texas—are already "majority minority." Racial and ethnic minority patients are more likely than majority-group patients to experience cultural and linguistic barriers when attempting to get the health care they need and often express greater satisfaction when they receive care from a provider of the same background.[55] To help health-care systems to address the needs of an increasingly diverse patient population, state and federal governments should:

- Require cultural competency training for all health-care professionals as a condition of licensure. New Jersey did so in 2005 when it mandated that physicians receive minimum standards of cross-cultural education.
- Support culturally competent health-care services by appropriately reimbursing language interpretation and translation, and by rewarding culturally competent practices consistent with the federal Cultural and Linguistic Access Standards, promulgated in 2001.
- Take steps to increase the racial and ethnic diversity of health-care providers by reducing or eliminating financial barriers to health professions education for low-income students, strengthening magnet science programs in urban high schools, and, consistent with the U.S. Supreme Court's ruling in the 2004 *Gutter v. Bollinger* decision, supporting the consideration of applicants' race or ethnicity as one of many relevant factors in higher-education admissions decisions.

Empowering Patients and Communities

Too often in U.S. health care, patients are expected to make sound decisions and advocate for their needs without the knowledge and power necessary to do so. Such an approach can be particularly problematic for communities of color, who face lower levels of health literacy and who often—for historical and cultural reasons—feel less empowered to aggressively advocate for their health-care needs than more socially and educationally advantaged groups. Moreover, governments have the power to lessen the impact of a market-driven health-care industry that has tended to overlook the needs of low-income communities and communities of color in favor of wealthier communities that promise lower financial risks and greater financial reward. State and federal governments should give all communities the power to make recommendations and weigh in on decisions regarding health-care policies that affect them. To accomplish these goals, state and federal governments should:

- Develop and assess the efficacy of patient-education programs, such as health literacy and navigation programs, and replicate those proven effective;
- Support the training of and reimbursement for community health workers, sometimes also known as "lay health navigators," or *promotores*, who can serve as a liaison between health-care institutions and their patients;
- Promote and (in most cases) reinvigorate community health planning, in which members of the community identify their needs and assist policymakers in planning, implementing, and evaluating the effectiveness of public health-care systems.

Strengthening Program and Policy Infrastructure

State health agencies and policy processes must be informed by sound research as well as the judgment and opinions of communities. They can also benefit from coordination and strategic planning of state health-disparities reduction efforts. The state program and policy infrastructure for health-care equity should:

- Promote the use of health impact assessments, which ensure that all state initiatives in areas outside the health-care delivery sector—such as transportation, housing, and environmental protection—are assessed to determine their potential impact on the health status of affected communities;
- Establish or strengthen state offices of minority health, to improve planning and coordination of state health-disparities reduction efforts;
- Convene and involve a wide array of stakeholders (business, labor, faith, education, community groups) to work toward solutions to health-care inequality.

Addressing Social, Economic, and Behavioral Determinants of Health

Social and economic inequality among racial and ethnic groups and other marginalized populations is the most significant underlying factor behind most health status inequality. Racial and ethnic discrimination and segregation perpetuate, and in some cases deepen, these gaps. Health care, therefore, cannot eliminate health status gaps between population groups. State and federal efforts should look to a broad range of social and economic policy when crafting strategies to improve and equalize health status for all, and state health agencies should play a leadership role in coordinating these efforts. And government can play a large role in providing incentives for efforts to improve health conditions in a community and more effectively punish acts that weaken community health conditions. These include efforts to:

- Improve the coordination of relevant state and federal agencies that should address determinants of health inequality (for example, in education, housing, employment, criminal justice);

- Create incentives for better food resources and options in underserved communities (for example, grocery chains, farmers' markets, food co-ops);
- Develop community-level interventions for health-behavior promotion (for example, smoking cessation, exercise);
- Address environmental racism (for example, aggressive monitoring, enforcement of environmental degradation laws).

6

Measuring the Extent and Forms of Discrimination in the Marketplace

Lessons from Paired-Testing Research

Margery Austin Turner and Carla Herbig

The ideal of opportunity in the United States is undermined when people experience discrimination based on their race, ethnicity, disability, or other fundamental attributes. Discrimination can deny people choices about where to live and where to send their children to school; it can deny them access to jobs for which they are qualified or limit their wages or advancement prospects; and it can deny them access to the capital necessary to invest in a home or business. By limiting access to housing, neighborhoods, jobs, and capital, discrimination can help sustain—or even exacerbate—inequality of income, wealth, and educational achievement.

Some have argued that little discrimination persists in the United States today—that unequal outcomes are attributable instead to differences in people's qualifications or their behavior and effort.[1] Certainly, no single factor explains the persistence of social and economic inequality. But this chapter summarizes compelling evidence from rigorous paired-testing research that discrimination remains a serious problem in housing, employment, lending, and other critical economic sectors. If we hope to achieve the American ideal of opportunity for all, we need to systematically monitor the incidence and forms of discrimination, refine our tools for combating it, and take vigorous action against it.

What Is Paired Testing?

Paired testing is a powerful tool for observing discrimination in action. In a paired test, two individuals—for example, one white and the other minority—pose as equally qualified home seekers, job applicants, customers, or clients. Both testers are carefully trained to make the same inquiries, express the same preferences, and offer the same qualifications and needs. From the perspective of the housing provider, employer, or salesperson they visit, the only difference between the two is their race or ethnicity, and they should therefore receive the same information and assistance. Systematic differences in treatment—telling the minority customer that an apartment is no longer available when the white client is told he could move in next month, for example—provide direct evidence of discrimination.

The paired-testing methodology originated as a tool for fair-housing enforcement, detecting and documenting individual instances of discrimination. It often provides powerful evidence, easily understandable by juries and the general public, of individual instances in which minorities are denied equal access to housing opportunities. Since the late 1970s, paired testing has also been used to rigorously measure the prevalence of discrimination across the housing market as a whole. And, more recently, this methodology has been adapted to rigorously measure discrimination in mortgage lending, home insurance, hiring, automobile sales, and some other market transactions. When a large number of consistent and comparable tests are conducted for a representative sample of businesses or employers, the results control for differences between white and minority customers and directly measure patterns of adverse treatment based on race or ethnicity. Additional information about the use of paired testing as a research methodology is provided at the end of this chapter.

Critics of paired testing have raised ethical and legal issues, arguing that this methodology deceives or entraps research subjects and may invade the privacy rights of the person or office being tested.[2] Is it unethical to intrude on someone's business without that person's knowledge? Is that intrusion harmful because of the cost of interacting with role players—even if the cost is only lost time? While these are valid concerns, a convincing argument can be made that paired testing is often the only feasible strategy for detecting and measuring discrimination and that the benefits far outweigh the drawbacks. Nonetheless, most carefully designed testing studies intentionally involve as limited an intrusion as possible, taking up the minimum amount of time necessary. And in terms of privacy, most of the studies discussed here involve responding to offers (for homes, apartments, jobs, and services) that were publicly advertised and that are subject to laws or regulations barring discrimination. As for such studies constituting entrapment, there is no lure or incentive for people to act any differently from the way they would otherwise.[3]

Rigorous paired-testing studies have systematically documented the stubborn persistence of discrimination against minorities in both housing and hiring. The largest and most comprehensive of these studies have been sponsored by the U.S. Department of Housing and Urban Development (HUD) to measure the extent and forms of discrimination against minority home seekers over time. Several smaller studies, most also sponsored by HUD, focus on home-mortgage lending and the provision of home insurance. Other studies have extended the paired-testing methodology to measure discrimination in employment, although none of these have been national in scope and none have tracked change in patterns of discrimination over time. This section reviews the findings from rigorous research testing studies on discrimination against minorities in housing and hiring and discusses their implications for policy and action.[4]

Testing for Discrimination in Housing Markets

HUD recognized the potential of the paired-testing methodology as a research tool at a time when it was just emerging as an investigative and enforcement strategy. Specifically, HUD funded the 1977 Housing Market Practices Study, which provided powerful evidence of the prevalence of discrimination against African American home seekers[5] and helped build the case for strengthening the enforcement of federal fair-housing protections in the 1988 Fair Housing Act Amendments. Roughly a decade later, HUD launched the 1989 Housing Discrimination Study, which extended those initial national estimates to cover Hispanics and concluded that overall levels of adverse treatment against African Americans had remained essentially unchanged since 1977.[6] Over the subsequent decade, this evidence played an important role in building public knowledge about the persistence of housing discrimination, making the case for more enforcement resources and suggesting areas where heightened enforcement efforts may be needed.[7]

In 2000, HUD commissioned the third and most ambitious of its national paired-testing studies. HDS 2000 produced two major sets of findings, both of which offer important lessons for public policy. First, the study provided rigorous estimates of the change since 1989 in discrimination against African Americans and Hispanics in metropolitan housing markets nationwide, offering insight on the extent to which the nation is making progress in the fight against discrimination. Second, HDS 2000 provided up-to-date estimates of the incidence of discrimination, including the first national estimates of discrimination against Asians and Pacific Islanders and the first rigorous estimates of discrimination against Native Americans searching for housing outside of native lands.

Evidence of Progress

Between 1989 and 2000, the incidence of discrimination against African Americans declined significantly, in both rental and sales markets nationwide. The incidence of discrimination against Hispanic home buyers also declined, but no significant change occurred for Hispanic renters.

More specifically, the incidence of discrimination against African American renters declined from 26 percent in 1989 to 22 percent in 2000, while discrimination against Hispanic renters stayed essentially unchanged at 26 percent.[8] The decline in adverse treatment against black renters reflects the fact that blacks are now much more likely to be told about the same number of available units as comparable white renters and to be able to inspect the same number of units. Hispanics appear no better off than in 1989 on these indicators. They are now more likely than in 1989 to be quoted a higher rent compared to non-Hispanic whites when asking about the same unit. On the other hand, agents are more likely than in 1989 to encourage Hispanics to apply by asking them to complete an application and/or make future contact.

In metropolitan sales markets, both African Americans and Hispanics have experienced quite dramatic declines in discrimination since 1989. Specifically, the incidence of discrimination dropped from 29 percent in 1989 to 17 percent in 2000 for African American home buyers and from 27 percent to 20 percent for Hispanic home buyers. These overall reductions in sales market discrimination reflect more complex changes in patterns of discrimination on individual treatment measures. For African Americans, the decline in adverse treatment is largest with respect to housing availability; black home buyers are more likely to be told about the same number of available homes as whites than they were in 1989. However, black home buyers are also more likely to be steered to racially mixed neighborhoods (while comparable whites are steered to predominantly white neighborhoods) compared to 1989. In other words, they may find out about just as many homes as comparable whites, but not necessarily in the same neighborhoods.

Hispanic home buyers are also much more likely now than in 1989 to be told about and to inspect the same number of available homes as non-Hispanic whites. They are also more likely to receive equal levels of follow-up contact from real estate agents. However, over the course of the 1990s, agents appear to have expanded the assistance and information about financing that they provide to white customers, but not Hispanics, leading to an increase in the level of adverse treatment experienced by Hispanics on measures of financing assistance.

Persistence of Discrimination

Despite the significant progress since 1989, levels of discrimination against African American and Hispanic home seekers remain unacceptably high. Moreover, HDS 2000 shows (for the first time) that Asians and Pacific Islanders also face significant levels of adverse treatment nationwide and that Native American renters may face even higher rates of discrimination than other groups (based on evidence from three states).

In the rental market, estimates of discrimination are relatively similar across racial and ethnic groups, ranging from 20 percent for blacks to 29 percent for Native Americans. In the sales market, levels of discrimination are somewhat lower, but still significant—ranging from 17 percent for African Americans to 20 percent for Asians.

Patterns of Discriminatory Treatment

Although overall summary measures are useful for estimating how big the problem of discrimination is, policymakers and practitioners should focus on individual treatment measures to develop strategies for reducing discrimination. In the rental market, the most frequent form of discrimination against blacks, Hispanics, and Native Americans is denial of information about available housing units. This is a critically important form of discrimination because it so clearly limits the options from which minority home seekers can choose. The opportunity to actually inspect available units also represents an extremely damaging form of discrimination and estimates of discrimination against blacks and Hispanics are also statistically significant on this measure. For Asian renters, estimates of discrimination are generally not statistically significant. Where they are—in the area of agent encouragement—the direction sometimes points toward more favorable treatment of Asians than whites.

Patterns of discrimination look quite different in metropolitan sales markets. African American home buyers still face some discrimination with respect to information about available homes and opportunities to inspect homes. In addition, agents steer black customers to homes in less predominantly white neighborhoods, provide less information and assistance with financing, and offer less encouragement overall. Hispanic home buyers also face some discrimination with respect to information about available homes, but the major obstacle they face appears to be the lack of assistance with financing compared to equally qualified white testers. Finally, estimates of discrimination against Asian home buyers are shockingly high, particularly given the mixed pattern observed in the rental market. Asian home buyers face high levels of discrimination with respect to information about available homes (11 percent), opportunities to inspect homes (19 percent), and assistance with financing (15 percent).

Telephone Inquiries

In all of the HUD-funded discrimination studies, testers visited real estate or rental agents *in person*. Although advance telephone calls were often required to make appointments, a test was not considered complete until both testers had been seen by the real estate or rental agent. Critics of this approach have argued that it understates the extent of discrimination that minorities face because real estate and rental agents may screen phone inquiries and messages and avoid making appointments with people they believe to be minorities.

Two recent studies have focused on discrimination at the telephone inquiry stage. Purnell, Idsardi, and Baugh conducted a carefully designed set of telephone tests, in which testers with prototypically white, black, and Hispanic accents and patterns of speech called landlords to inquire about apartments recently advertised as available for rent.[9] Similarly, Massey and Lundy directed a study involving 477 telephone inquiries to landlords about advertised rental units, comparing the treatment of male and female speakers of standard American English, black-accented English, and black vernacular.[10] This study also provides evidence of strong and persistent racial discrimination. For example, Massey and Lundy conclude that, other things being equal, the likelihood of reaching a rental agent and being told about an available unit declined from a high of 95 percent for a man speaking standard American English to a low of 60 percent for a woman speaking black vernacular.[11]

Home Insurance

In 1996, HUD funded the Urban Institute to conduct an exploratory pilot study to determine whether the paired-testing methodology could be effectively adapted to measure possible discrimination by home insurance providers against homes located in minority neighborhoods. The motivation for the study was evidence of differential outcomes for minorities relative to whites, but no credible evidence on the extent to which discriminatory treatment might be a contributing factor. More specifically, previous research had documented that home owners in minority neighborhoods had more difficulty obtaining home insurance, received inferior coverage, or had to pay more for full coverage than home owners in white neighborhoods.

The central methodological challenge involved in extending paired testing into the insurance area was the need to match homes and neighborhoods, as opposed to individual people. More specifically, researchers had to identify homes of comparable age, construction type, and condition in neighborhoods that were similar in all respects except their racial or ethnic composition. Testing for this study was conducted in three metropolitan areas, but in one of the three the testing effort was detected by insurance providers and had to be terminated.

Results from this exploratory testing effort did not find systematic patterns of adverse treatment by home insurance providers against properties in minority neighborhoods. The study did, however, raise concerns about possible disparate impacts from the rating-area boundaries established by insurance companies.[12]

Mortgage Lending

The Urban Institute's 2002 lender testing study adapted the paired-testing methodology to measure discrimination by mortgage lending institutions. The mortgage lending industry is extremely diverse and the process of applying for a mortgage loan is complex. Several different types of institutions provide home-mortgage loans; their application and approval processes differ; potential borrowers qualify for very different types of products and may apply to lenders at different stages in their housing search. This complexity led Urban Institute researchers to implement a two-phased process for developing and validating new paired-testing protocols.

First, an *exploratory phase* involved the design and implementation of many different testing scenarios, including, for example, tests targeted to mortgage brokers as opposed to actual lending institutions, tests of mobile-home dealers and new housing developments, tests in which testers had a specific home and mortgage amount in mind, and tests where testers had not yet started their housing search.[13] The purpose of this exploratory phase was to assess the feasibility of a wide range of testing scenarios and to determine what kinds of differential treatment they might reveal. No statistical inferences were drawn because the number of tests conducted for any single scenario was too small.

The exploratory phase confirmed that it is feasible to design and conduct tests for mortgage lending discrimination and led to the design of a proven set of protocols that were implemented in the project's pilot phase. In the *pilot phase*, one hundred black-white tests and one hundred Hispanic-

Anglo tests were conducted in each of two metropolitan areas—Los Angeles and Chicago. Testers visited mortgage lending institutions in person to inquire about how much they could qualify to borrow and what types of products might be available to them.

Results indicate that in both metropolitan areas, African American and Hispanic home seekers face a significant risk of being denied information that comparable white customers receive. Minority home seekers were denied basic information about how much they could afford to borrow, told about fewer loan products, offered less "coaching" about how to qualify for mortgage financing, or received less aggressive follow-up from loan officers. The incidence of unfavorable treatment varied considerably across indicators, ranging from 10 to 15 percent of tests in which minorities were denied basic information that their white partners received to as high as 50 percent of tests in which whites received more "coaching" in how to qualify for financing than their minority partners.[14]

Testing for Discrimination in Hiring

At about the time that HUD's second national housing discrimination study was completed, researchers began to explore the feasibility of extending the paired-testing methodology to measure discrimination in hiring. Data showed that young Hispanic and African American men were substantially less likely than whites to be employed, even after controlling for basic educational achievement. But available data could not answer questions about the extent to which these differences might be attributable to discrimination by employers, as opposed to differences between African Americans and whites in qualifications, skills, or job search and application strategies. Paired testing seemed particularly well suited to determining whether and to what extent unequal treatment of well-qualified minority candidates (relative to equally qualified white candidates) might provide some of the explanation.

Discrimination Against Entry-Level Job Seekers

Building on the fair-housing experience, the paired-testing methodology was extended to test for discrimination in hiring. Two pilot studies—one focusing on the treatment of Hispanic men and the other on the treatment of African American men—were conducted early in the 1990s; these studies found significant discrimination in hiring for entry-level job openings. In these studies, pairs of young men—one African American or Hispanic and the other white—were matched on major characteristics relevant to the hiring decision; they then applied for entry-level positions advertised in the newspaper. Unfavorable treatment of African American and Hispanic applicants was recorded whenever they were unable to advance as far in the hiring process as their white counterparts.

Adapting the paired-testing methodology to the hiring process required a number of careful modifications and innovations. For example, tests were designed to measure discrimination at three distinct steps in the hiring process: application, interview, and offer. Each of these steps involved interaction between testers and employers, either in person or through follow-up telephone calls. Follow-up calls by both testers on a team had to be carefully scheduled and monitored to ensure that neither tester appeared more eager, prompt, or responsive than his partner. In addition, because an applicant's dress, demeanor, articulateness, and enthusiasm are all relevant to the hiring decision, tester pairs had to be matched and trained to present themselves and behave similarly.

These studies found significant levels of discrimination against both African American and Hispanic job seekers. Minorities were less likely than their white partners to be able to submit an application, to be interviewed, and to be offered a job. Overall, white applicants advanced further in the hiring process than their black counterparts 20 percent of the time (compared to only 7 percent in which blacks advanced further), and whites got job offers while their black partners did not in 15 percent of tests (compared to 5 percent in which only the black received a job offer).[15] Adverse treatment of Hispanic applicants occurred even more often. Anglo applicants advanced further in the hiring process than their Hispanic partners in 31 percent of tests (compared to only 11 percent in which Hispanics advanced further), and Anglos got job offers while their Hispanic partners did not in 22 percent of tests (compared to 8 percent in which only the Hispanic was offered a job).[16] In addition, the black-white testing study found that black applicants encountered more difficulty in applying for jobs and received less encouragement in the application and interview process, relative to equally qualified white applicants.[17]

A third paired-testing study of entry-level hiring discrimination was conducted in Denver at about the same time as these two Urban Institute studies. The Denver study was similar in design, but implemented somewhat different tester recruitment and compensation strategies. This study found no evidence of systematic discrimination against either African American or Hispanic applicants for entry-level job openings. One possible explanation may be that the African American and Hispanic testers may have been more aggressive than their white partners in their interactions with potential employers. Another possibility, however, is that blacks and Hispanics face different levels of discrimination in different metropolitan areas, based in part on employers' perceptions of the capabilities of minority workers.[18]

Two more recent studies have used the paired-testing methodology to explore the extent to which having a criminal record affects the likelihood of success in the job application process, and whether these effects differ for blacks and whites. In these studies—one conducted in Milwaukee and the other in New York City—tester pairs were matched on race, with one member of each pair posing as a person with a criminal record. Results indicate that a criminal record poses a serious barrier in the hiring process. For example, for white testers in Milwaukee, having a criminal record reduced the likelihood of receiving a callback from an employer by 50 percent. In addition, however, race plays a major role. In fact, in Milwaukee, the likelihood of receiving a callback was slightly higher for whites with a criminal record than for blacks with no criminal record. And having a criminal record reduced a black tester's chance of receiving a callback by 64 percent.[19]

The New York City study implemented a more complex methodology involving white, black, and Hispanic testers. Some tests compared the treatment of black or Hispanic applicants to the treatment of white applicants, none with criminal records. Other tests compared the treatment of white applicants with criminal records to black and Hispanic applicants with no criminal record. And some compared the treatment of same-race pairs, where one tester was assigned a criminal record. Findings from this study confirm that—in the absence of any criminal record—the chance of getting called back by an employer is lower for Hispanics than for equally qualified whites, and lowest for African Americans. Moreover, the impact of a criminal record is greater for blacks than for whites. And finally, the disadvantage associated with being black or Hispanic (without a criminal record) is about the same as the disadvantage associated with a criminal record for whites.[20]

Using Résumés to Test for Discrimination

Most of the employment testing studies discussed above involve in-person visits by individuals posing as job applicants. Matching testers effectively on tangible and intangible factors that might be relevant to the hiring decision represents a significant challenge for studies of this type. And because it is difficult for testers to pose as credible candidates for higher-level or more technical positions, these studies have focused on entry-level, low-skill job openings.

Bertrand and Mullainathan developed an alternative testing strategy, submitting résumés by mail for a wide range of job openings, with each résumé assigned a distinctively "black-sounding" or "white-sounding" name. Examples of the names include Emily Walsh and Lakisha Washington, or Brendan Baker and Jamal Jones. The assignment of names was based on empirical analysis of data from birth certificates of all babies born in Massachusetts over a five-year period. Four résumés—one high-quality and one low-quality with both black-sounding and white-sounding names—were submitted for each of over 1,300 job openings in Chicago and Boston, including a wide range of occupations and skill levels. Résumés with white-sounding names were 50 percent more likely than those with black-sounding names to generate callbacks from employers. Moreover, having better credentials significantly improved the rate of callbacks for the résumés with white-sounding names, but not for the résumés with black-sounding names.[21]

A similar methodology was implemented by the Discrimination Research Center, which sent out six thousand nearly identical résumés to temporary employment agencies in California. The matched-pair tests, using fabricated applicants with ethnically identifiable names, found that Asian Americans (especially those with Arab-sounding names) were most likely to receive unfavorable treatment.[22]

Combating Discrimination in Housing and Hiring

What insights do the findings from rigorous paired-testing research offer for policymakers and practitioners working to combat discrimination? First, and perhaps most important, these studies provide compelling evidence that discrimination against minorities persists in both housing and employment—evidence that efforts to combat discrimination are still needed. By directly documenting unequal treatment of equally qualified whites and minorities, paired testing clearly demonstrates that our country has not yet achieved its ideals of equal access to opportunity.

Although discrimination is certainly not the only source of racial and ethnic inequality in housing and home ownership or employment and earnings, the paired-testing studies reviewed here show that it certainly contributes. African American are steered away from homes they could afford to buy in predominantly white, high-income neighborhoods; Native Americans are denied information about available rental apartments; Hispanic home seekers don't receive assistance to qualify for a mortgage loan; and black and Hispanic job applicants are significantly less likely to be called back or invited for an interview than whites with the same qualifications.

Paired testing does not tell us *why* employers, real estate agents, landlords, or mortgage loan officers discriminate. In some cases, discrimination may be intentional; a landlord might not want a Hispanic tenant or an employer might want to keep his workforce all-white. Analysis of testing results suggests, however, that housing providers and employers may simply assume minorities are less qualified than whites or that they prefer to live in different types of neighborhoods. Another possibility consistent with the results of testing studies is that some whites may be less comfortable interacting at length with minority customers or job applicants and therefore spend less time with minorities, giving them less information, assistance, and encouragement.

The three waves of HUD-sponsored testing in metropolitan housing markets also teaches us that patterns of discrimination change over time. The significant reductions in discrimination against African American renters and home buyers and against Hispanic home buyers clearly suggest that progress is possible—that sustained investments in education and enforcement can make a difference. But these results also teach us that patterns of discrimination may evolve over time. While African Americans are now less likely to be denied information about available homes than they were in 1989, they are more likely to be steered away from predominantly white, high-income neighborhoods. And while outright "door slamming" against minority customers is rare, housing providers may now be engaging in more subtle forms of discrimination. Thus, strategies for measuring and combating discrimination may have to evolve over time to address changing practices.

Discrimination in both housing and employment is extremely difficult for its victims to detect. In the testing studies conducted over the last fifteen years, almost no housing providers or employers have explicitly told minorities that they were not welcome or would not be served because of their race or ethnicity. In fact, most minority testers have reported that they were treated courteously and given at least some information. Typically, minority testers have no reason to suspect that they were treated less favorably than their white partners. Instead, white testers are the ones who sometimes report that a housing provider or employer said something disparaging about an earlier minority applicant.

The finding that victims of discrimination are unlikely to be aware that their rights have been violated means that complaints cannot be relied upon as the primary mechanism for detecting and combating discriminatory practices in either housing or employment. Certainly, individuals who suspect that they have been discriminated against should be encouraged to complain, and both public and private agencies should be available to assist them in pursuing their complaints. But fair-housing and equal-rights organizations should also conduct systemic testing programs in order to detect discrimination, target particular housing providers or employers for further investigation and possible enforcement action, publicize instances in which discrimination is found to have occurred, and thereby deter further discrimination. Housing discrimination won't end until violators know they are likely to be caught and penalized.

Public education provides another essential step toward a solution. A recent Urban Institute survey found that almost 50 percent of American adults don't know that steering home buyers to neighborhoods on the basis of race is illegal, and more than four out of ten are unaware of key protections for the disabled and for families with children. People who may be victims of discrimination need to know their rights; housing providers and employers need to understand what actions are prohibited; and all of us need to speak out against practices that limit freedom of choice and pose barriers to opportunity.

Over the long term, one would hope that discrimination would abate not only because of the fear of detection and the threat of penalties, but because of changing attitudes about minority neighbors, customers, co-workers, and employees.

Over the last half century, white Americans' perceptions of minorities have become steadily less pejorative. But many white people still see African Americans and Hispanics as less well educated, poorer, less hardworking, and more likely to commit crimes, perceptions that seem likely to contribute to ongoing discrimination in both housing and employment.[23]

Future Research Priorities

Although we have learned a lot from the paired-testing research that has been conducted over the last three decades, this research has been quite narrowly focused. Testing for discrimination in housing has been almost entirely limited to private housing located in large metropolitan areas and to the federally protected classes of race and national origin. Testing for employment discrimination has been even more limited in scope; no studies have attempted to measure the incidence of hiring discrimination nationwide or change over time and, again, the focus has been almost exclusively on adverse treatment of racial and ethnic minorities.

Smaller-scale projects, often implemented for advocacy or enforcement purposes, illustrate the potential for paired testing to be extended much more broadly: to explore other segments of the housing market, to track employment discrimination more systematically, to measure the extent to which other protected classes experience discrimination, and to test for discrimination in other market transactions. For example, a telephone-testing project implemented in the Chicago rental market found that elderly-sounding testers, especially women, experienced unfavorable treatment.[24] Another exploratory telephone-testing effort conducted in Washington, D.C., revealed that landlords often refuse to accept Section 8 housing choice vouchers, even though doing so is a violation of the city's fair-housing laws.[25] Two small-scale studies found significant discrimination against women applying for advertised job openings, including offers of lower-paying jobs to female applicants than to equally qualified men.[26] And a few exploratory projects have adapted the basic paired-testing methodology to the treatment customers receive in bars, restaurants, car dealerships, and other consumer transactions.

This section discusses opportunities to extend paired-testing research, both within the housing and hiring arenas and beyond—including health care, consumer credit, and public accommodations. We briefly review evidence suggesting the need for more systematic testing studies and describe innovative strategies for adapting the basic paired-testing methodology to different types of transactions. Over time, thorough and rigorous testing research should help us establish reliable measures of discrimination—on local, regional, and national levels—for a broad section of the U.S. population across a variety of sectors. Moreover, paired-testing research can and should work hand in hand with enforcement testing to expand our knowledge and disseminate the results as widely as possible.

Next Steps in Testing for Housing Discrimination

Paired testing is so well established as a tool for measuring and tracking discrimination in both rental and sales markets that it is surprising no systematic research has yet been conducted on the full range of groups protected under the federal Fair Housing Act or under state and local fair housing statutes, on housing markets in rural or nonmetropolitan areas, or on publicly assisted housing.[27] Evidence clearly indicates a need for rigorous testing research in all of these areas, and although some modifications to conventional protocols would be required, paired testing is clearly feasible for all of these purposes.

In addition, almost all housing discrimination testing conducted to date has been limited to the "initial inquiry" stage of the home-seeking process, in part because of legal concerns regarding the falsification of lease applications or sales documents. However, discrimination can and does occur at every stage of the search process. Some argue, in fact, that even more discrimination occurs at these later stages and, thus, future testing efforts should attempt to go beyond the initial inquiry stage. For example, rental testers could conduct callback follow-up tests of housing providers to better establish intent to rent a unit, and sales testers could be matched on their real credit scores so that lenders are able to provide a thorough prequalification, which could then be compared.

National Origin

Although the Fair Housing Act offers far-reaching protections, major paired-testing studies in housing have focused primarily on race and ethnicity. And until recently the only racial and ethnic groups included were African Americans and Hispanics. HDS 2000 finally expanded these categories to include other ethnic groups—specifically Asian and Pacific Islanders and Native Americans—and, in fact, found the incidence of discrimination against these groups to be quite high. In addition to high levels of disparate treatment, the study found that housing providers often made discriminatory remarks directly to the Asian/Pacific Islander and Native American testers or made racist comments about them to their white tester partners. There was also evidence that in some cities particular subgroups within the Asian American population (for example, Korean, Chinese, South Asians) were being specifically targeted for unfavorable treatment.

There is reason to believe that discrimination against certain ethnic or national-origin groups has increased alarmingly since 9/11. The Department of Justice has litigated several cases of discrimination against persons of Middle Eastern descent in housing and public accommodations since that date. Similarly, as suggested by the résumé-testing study cited above, persons of Middle Eastern descent may be especially targeted for discrimination in employment. Other immigrant groups also warrant further attention. HUD reports that complaints by Hispanics have increased 31 percent over the last year, with many of these complaints coming from recent immigrants.[28] Although this increase is substantial, it still may understate actual levels of discrimination because many new immigrants may not be aware of their fair-housing rights or know how or where to file a complaint, or they may be reluctant or afraid to complain, fearing repercussion.

New immigrants may also face additional barriers because of discrimination based on language, which can serve as a proxy for other forms of discrimination, such as national origin.[29] Several advocacy groups have conducted paired telephone tests to compare the treatment of accented testers with nonaccented partners.[30] All have uncovered disparate treatment favoring the tester without an accent. However, it is not clear from these tests if specific types of accents, specifically those of racial minorities, are more or less likely to be targeted for discrimination than others. That is, no testing has been conducted using white testers with accents paired with minority testers with accents (for example, British or Russian accents versus Spanish or Korean accents). Implementing such a methodology might help establish more clearly the connection between language and racial discrimination.[31]

Disability and Familial Status

As noted earlier, the Fair Housing Act, as amended in 1988, bars discrimination on the basis of familial status and disability (handicap); these are the only protected classes under the act with provisions for specific members. Only persons with children and persons who are disabled (or who have associations with such persons) are protected under the act. Because these provisions clearly indicate which members have standing, it is not surprising that these two protected classes have the second- and third-highest percentage of all fair-housing complaints after race.[32] The 2004 National Fair Housing Alliance "Fair Housing Trends" report noted that complaints from persons with disabilities increased for all reporting agencies.[33] At the Department of Justice, for example, disability complaints rose from 38 percent to 61 percent.

Very little enforcement testing has focused on disability, in part because many fair-housing groups lack experience with disability issues and few disability advocacy groups conduct testing at all. One pilot research study has been conducted to measure discrimination against disabled persons seeking rental housing, and the results from this study are staggering.[34] The Disability Discrimination Study (DDS) found high levels of disparate treatment in the Chicago metro area against deaf people inquiring about rental housing over the telephone (using TTY devices) and against physically disabled people inquiring about rental housing in person. Specifically, in almost half of all tests, deaf people received less favorable treatment compared to their nondisabled partners. In one out of every four tests, deaf testers were refused housing information altogether. Physically disabled people received unfavorable treatment in up to one-third of the tests and were often not told about all units that were available and were refused the opportunity to inspect units.

In addition to producing these disturbing results, DDS developed exploratory testing methodologies that helped to ensure appropriate protocols, reporting forms, and tester training. The exploratory testing targeted four types of disability (deaf, blind, mentally ill, physically disabled) in different housing circumstances (private market, low-income housing tax credit properties, elderly housing). Although the number of exploratory tests was small, the study did find evidence of disparate treatment across all disability types. For example, blind testers who made their visits accompanied by their guide dog were sometimes refused entry by housing providers with whom they had appointments. Testers with cognitive or mental disabilities were sometimes made to wait much longer than their nondisabled partners when attempting to gather information or inspect units. All of the exploratory tests that showed any disparate treatment favored the nondisabled tester. But because the DDS tests were conducted in only two metro areas and the number of tests was very small for each type, no national estimates could be derived from these results. Clearly, more research needs to be conducted for other disability types, for other housing circumstances, and in other metro areas.

Complaints from families with children are the third most often reported by public agencies and private fair-housing groups.[35] The types of discrimination facing families with children include outright refusals, for example, when the housing provider says that an available unit simply will not be rented to a family with children or that the unit or building is not "safe" for children. Families with children are also often steered to less desirable units on lower floors or in the back of the development. Some housing providers advertise their units as being for "adults only," even though the development is not legally so designated. Some municipalities are discouraging and even restricting housing for families, claiming burden on schools and city services.[36] They sometimes impose quotas on families in particular developments or pass ordinances that prevent developers from building housing for families at all. A number of recent court cases have struck down such ordinances, but this has not stopped their proliferation. Finally, the issue of discrimination against families with children is far off the radar screen of the general public, in part because many people do not even know that discrimination against them is illegal.[37]

Often, families with children simply do not complain. They may not know their fair-housing rights, they do not want to or cannot take the time to complain, or they are afraid of repercussions. Many families with children are among the most vulnerable populations, including low-income households, immigrants, and single-parent families who are ill-equipped to handle the extra burden of fighting discrimination. These barriers, coupled with a lack of any testing data, severely limit our knowledge on the extent to which discrimination against families with children occurs, what forms it takes, and how many and which families are being most affected. The need for rigorous paired-testing research on discrimination against families with children is especially intense in communities where low-income and minority families with children are being relocated from distressed public housing developments. Many families who are given vouchers to move to private housing report that the discrimination on the part of housing providers severely limits their housing choice.[38]

Gender

As with disability and familial status, other federally protected classes have been neglected in paired testing. In the case of discrimination based on gender, complaints by women

and subsequent lawsuits have centered primarily around issues of sexual harassment by housing providers in the rental
market, denials of home loans in sales, or adverse terms in
lending. However, no housing testing studies have focused exclusively on disparate treatment against women in rental,
sales, or lending.

State and Locally Protected Classes

Groups protected under state and local fair-housing laws have
also been neglected by paired-testing research. Depending on
location, these protections cover discrimination based on age,
sexual orientation, and source of income. Perhaps because of
the aging of the general population, there appears to be an increasing interest in discrimination against older persons. For
example, the Perisphere Institute conducted over 250 tests of
housing providers in the Chicago rental market using testers
who were in their forties matched with testers who were
senior citizens. They found that elderly testers, especially
women, were often denied the opportunity to inspect units,
were quoted higher security deposits, and were offered less
favorable lease terms. After the testing was completed, study
researchers asked some of the housing providers why they
had discriminated against the older testers. Many said they
did not want their developments to become "retirement
homes." Several also noted that they were anticipating that
elderly tenants would most likely become mentally or physically disabled.[39]

Indeed, there is reason for concern that the disabled elderly
may face particularly acute discrimination in housing. Tests
conducted by fair-housing groups and others consistently find
that when elderly persons who use wheelchairs search for
housing, they are often denied units in private-market rental
developments under the assumption that they are unable to

take care of themselves. Similarly, they are denied access to home ownership opportunities in "active living" communities, and when searching for facilities that offer continuum-of-care options, disabled elderly are often relegated to the assisted-living section of the development, even though they are perfectly capable of living independently.

Although sexual orientation, like age, is not a protected class under federal law, many localities and states provide legal protections. According to a 2005 report by the National Gay and Lesbian Task Force, thirteen states and the District of Columbia have laws protecting people from housing discrimination based on sexual orientation, and close to two hundred cities and counties also provide their own protections.[40] A 2001 Kaiser Foundation study found that 34 percent of gay people nationwide report having been turned away from renting or buying a home because of their sexual orientation, or know someone who has.[41] A survey administered in Topeka, Kansas, found that approximately 20 percent of gay men and lesbians reported personally experiencing housing discrimination in buying or renting a home or securing renters' or home owner's insurance. One in five also reported having observed discrimination of other gay and lesbian home seekers.[42]

Nonmetro and Rural Areas

To date, paired-testing research has been limited primarily to large metropolitan areas. But the housing market is, of course, much broader than that, and discrimination testing efforts should reflect this. Although the number of minorities living in nonmetro areas remains relatively small, the increase in their population over the last decade has been dramatic. Between 1990 and 2000, the total nonmetro population increased by only 10 percent, while the minority population in these areas climbed almost 30 percent; the nonmetro Hispanic population increased 70 percent, and the nonmetro Asian population increased 56 percent. Some states, such as Colorado, Delaware, Idaho, Oregon, and Washington, saw increases in their minority populations of over 50 percent. And three of every four states experienced growth of 50 percent or more in the Hispanic nonmetro population.[43]

Not only are minority populations in nonmetro areas growing, there is strong evidence that many are living in housing and neighborhoods of poorer quality and in overcrowded conditions compared to whites.[44] And anecdotal evidence suggests that minorities living in nonmetro areas face high levels of housing discrimination.[45] In phase 3 of HDS 2000, researchers conducted tests for discrimination against Native American home seekers in a few midsized metropolitan areas (population under 100,000) that were selected because they represented areas of the sampled states (Minnesota, Montana, New Mexico) that had large Native American populations. The study found levels of discrimination that were higher for Native Americans than for any other racial or ethnic group for which tests were conducted previously. However, no comparable measures of discrimination against African Americans, Hispanics, or Asians in smaller metro areas are available. Clearly, more information about housing-market discrimination and its role in nonmetro communities is needed.

But testing in nonmetropolitan communities is extremely difficult. First, the housing market itself is quite small, so conducting enough tests for statistical significance without testing the same providers over and over is difficult. Moreover, drawing representative samples is challenging, because many housing units in nonmetro areas are not advertised in major newspapers, but are posted in the developments themselves or in other private spaces or are advertised only through word-of-mouth. In addition, testers are extremely hard to recruit in nonmetro areas, simply because everyone knows everyone else and because local testing organizations are often nonexistent. However, despite those barriers, paired testing could be accomplished by working with testers and testing organizations who are not from the area or by using the real personal and financial characteristics of local testers. As the number of minorities in nonmetro areas continues to increase, these and other testing options warrant careful consideration.

Low-Income Housing Tax Credit Program

The low-income housing tax credit program is currently the largest producer of affordable rental housing in the country, with approximately 95,000 units placed in service each year from 1995 through 2003.[46] Even though several laws and executive orders prohibit discrimination in federally funded housing, there is no information on whether any of these prohibitions are in effect with regard to LIHTC developments. Since it began in 1986, the program has operated with little consistent oversight.[47] Although many LIHTC properties are located in predominantly minority, high-poverty neighborhoods, other metro areas, particularly in the South and the Midwest, also have a significant number. We currently have little information about who is living in these units or whether there is equal access to them.

The Internal Revenue Service does not require such basic demographic data as race to be collected, and HUD's LIHTC database currently provides no information that could be used to assess whether these properties are in compliance with fair-housing laws. Further, the provisions of the Fair Housing Act are not directly incorporated into the LIHTC regulations, and the Department of the Treasury has provided little guid-

ance to the state finance agencies that run the programs locally.[48] In 2000, a memorandum of understanding was issued
between HUD, the Department of Justice, and the Department of the Treasury recognizing that all three agencies had
responsibility to enforce the provisions under various federal
laws that address fair housing as it pertains to LIHTC properties. The memorandum specifically called for the agencies to
"cooperate in research sponsored by either Department con-
cerning low-income housing tax credit properties" and "in
identifying and removing unlawful barriers to occupancy of
low-income housing tax credit properties by individuals
holding section 8 vouchers."[49] To date, no such research has
been conducted.

The Disability Discrimination Study conducted a handful
of tests at LIHTC properties. Although the results were in-
conclusive on the issue of disability discrimination, they did
provide anecdotal evidence that racial discrimination may
have been in effect. In a couple of tests, a white advance caller
secured information from the housing provider that LIHTC
units were available to rent. However, when minority testers
arrived at the properties only a few hours later, they were told
that nothing was available. Current paired-testing methods
could easily be adapted to accommodate testing of LIHTC
properties.

Housing Choice Vouchers

LIHTC properties, like all federally funded housing, must be
made available to families with federal housing vouchers.
Since the early 1980s, vouchers have been the federal government's primary means for providing housing assistance to
poor renters. Considerable evidence suggests that voucher
holders face discrimination when they search for housing,
whether because of their status as subsidy recipients or be-

cause of their race, ethnicity, or disability.[50] A recent survey administered to families participating in the Moving to Opportunity initiative asked respondents about their housing search experience. The MTO initiative randomly assigned families moving from public housing to one of three groups: experimental families who were required to use their vouchers to move to low-poverty neighborhoods, Section 8 families who were allowed to use their vouchers to move anywhere they chose, and a control group who did not receive a voucher and had no move requirement. The results of the survey found that although 3 percent of the control group reported encountering discrimination in their housing search, the incidence of such reports was significantly higher for the experimental and Section 8 groups.[51]

A 1997 case, *Green v. Sunpointe Associates, Ltd.*, found that a landlord's "no Section 8" policy had a disparate impact on, and was found to be a violation of the fair-housing rights of, African Americans, women, and children.[52] In 1998, the Fair Housing Council of Greater San Antonio sent African American, Hispanic, and white testers to visit apartment complexes with federal housing vouchers. In several instances, housing providers refused to accept the vouchers from the African American testers while accepting them from the others.[53] The Equal Rights Center in Washington, D.C., recently conducted telephone testing in which testers called housing providers to inquire if they would accept vouchers. The study found a high refusal rate, even though refusing to accept a housing voucher is a violation of the city's fair-housing laws. The Equal Rights Center postulated that this discrimination constituted de facto racial and ethnic discrimination, since the testers were all minority.[54] However, using matched pairs in a similar testing scenario would provide a more definitive result.

In their report on the uneven geography of opportunity,

the Civil Rights Project at Harvard University called for testing of housing choice vouchers to measure the incidence of discrimination against voucher holders in federally protected classes, as well as groups protected under state and local laws.[55] Established methods used to test for discrimination by private rental housing providers could easily be adapted for this purpose. It might be necessary to team with a local housing authority in order to provide testers with any special information or materials they may need to pose as voucher recipients, but it would certainly be in a housing authority's best interest to assist voucher recipients in their housing search.

Next Steps in Testing for Employment Discrimination

Although pilot studies have demonstrated that paired testing—both in person and via résumés—can effectively detect and measure hiring discrimination, no national employment discrimination study has ever been conducted, no measures of change have been produced—even for selected metro areas—and only a very limited number of protected groups have been studied. The Equal Employment Opportunity Commission issued a press release several years ago announcing a major employment discrimination testing study, but since then no information has been disseminated, suggesting that either the study was not conducted or its results have not been released to the public.[56]

Emerging areas of interest for paired-testing studies include issues such as discrimination against minority women, women in nontraditional jobs, and minority men and women in jobs that are above entry level. Changes in welfare policy have encouraged an increasing number of women (especially minority heads of household) to enter the workforce. In general, this is a positive development, but if hiring discrimination denies women access to employment opportunities, or steers them to lower-paying or less secure positions (such as part-time, split-shift, contract work, or jobs without benefits), their prospects for success may be significantly diminished.

Paired testing offers one of the few ways to obtain reliable information about the extent to which discrimination may be a barrier to women and minorities in achieving economic and social mobility. One recent innovative testing study of auto service shops found that women faced disparate treatment in almost half the tests. And when they *were* offered jobs, they were often offered lower-paying ones than those for which they had applied and were qualified.[57] Moreover, the résumé-testing methodology discussed earlier clearly has potential as a tool for measuring discrimination against both women and minorities in a wide range of occupations. This methodology could be rigorously implemented on a national scale at relatively low cost.

Paired Testing in Other Sectors

Although most paired testing conducted to date has focused on either housing or hiring discrimination, the methodology has the potential for much wider application. Indeed, a few scattered studies have adapted the methodology to other sectors. Here we discuss the need and the potential for paired-testing research in health care, consumer credit, and public accommodations.

Health Care

Racial and ethnic disparities in health and health care in the United States have been extensively documented. Several literature reviews on this topic document that minority groups, particularly blacks and Hispanics, experience poorer health outcomes and differential access to and use of critical health services.[58] But a recent comprehensive study by the Institute of Medicine points out that few studies have documented whether and to what extent racial and ethnic discrimination in health care exists. The authors recommend further research to "assess the relative contributions of provider biases, stereotyping, prejudice, and uncertainty in producing racial and ethnic disparities in diagnosis, treatment, and outcomes of care."[59]

Most research in health-care discrimination has approached the issue by using methods once removed from an actual clinical encounter, such as surveys of patients and physicians, review of patient files, or simulations of the diagnostic review process. These approaches cannot unambiguously answer questions about the independent effects of race or ethnicity or any other protected class. No research to date has applied the paired-testing methodology to directly observe and measure the treatment of racial and ethnic minorities relative to comparable whites seeking health care.

Paired testing can provide a powerful tool for observing discrimination in health care, for measuring its prevalence, and for better understanding the forms it takes. But although it offers tremendous potential, extending it to the field of health care also poses significant challenges. Careful consideration would be required to design credible test protocols that effectively capture important forms of treatment by health-care providers, protect the privacy of physicians and other health-care providers, minimize the costs incurred by these providers, effectively match testers with respect to health conditions and needs, protect testers from invasive or harmful tests and procedures, and control for and assess the impacts of different types of medical insurance.

One relatively easy approach to health-care testing would be to focus on the initial inquiry stage, when patients first contact the office of a health-care provider to make an appointment. For many people, simply securing an appointment with a health-care provider is a crucial first step toward a successful health outcome. Patients who are not adequately served at this initial stage may delay necessary health screenings or forgo health care altogether. Conducting matched-pair testing at this stage could focus primarily on two categories— service and information—and might include such basic indicators as whether the tester was able to secure the appointment, whether the tester was able to secure the appointment with the physician requested, when the appointment was scheduled for, and the type of information the tester was asked to provide.

In the more than one hundred studies it reviewed, the Institute of Medicine found that even routine treatments for common health problems differed based on race and ethnicity. Such disparate treatment, even at this lowest level of health care, could contribute to the wide health disparities between minorities and whites. So in addition to testing at the initial appointment stage, more complex testing should also be conducted at the initial office visit. Testers could be assigned to meet with a physician to discuss a common, non-life-threatening health concern for which further medical advice and/or additional services would generally be recommended (for example, headache, fatigue, excess weight). Treatment indicators for office visit tests could be grouped into four categories—service, information, treatment, and follow-up—and could include measures of how long the tester waited in the examination room for the physician to arrive, the length of time the physician met with the tester, what information the physician offered to the tester, what procedures were performed, whether the physician provided the tester with any written materials or free samples of medications, whether the physician referred the tester to another health-care provider, and whether or not there was any contact from the physician or office staff following the visit.

Although paired testing may not be an appropriate or feasible methodology for assessing potential discrimination in all phases of health care, it has potential as a tool for detecting and measuring discrimination in at least some primary-care settings. Given the serious consequences of racial and ethnic disparities in health outcomes, extending the paired-testing methodology to the health-care arena is a high priority.

Consumer Credit

Several recent high-profile stories have reported on discrimination in consumer credit and public accommodations.[60] It seems that even the rich and famous can be victims of discrimination. Although the consequences to victims may not be as severe as in other areas, such as housing, employment, or health care, day-to-day experiences with discrimination are certainly damaging to minorities and undermine the ideal of equal access to publicly available goods and services.

Considerable evidence suggests that minority communities tend to be underserved by traditional financial institutions and targeted instead by check-cashing and payday loan providers. But individual minority customers may also face direct disparate treatment by established credit providers. For example, a 2004 study that examined almost 400,000 customers of American Honda Finance found that African Americans consistently paid more for car loans than white customers with the same credit ratings.[61] In addition to standard charges based on credit risk factors, lenders may also add cost markups not based on any objective factors. These markups are extremely common among auto finance lenders, and dealers often benefit directly from them.[62]

In a press conference held in April 2003, civil rights

lawyers announced a nationwide class-action suit against lenders for the Honda and Toyota motor corporations. The suits alleged that African American and Hispanic car buyers were the victims of discriminatory loan markups. The auto loan companies were accused of charging minority customers higher interest rates on loans than white customers with similar credit ratings. Minority borrowers were charged, on average, twice as much as white buyers. One Hispanic customer was charged 20.75 percent interest after markup.[63] A Consumer Federation of America 2004 press release noted recent legal actions filed against several auto financing companies. But despite this legal action, some of the named finance corporations refused to change this practice.[64]

Auto financing is not the only consumer credit sector for which discrimination has been documented. Such disparities have also been uncovered in mobile-home sales and among popular retailers. For example, lawsuits were filed against Kaybee Toys and Footlocker because they refused to accept personal checks from African American customers while accepting them from comparable whites. Discrimination in consumer credit certainly can have as deleterious financial effects as other types of discrimination. But instances of this kind of discrimination usually come to light only after a victim files a complaint. As with other forms of discrimination, people often do not know that they have been victimized. We do not know the extent to which this type of discrimination occurs, which businesses are involved, or who its victims are. The use of systematic paired testing in this area could go a long way toward educating consumers and businesses alike.

Public Accommodations

Some of the highest-profile discrimination cases have involved public accommodations.[65] Litigation in this area has been based on national origin, disability, and gender and has extended from high-priced lodging, such as the Adam's Mark hotels, to the economy chains of Econolodge and Best Western. Complaints have focused on restaurant chains, such as Denny's and Cracker Barrel, but also to delivery services, such as Domino's Pizza. And cases have been filed against nightclubs, sports facilities, taxicab companies, car-rental agencies, airlines, and retail outlets. These cases strongly suggest that public accommodations discrimination is a recurrent and pervasive problem. Yet there has been only limited research on its extent, severity, or effects. One exploratory study conducted by the New Orleans Fair Housing Council paired young African American and white males and sent them to a number of bars and nightclubs on Bourbon Street. That study found that the African American men were more likely to be charged higher prices for drinks than their white partners. In addition, they were told that a drink minimum and a dress code were enforced, whereas their white partners were not informed of these requirements. Systematic testing of this type can and should be conducted more broadly, focusing on the incidence of discrimination based on race, ethnicity, gender, and other protected classes in representative samples of public accommodations and transactions.

Probably the most notable public accommodations litigation was against Denny's; two lawsuits were filed in the 1990s. The first lawsuit was brought in 1991 on behalf of a group of young African Americans who were required to pay for their meals before being allowed to order. Two years later, a second suit was filed on behalf of a group of African American Secret Service agents in Annapolis, Maryland. The plaintiffs in this case alleged that Denny's provided unequal treatment, resulting in African American customers having to pay ahead for their meals; being denied restaurant promotions, such as free birthday meals; having to wait long periods of time for service; and other discriminatory treatment. The case resulted in a $34.8 million settlement and a consent decree that required Denny's to provide training for all its managers and wait staff and to investigate customer complaints.[66]

The Justice Department has filed similar cases against other large corporations. The Adam's Mark hotel chain was charged with racial discrimination, the first such suit filed against an entire hotel chain. Investigators found that the company had a policy of minimizing the number of black guests in its hotels by charging them higher rates, renting them inferior rooms, and restricting their access to services provided to other guests. The investigation was triggered by a class-action suit filed by five African Americans who were guests of the Daytona Beach Adam's Mark during the black college reunion. In addition to the above allegations, the suit charged that the hotel required black guests to wear orange wristbands and prohibited them from having black visitors. The suit also charged that rooms rented to blacks had been "stripped down" and lacked such basic amenities as telephones and maid service; pictures had been removed from the walls, and room minibars were locked.[67] Then attorney general Janet Reno said at a news conference about the case, "It is hard to believe that thirty-five years after the Civil Rights Act was passed by Congress, this type of discrimination still exists."[68]

Future Paired-Testing Research: Beyond What We Already Know

If, as a nation, we hope to move forward toward ensuring equal access to economic opportunities for minorities and other protected groups, we need reliable information about the incidence of discrimination, the forms it takes, and the extent to which it is changing over time. Paired testing provides a valuable research tool for gathering rigorous information of this kind. The potential of paired-testing research has been proven in the housing arena, where national estimates of the incidence of discrimination have helped inform public debate about the need for stronger enforcement, about progress over time, and about the need to target fair-housing education and assistance to Hispanics, Asians, and Native Americans as well as African Americans.

The same kind of rigorous paired-testing studies can and should be implemented in other areas as well, including unexplored segments of the housing market, but also hiring, health care, consumer credit, and public accommodations. Although paired testing is not the only research methodology worth pursuing, pilot and exploratory studies have proven that it can be effectively adapted to a wide range of transactions and provides direct and credible evidence of unequal treatment.

Finally, future paired-testing research can build on experience to date in two important ways. First, reports that present paired-testing results should combine statistically rigorous estimates of the *incidence* of discriminatory practices with qualitative narratives that offer greater insight into the *forms* that discrimination can take, why it may be occurring, and what steps might be required to combat it. Recent research reports on mortgage-lending discrimination and discrimination against disabled renters have integrated quantitative and qualitative results in this way, making the findings more meaningful to the public and policymakers. In addition, researchers and civil rights practitioners can and should collaborate, planning and implementing rigorous paired-testing studies in conjunction with public education and enforcement initiatives. Although research and enforcement testing differ in important ways, they can be mutually reinforcing, producing not only generalizable estimates of the incidence of discrimination, but also convincing evidence of specific violations.

Appendix: The Use of Paired Testing as a Research Tool

Although research testing shares common origins with enforcement testing, it differs in several important ways. Because its goal is to measure the prevalence of discrimination across the market as a whole, research testing usually covers a representative sample of businesses or employers, rather than targeting attention to those where discrimination is suspected. In addition, to produce generalizable results, research testing requires a fairly large number of tests, covering many different businesses, rather than multiple tests to clearly establish discrimination by a single business. In order to generate results that can be aggregated across many tests, research protocols have to be rigidly consistent for every test, whereas the best enforcement protocols are flexible enough to respond to circumstances that arise in particular tests. Finally, research testing report forms require predefined, closed-ended responses that can be consistently compared across many tests, rather than detailed and nuanced narratives that convey exactly what happened in an individual test.

To illustrate, local fair-housing organizations often send testers to visit rental properties about which they have received complaints. If an initial test finds evidence that minorities are treated less favorably than whites, the organization may send additional pairs, in order to confirm the initial results and compile the most convincing evidence of discrimination. If the complaint (or the initial test) suggested that the property manager required a higher security deposit from minority tenants, testers would be specially instructed to inquire about security deposits for each unit under consideration. Research tests, on the other hand, are typically distributed across many housing providers, including those for whom no complaints have been received. Unless a provider owns or manages a large share of units on the market, he or she is unlikely to be tested multiple times. And even if testers suspect that they may have experienced unfavorable treatment, they must adhere to standardized protocols so that the results of many tests can be pooled and statistically analyzed.

The protocols and reporting forms required for the most rigorous and unassailable research testing would not make for effective enforcement testing. Nonetheless, research testing can inform and support ongoing enforcement-testing efforts, not only by raising public awareness about the extent and forms of discrimination but by identifying neighborhoods or types of businesses where discrimination may be particularly prevalent and focusing attention on places where people did not realize discrimination was occurring. In addition, new testing strategies developed for research testing can be adapted for effective use in enforcement testing as well.

Although paired testing has tremendous power and potential, the methodology also has significant limitations. Probably the major constraint on the use of this methodology is its cost. Because rigorous, in-person paired testing is labor-intensive, cost considerations may limit sample sizes and the extent to which results can be generalized. In addition, there may be some areas where the methodology cannot be applied for practical reasons. For example, it may not be feasible to design reliable testing protocols to measure discrimination in complex transactions that require specialized knowledge or credentials on the part of a customer or applicant. And discrimination against established tenants, employees, or customers (such as lease renewals or promotions) probably cannot be captured through paired testing.

7

Finding America
Creating Educational Opportunity
for Our Newest Citizens

Edward E. Telles and Vilma Ortiz

On May 1, 2006, hundreds of thousands of marchers took to the streets in several major cities to protest proposed immigration reforms by the U.S. Congress. Immigrants, immigration activists, and a wide range of their supporters flexed their economic muscle and boycotted commerce, work, and school to state their opposition to tighter restrictions on immigration. Immigrant activists contended that both legal and illegal immigrants contribute to the U.S. economy and improve the economic status of all Americans, but many wish to deny them entry. Like millions of immigrants before them, these immigrants came to the United States to work. At the same time that many U.S. lawmakers seek to make illegal immigration a felony and build an additional 700 miles of security fence along the U.S.-Mexico border, others seek ways to provide legal status to undocumented immigrants.

In their two-volume series, published by the National Academy of Sciences, James Smith and Barry Edmonston point out that even when legal and illegal immigration are combined, current levels of immigration, as a percent of the total population, are still below the levels reached at any time during the eighty-year period from 1850 to 1930.[1] The study found that immigration overall is beneficial to the U.S.

economy and to native-born workers, although there may be a small negative impact on the least educated. Labor markets are dynamic and very complex and immigrants often complement native workers by preserving entire industries in the United States, creating more jobs while providing American consumers with low-cost goods and services. There are no fiscal costs at the federal level, but states with large numbers of immigrants do spend disproportionately on education for immigrant children. This, however, may be a good investment; the American population is aging, fertility is below the replacement level, and educational levels are rising, thus economists predict that our economy will need millions of additional workers to keep growing as it has for decades.

Competition from immigrants, a small negative impact on low-skilled American workers, is a legitimate cause for concern. However, the National Academy of Sciences report and other analyses also make clear that the effects of free trade are just as harmful to the least educated workers as competition from immigrants, and that both free trade and immigration have been a boon for the large majority of Americans. For poorly educated Americans, greater investments in schooling would do more to improve their situation than ending or sharply curtailing immigration.

History

Even though a large proportion of today's Latino population arrived only in recent decades, the Latin American presence in the United States greatly predates the recent large wave of immigration. Spanish roots in this country predate the first English colony by nearly a century.[2] This historical imprint can still be felt in the Southwest and the Southeast, in places like Los Angeles, San Antonio, Santa Fe, Arizona, Nevada, Colorado, and Florida.

The transition to American rule occurred well before the onset of the twentieth century. Nowhere was this more dramatic than in the Southwest, where nearly half of Mexico's land was ceded to the United States in 1848 at the end of the Mexican-American War. Under the Treaty of Guadalupe Hidalgo, Mexicans in the territory, some 80,000 to 100,000, were granted U.S. citizenship while being allowed to retain cultural and linguistic rights. But in reality their lands were usurped by the incoming Yankees and they were victims of fierce discrimination, including lynchings, segregation, and poll taxes. They had become foreigners in their own lands.

After 1848 there was a small but steady stream of unregulated immigration back and forth from Mexico, which shares a 2,000-mile border with the United States. With breakdown in the political and economic order in Mexico in the early twentieth century, immigration to the United States increased markedly. From about 1907 until the Depression in 1929, a period which included the Mexican Revolution, as much as one-tenth of the Mexican population immigrated to the United States.

The 1930s were marked by the Depression in the United States and the forced repatriation of Mexican immigrants and, often, their U.S.-born children. Hundreds of thousands of Mexicans and Mexican Americans were repatriated in that period. In 1942, soon after the United States entered World War II, the U.S. and Mexican governments negotiated the bracero, or "guest worker," program to meet American needs for agricultural workers. The war effort had attracted many rural American workers to the cities and the war itself. Mexican laborers from deep in their country's interior were recruited and matched with agricultural employers for fixed terms in this guest worker program, which lasted until 1964.

The war and its aftermath prompted immigration from the Spanish-speaking Caribbean as well. Many people arrived from Puerto Rico, Cuba, and the Dominican Republic. They came for different reasons, and their reception varied widely. Puerto Ricans, who are not immigrants but U.S. citizens by birth, came to the U.S. mainland in large numbers to work as manual laborers, filling bottom-rung jobs. Because of Puerto Rico's unique commonwealth status, they could enter and depart the mainland freely. By 1950, Puerto Ricans on the mainland numbered 300,000, up from only 53,000 in 1930. Since then, the social networks between origin and destination have become well established, and, with the ease of air travel, migration became virtually nonstop. By 2000, there were 3.5 million Puerto Ricans on the mainland—almost as many as on the island itself.

The Cuban Revolution of 1959 marked the beginning of a large-scale exodus of mostly upper and middle-class Cubans from that Caribbean island. Cuban immigration had several distinct phases, as it would be interrupted by periods of visa restriction by the United States and the will and ability of the Cuban government to largely prevent outmigration. The Cuban immigrants of the 1960s were granted status as political refugees and their settlement was greatly assisted by the U.S. government. As recipients of this favorable reception, with the high levels of human and business capital of the immigrant generation and with a largely white identity and phenotype, Cuban Americans have, not surprisingly, accommodated well to U.S. society. By 2000, the Cuban origin population would number 1.3 million with the majority continuously residing in south Florida.

With the Immigration Act of 1965 and two subsequent amendments, in 1968 and 1972, the second wave of mass immigration to the United States began. This time it was dominated by Latin Americans and Asians, unlike the first wave at the turn of the twentieth century, which was primarily European. The new legislation ended immigration restrictions on

Eastern Hemisphere countries, created uniform numerical ceilings across all countries, and emphasized family reunification as a basis for immigration and the official end to the bracero program. These laws prompted a large increase in immigration from Asia and a diversification of legal immigrants from Latin America. For example, large numbers of immigrants from the Dominican Republic began to arrive in the United States in the 1960s, as a result of large political transformations in that country. Asian immigration, unlike most immigration from Latin America, tended to be almost all legal and highly skilled, and often used the new provisions of family reunification. For the most part, the high human capital of Asian immigrants, like the Cubans, allowed them to enter U.S. labor markets at the middle or high end and send their children to private or relatively well-resourced public schools.

The per-country limits also severely curtailed visas previously available for Mexican immigrants right at the time that the bracero program ended, even though visas well in excess of the national quota were allowed for Cuban and other "political refugees." With increasing restrictions on Mexican immigration after 1965 and a sudden surge in the Mexican population in the 1970s, the era of undocumented immigration began.[3] Despite an amnesty law for undocumented immigrants in 1986, the number of undocumented immigrants continued to mount; by 2004, there were fully 10.3 million undocumented immigrants in the United States, mostly from Mexico.

Contemporary Demography

Recent years have seen a surge in undocumented immigration and a diversification in national origins of immigrants from Latin America, largely due to changing legislation.[4] The composition of the Latino population is no longer dominated by the three traditional groups—Mexicans, Puerto Ricans, and Cubans; countries with few immigrants in the past are now well represented in the United States. Dominicans in particular are now more numerous than Cubans, and Salvadorans and Guatemalans are not far behind. Still, Mexicans continue to constitute the majority of both the U.S.-born and the immigrant Latino population.

Until the past decade, the traditional Latino subgroups have been concentrated in different regions. Nearly all of the Mexican-origin population resided in the five southwestern states and Chicago; Puerto Ricans were in the Northeast and Chicago; the majority of Cubans were in south Florida. This has changed dramatically since the 1990s. With the growing demand for cheap labor throughout the country and the ease of travel for legalized immigrants after the amnesty program in 1986, and the saturation of ethnically concentrated labor markets, Latino immigrants have chosen to live and work in new destinations such as Kentucky, North Carolina, and Georgia, states where their co-ethnics had rarely lived in before. As a result, Latinos, especially the Mexican-origin population, have become increasingly visible throughout the country and a potential "Hispanic problem" has become an important issue in the national debate.

Another important demographic feature of the Latino population is its youth. Immigrants tend to be young and have relatively high birthrates. In contrast to an aging U.S. population overall, fully 65 percent of the Latino population is under 35 and 40 percent is under age 20. The U.S. baby boom after World War II has created a bulge in the U.S. population that will soon be nearing retirement age. Latinos have thus largely supplanted non-Hispanic whites and blacks as entrants into the labor force and also constitute large numbers of the school-age population. In some of the nation's largest school districts, including the two biggest, New York and Los Angeles, Latinos now comprise the majority of students. These students are largely, but not exclusively, second-generation—the children of those immigrants that have come to fill low-level jobs in the United States.

Latinos now comprise the largest minority population in the United States. At 14 percent of all Americans, they have surpassed African Americans in population size and are projected to become fully 20 percent of all Americans in 2025. Whereas the entire Latino population was 4 million in 1950, it is now 44 million, larger than any Latin American country except Mexico and Brazil.[5] The Latino future will be an important part of the American future. Their educational and job prospects, as well as how they will be integrated in American society, are of vital national concern. Deteriorating resources for funding public schools and an increasingly polarized labor market suggest that there may be significant problems ahead.

Roughly half of the Latino growth rate since 1980 has been fueled by immigration,[6] and immigrants comprise nearly half of all adult Latinos in this country.[7] Immigration from Latin America results from a complex set of factors, including the economic and political attraction of the United States relative to poorer Latin American countries and the social networks that increasingly tie employers and workers across national borders. Such factors vary among Latin American countries. Immigrants from Mexico, for example, are primarily economic migrants. Immigration for Cubans has been almost entirely political since 1959. Since the 1970s, immigration from El Salvador, Guatemala, and the Dominican Republic has been driven by both economic and political conditions. Since most immigrants from Latin America now arrive as labor immigrants to fill the lowest-paying jobs, their average status tends to be near the bottom of the social hierarchy. Their lowly economic position and their large numbers relative to the immigrant population as a whole lowers the status of the Latino population as a whole, even though their U.S.-born descendants tend to have more education and higher incomes.

The majority of immigrants from Latin America do manual labor and are among the lowest-paid American workers.* Their work is essential for many industries in the United States: native workers are unwilling to accept these low-paid jobs, and employers contend that they need to keep wages low in order to remain competitive and in the United States. Entire industrial sectors depend on their labor, including agriculture, cattle raising, meatpacking, hotels, restaurants, manufacturing, and, increasingly, construction. The low wages and hazardous conditions in these jobs are made worse by especially poor access to appropriate and timely health care.[8] Although this has long been the case for the lowest-paid workers in the United States, the situation has worsened because recent legislation further restricts public health benefits for immigrants and noncitizens. American society can and should improve the working conditions, health care, and other conditions faced by immigrants, even though the overall education and social status of these adults are unlikely to change little during their lifetimes. This of course is a contentious point but one that needs to be recognized if we value the contribution of these workers to American society and truly subscribe to American values of opportunity and compassion.

Rather than elaborate on the experiences of immigrants,

---

* Cuban immigrants are exceptions in that their origins are political and they tend to be middle-class. Also, immigrants from some South American countries, like Argentina and Colombia, are often middle-class but their numbers are relatively small.

this chapter focuses instead on some of the challenges in successfully incorporating their descendants into American society. The children of these immigrants generally move up the social and economic hierarchy; for the most part, they do not continue in the jobs of their parents. Since these children are educated in American schools, socialized in American ways, and almost universally speak English, we expect them to fully enjoy the benefits of U.S. citizenship.

The available evidence suggests that the children and grandchildren of these immigrants are not likely to do as well as the white Anglo population, although they seem to be better off, on average, than African Americans. It remains to be seen whether today's U.S.-born Latinos can repeat the experience of European immigrant groups of the early twentieth century, whose descendants became fully incorporated into American society by the second or third generation. Rather, like African Americans, this population risks being marginalized. This seems to be a distinct possibility as the Latino population grows and becomes an ever larger segment of the total U.S. population.[9] The fate of these young Americans is already being shaped in our schools.

A Portrait of Latino Education

The educational levels of Latinos are among the lowest in the country. Fully one-fourth of Latino adults over age 25 have less than a ninth-grade education, while only 11 percent have a bachelor's degree.[10] The Mexican-origin population, which constitutes two-thirds of all Latinos, has the lowest levels of educational attainment among all Latino national groups. These figures, though, include immigrants, many of whom came to the United States well after completing their educations. Certainly, there is little that can be done to change the educational levels of immigrants. However, the education of their descendants is a different story and should be a cause for major national concern.

Even though they tend to be more educated than their parents, the U.S.-born Latino population fails to achieve anywhere near the national norms. Nearly half of Latino high school students in the United States fail to graduate from high school on time.[11] High school dropout rates for the Mexican-origin population in states like California and Texas are the highest of any ethnic group. Given the growing size of this population and the worsening job prospects and wages of the lowest-educated workers in the United States over the past thirty years, this is a worrisome sign of an underclass in the making. Economically, while the savings on educational investment today may be great, the longer-term costs to this nation may be much greater: high school dropouts are the most likely candidates for unemployment and incarceration, and their productive potential is not allowed to blossom, dragging down American economic competitiveness. Just as important, the state of Latino education, like that for African Americans, threatens the values of equity and fairness that our democracy greatly cherishes.

Noted educational analyst Jonathon Kozol writes about the sorry state of U.S. schools and their resegregation in his 2005 book *The Shame of the Nation*.[12] Approximately 75 percent of Hispanic students attend schools with over 50 percent minority populations, and just over 35 percent attend schools with over 90 percent minority student populations.[13] These "apartheid" schools tend to be the most underfunded, with few advanced courses and the most low-level technical courses. Furthermore, when advanced courses are offered, both Latino and African American students are more likely to be tracked into low-level curriculum sequences. The deterioration of poorly resourced public schools has coincided with a surge in the school-age population resulting from immigration.

The state of education for Latinos in the United States has largely been ignored. Many Americans believe the immigrants, especially the undocumented, who have come to the United States in search of economic opportunities should be prepared to accept the working conditions found here. It would be difficult to argue, though, that their children should be similarly denied opportunities. Their children are citizens and, according to the opportunity principles of our society, they should be afforded the same chance for mobility as the rest of society. Despite this, a group of state legislators in Texas has recently proposed that they would deny public services to the U.S.-born children of undocumented immigrants.

A growing chorus of academics, policy wonks, and journalists argue that the low status of the Mexican-origin population is due to a large number of immigrants with little human capital and that their descendants will eventually move up into the ranks of average white Americans. They will copy the cycle of the slowest assimilating European groups, but assimilate they will. But this is likely only if they are given the same opportunities. The evidence suggests that educational opportunity leaves much to be desired and Mexican Americans seem to share the fate of African Americans, who have also been marginalized in U.S. society.

Latinos, both immigrant and native, tend to have occupational levels and incomes well below the national average—primarily because of their low levels of education. Much of the research has focused on Mexican Americans, by far the largest subgroup. The bulk of research shows that Mexicans have similar incomes per year of schooling as non-Hispanic whites. Research shows that African Americans experience direct labor market discrimination: their incomes are markedly lower than Latinos' and whites', even when they have the same level of schooling.[14]* On the other hand, average educational levels for U.S.-born Mexican Americans are lower, and high school dropout rates are higher, than those of blacks and whites.[15] The economic disadvantage of the Mexican-origin population therefore lies not in returns to human capital but in the *accumulation* of human capital itself.[16] In other words, their level of education places them in the lower ranks of the American socioeconomic structure. Thus, it is not surprising that educational attainment is the most important issue facing Latinos today, according to most public opinion polls.[17]

Table 7-1 describes relative educational levels among U.S.-born persons in New Mexico, Arizona, Colorado, Texas, and California, where Mexican Americans are concentrated. The table shows that both in 1970, when there was little immigration, and in 2000 Mexican Americans had lower levels of schooling than non-Hispanic whites (Anglos), African Americans, or Asian Americans. As late as 2000, the average years of schooling completed by Mexican Americans was barely over high school graduation levels. Indeed, only 74 percent of the population graduated from high school, compared to 90 percent of Anglos, 84 percent of blacks, and 95 percent of Asian Americans. At a higher level, only 13 percent completed college, the lowest of all the groups. The 1970 figures, when a large number of the U.S.-born were mostly third generation (i.e., the grandchildren of immigrants), were similarly the lowest among all the groups.

Assimilation scholars often claim that it takes three and possibly four generations for the descendants of low-status immigrant groups to become "average Americans."[18] They

---

* However, at least two important studies based on data from the 1970s showed that the Mexican-origin population was less effective than blacks in translating education into occupational status. See Featherman and Hauser, note 16, and Niedert and Farley, note 15.

TABLE 7-1

**Schooling statistics by race for the U.S.-born
in the five Southwest states, 1970 and 2000**

	1970	2000
Years of School		
Mexican Origin	9.7	12.3
White	12.3	14.1
African American	10.9	13.2
Asian American	—	14.7
Percent High School Graduate		
Mexican Origin	44	74
White	75	90
African American	54	84
Asian American	—	95
Percent College Graduate		
Mexican Origin	3	13
White	15	35
African American	5	17
Asian American	—	54

Note: Asian Americans are not reported in 1970 since their numbers were fairly small. The size of the Asian American population has multiplied several times since then because of the contemporary wave of immigration.

Source: Authors' tabulations, 1970 U.S. Census and 2000 U.S. Census, public use micro-data samples; 1970 figures are for ages 18–54, 2000 figures are for ages 35–54.

reason that if Polish, Irish, and Italian ethnics were able to move up the success ladder within three generations, then Latinos will do the same. They argue that Mexican incorporation might take longer because of the especially low human capital and illegality of many of their immigrant ancestors. Only African Americans have been unable to move up the ladder because of extensive racism, which has locked them in place many generations after their ancestors were brought from Africa. Indeed, their enslavement is often cited as the cause of the problem, although social scientists often point to the effects of ongoing institutional discrimination.[19]

Intergenerational Experiences

Most analysts argue that Mexican educational attainment improves from immigrant parents to their children but stalls between the second and third generations, even though the parents of the third generation have significantly more education and resources to pass on to their children than their own immigrant parents had.[20] (Alba et al. did find improvements between the second and third generations using the National Longitudinal Survey of Youth but not the National Educational Longitudinal Study.)[21]

Explanations for stagnation by the second generation often involve immigrant optimism hypotheses, in which the relatively ambitious immigrant parents, who themselves suffered from low human capital, believe in the American dream and drive themselves and their children to do well in school, while second-generation parents perceive greater limits on their success in the United States.[22] Others contend that the second-generation schooling advantage might be from their resistance to assimilation and their ability to mobilize ethnicity as a positive resource to escape schools' sorting of minorities into disadvantaged strata.[23] Unfortunately, the poor state of education for Latinos largely determines their economic success throughout their adult lives, and this disadvantage is consequently passed on to their own children.

The educational disadvantage of Latinos begins at a very young age and accumulates throughout the schooling cycle. First of all, they often begin without the social and economic resources that other students have, especially if they come from immigrant families with relatively low rates of literacy and if they are unfamiliar with the English language and American schools and norms and values. From the very beginning, Latino children are the least likely of all groups to attend preschool, even though they may need it the most.

These disadvantages are coupled with poor school, library, and other infrastructural resources and an early disencouragement and disengagement from academic activities for a host of reasons. These include attendance at schools with the highest levels of poverty, low teacher expectations, and the largest number of inexperienced or uncertified teachers. In majority-white schools, discriminatory aggressions against minority students,[24] a feeling that Asian and white students are born smarter,[25] and an internalized belief in common racial stereotypes[26] further lower students' own expectations. Also, the low number of Latino teachers makes it difficult for students to share connections or identities with teachers and thus view them as concerned adults or role models.[27]

Mexican American educational disadvantage throughout the twentieth century has been blamed on discrimination and negative stereotyping.[28] At different points in history, such attitudes have been reinforced by legal determinations of Mexican Americans as nonwhite citizens, segregation into separate schools, and persistent tracking into inferior curricula within schools.[29] Segregated schools receive lower levels of funding, fewer experienced teachers, and poorer facilities in comparison with mostly white schools.[30] In more integrated schools, Mexican-origin students are disproportionately tracked into low-ability curricula.[31] Both segregation and tracking as well as other forms of educational discrimination, including lower teacher expectations, cause Mexican Americans to suffer from greater stress and susceptibility to stereotyping and feelings of inferiority and insecurity.[32]

In response to such structural and individual discriminations, Ogbu argued the development of oppositional identities by nonimmigrant and nonwhite children that impede school success.[33] According to both Matute-Bianchi and Fernandez, U.S.-born Mexican Americans have discovered that the social environment in which they have grown up is adverse to their success; they thus feel that pressure on their children to succeed is largely fruitless.[34] Also, the historical claims of Mexican Americans to the U.S. territory they live on, unlike any other U.S. group, buttress an oppositional identity. Portes and Rumbaut similarly blame downward mobility from the second to the third generation on a "particularly adverse social context" for Mexicans, in which the immigrant drive and optimism weakens by the third generation.[35] For these authors, the educational underperformance of Mexican Americans over several generations since immigration is mostly the result of a process of racialization, in which "assimilation" is toward the African American instead of a white norm.

Change Across the Generations

For Latinos, the experience of Mexicans who immigrate to the United States in the early twentieth century or before provide an example of the multigenerational success or failure of one group in schools. In a study sponsored largely by the National Institute of Child and Human Development (NICHD), we tracked a random sample of second-, third-, and fourth-generation Mexican Americans and examined their educational experience, among other things. Our study takes advantage of the long-term presence of Mexican-origin population in the United States, dating back at least to the mass immigration from eastern and central Europe in the early twentieth century. Our data overcome the limitations of many previous studies because we have information from parents as well as their children regardless of whether the children themselves claim that identity, and we have a fourth generation. Educational attainment is measured using years of schooling, percent of high school graduates, and percent of college graduates.

Figure 7-1 shows generational progress in the mean years of schooling from the parents of the original respondent (grandparents) to original respondents (parents) to children of original respondents (grandchildren). Both cohorts reveal substantial improvements in education for each succeeding generation, which roughly represent education in the 1900s–1930s for grandparents, 1930s–1950s for parents, and 1950s–1980s for grandchildren. Immigrant grandparents had an average of 4.1 years of schooling while their U.S.-born

FIG. 7-1
Average years of schooling for Mexican American grandparents, parents, and children by generation since immigration

Generation Since Immigration	Grandparents	Parents	Children
1	4.1	7.4	—
2	6.1	10.0	13.1
3	—	10.4	13.1
4+	—	—	12.4
Years in school	1900s–1930s	1930s–1950s	1950s–1980s
Anglo Average	9.5	12.5	14.2

Source: Authors' tabulations, Mexican American Study Project.

children more than doubled these levels to 10.0 years, and, finally, their third-generation grandchildren tripled their own educational levels, to 13.1 years. Similarly, second-generation grandparents would have seen great gains in schooling for their children (from 6.1 to 10.4 years) and grandchildren (12.4 years). Seen in this way, schooling improved greatly across the generations.

Schooling also improved for the U.S. population among the same cohorts, so we also show the deficit in years of schooling for each group compared to U.S.-born non-Hispanic whites. The reference group for grandchildren is 35- to 54-year-old non-Hispanic whites in the 2000 census, for parents, 20- to 54-year-old non-Hispanic whites in the 1970 census, and for grandparents, all non-Hispanic whites in the 1950 census. All reference groups are for Los Angeles and San Antonio separately. While immigrant grandparents have 4.1 years of education and the second-generation grandparents have 6.1 years, their Anglo counterparts have 9.5 years of education (a deficit of −5.2 and −3.4, respectively). Among the grandchildren, both the second and third generation have 13.1 years of schooling and the fourth generation has 12.4 years, compared to 14.2 years of schooling for Anglos (indicating a deficit between 1 and 2 percent). Seen as a deficit, improvements were also made from grandparents to grandchildren. The shortfall compared to non-Hispanic whites was reduced from 5.2 for immigrant grandparents to 1.3 for their grandchildren and 4.4 for U.S.-born grandparents to 1.6 for their grandchildren.

However, despite the emphasis on improving the poor state of education and achieving equality for Mexican Americans throughout the twentieth century, their schooling remains frustratingly low. The dramatic result is that this is true for the fourth generation, who may be the first generation not exposed to immigrant relatives and whose ancestral tie to

Mexico is predominantly through their great-grandparents. There is no assimilation even by the fourth generation. To make matters worse, the expectation that assimilation improves across generations is turned on its head for the children of the original respondents. The fourth generation, regardless of whether it identifies as Mexican American, has fewer years of schooling, on average, than the second or third generation.

As we showed earlier, Mexican Americans continue to have lower high school graduation rates—or, conversely, higher dropout rates—than any other major ethnic group in the United States. Like average years of schooling, there are large improvements in high school graduation rates from immigrant parents to their U.S.-born children, reflecting a general increase over time throughout the United States. Table 7-2 shows that only a minority of original respondents completed high school, while about four-fifths of children did.* Told from the perspective of generations since immigration, improvements are not as clear. For the parents, high school graduation levels vary from 30 percent in the first generation, to 48 percent in the second, to 57 percent for the third generation, suggesting a smooth generational improvement. However, the deficit for even the third generation remains very large, as fully 75 percent of non-Hispanic whites graduate from high school for roughly the same cohort. For the chil-

---

* Estimates of the rate of high school dropouts vary widely. For example, California estimates a high school dropout rate of 13 percent, but the Civil Rights Project of Harvard University estimates a high school graduation rate of 71 percent for that state. Both numbers exclude persons who received the General Equivalency Diploma (GED), since they generally dropped out but later took the exam to receive equivalency credit. However, while the California state numbers consider dropouts to be students known to be leaving school altogether, Harvard figures consider students who may have transferred to other schools as nongraduates. The high school graduation rate for Latinos using the Harvard methodology is 40 percent.

TABLE 7-2
High school and college for Mexican American parents and children by generation since immigration

	Parents			Children		
	Gen. 1	Gen. 2	Gen. 3	Gen. 2	Gen. 3	Gen. 4
Percent High School Graduate	30	48	57	84	87	73
Percent College Graduate	7	6	5	13	14	6

Source: Authors' tabulations, Mexican American Study Project.

dren of the original respondents, the fourth generation has the lowest graduation rates, at 73 percent, which compares to 87 percent for the third and 84 percent for the second. Thus, there are clear improvements from parents to children in graduation from high school, but the improvements are particularly great for immigrants whose children gain tremendously while the children of the original third generation experience relatively small gains. The deficit in high school graduation has declined from parents to children; this is largely due to a ceiling effect, as non-Hispanic white rates are at 90 percent, which is close to the maximum. Nevertheless, only 73 percent of fourth-generation Mexican Americans graduate from high school, which is fully 17 percent less than for U.S.-born non-Hispanic whites.

Finally, Table 7-2 shows the other important benchmark in the educational pipeline: college completion. While less than 7 percent of Mexican Americans in the original sample had a college education compared to 15 percent of non-Hispanic whites, that number increased to 6 to 14 percent for their children, roughly the amount that their Anglo peers had in the 1965 sample. However, by their children's time, the Anglo college completion rate had increased to 35 percent. Thus, the deficit in percentage of college completers was between

21 and 29 percent. Sadly, and in direct contradiction to the assimilation theory, the fourth generation had the largest deficit. Education assimilation was reversed.

Although the gap between the schooling of Mexican Americans and that of non-Hispanic whites has been closing throughout the past fifty years or so, it still exists. While many have assumed that such a gap remains because of the disadvantage of Hispanics being raised in immigrant households, the data here show that schooling outcomes stubbornly continue at low rates even into the fourth generation, a group who is unlikely to have ever known an immigrant in the family. The statistics presented thus far show that the educational progress of Mexican Americans does not improve over the generations. Given a small statistical margin of error, at best, our data show no improvement in education over the generations; at worst, they suggest a pattern of decline.

The educational experiences of these third- and fourth-generation Mexican Americans today may not be the same as those of the third- and fourth-generation descendants of all Latino immigrants today. Although the trends suggest improvements in Latino education, at least in the number of years they remain in school, relatively recent trends suggest things may get worse because the public educational system in the inner cities, where schools are increasingly segregated into all-black or all-Latino student bodies, have noticeably deteriorated in the past decade.[36] The tax base for schools is eroding and segregation has increased to pre–civil rights levels. Also, the surge in the number of undocumented immigrants, most of whom are Mexican, has further restricted access to services like medical care and education for their immigrant parents, further impairing the ability of the second generation's prospects for mobility. Hope for the descendants of these new Americans seems dim unless we can turn inner-city schools around and make them places where students' hearts and minds can be engaged.

To make matters worse, the labor market is increasingly polarized into good and bad jobs, the latter offering fewer ladders for mobility than they did in the first half of the twentieth century, when European immigrants and their children entered the labor force. The earnings of those with a high school education or less have decreased, while earnings for those with college educations have increased. Until the late 1970s, low-level jobs often offered decent pay and many opportunities for mobility into higher-paid and more secure jobs. With deindustrialization, today's jobs are less likely to lead to mobility. The middle rungs of the job ladders that immigrants and their children used to attain the American dream are fewer and farther apart.

The intergenerational mobility prospects for Mexican Americans have not been good in the past, and there are indications that they are likely to get even worse. The socioeconomic status of the descendants of immigrant groups like Cubans and most Asian nationalities are much better because the immigrants who landed on American shores tended to be in the middle class of their countries prior to immigration; their children have thus entered the American race for mobility in the fast lane. Puerto Ricans are a special case. They often enter at the bottom rungs but they are citizens. Their migration is more likely than any other group to be circular, even across generations, although third-generation Puerto Ricans on the mainland are no better off, perhaps even worse off, than their Mexican counterparts. Other Latin American flows, including Dominicans and Central Americans, as well as Southeast Asians, are likely to mimic the Mexican experience; these groups start at the bottom, are seen as nonwhite, and are often undocumented. In their studies of West

Indians, Waters and Kasinitz have found, sadly, that a large number of the descendants of these generally optimistic immigrants have begun to experience the full brunt of racial discrimination that has historically accrued to people of African ancestry in this country.[37] The future, though, is not certain. The chances that become available to these immigrants will largely depend on the extent to which values of fairness, participation, community, and human dignity become shared values among Americans.

Policy Choices

What should be done? The nation's current policies on immigration are contradictory. We depend on immigrants, yet at the same time we tell them to go away. The contradictions are especially sharp with respect to undocumented immigration. Undocumented immigrants receive the benefit of being charged college tuition as California residents, but they do not qualify for federal education loans. They can buy cars and car insurance, but in most states they cannot get driver's licenses. They can find jobs, often in federally funded hiring halls, but they cannot lawfully work.[38] The contradictions extend to our relations with Mexico, our neighbor and third largest trading partner, as Mexico-bashing becomes more popular.

We have millions of residents who are not supposed to be here by law, but, in economic terms at least, the country needs them as a source of cheap and willing labor. The very term "illegal" raises the specter of criminality and lack of control. However, the flow of undocumented immigrants is essentially a problem of an outdated visa system that does not meet the country's growing labor needs. Immigration reform needs to recognize that basic fact. A sudden end to immigration would mean disaster for many sectors of the American economy. Just as prohibition denied a strong American dependence on alcohol, our current immigration policy reflects a denial of another, but arguably more vital, kind of dependence.

However, we can achieve a practical outcome where almost everyone can benefit. A program with realistic quotas to meet labor needs would certainly be more fruitful than continued efforts to seal off the border, which cannot succeed in practical terms and serves merely to antagonize Mexico. A realistic program of entries would allow greater control over immigrants and the border. This should be combined with reforms that allow immigrants to choose either a path to citizenship or an easy return to their country of origin. Immigration reform has recently risen on the political agenda, and the ideas being proposed need to be carefully evaluated and discussed.

The disastrous state of much of public education today produces continuing educational disadvantages for many Latinos, and especially for Mexican Americans, further impeding their prospects for economic assimilation. Their future for at least the next twenty to thirty years depends largely on education today. Recent trends may signal an impending American underclass composed largely of U.S.-born Latinos. About half of Mexican-origin youth do not complete high school on time, apparently reversing improving trends in recent decades. While the lack of such an education could be overcome by manual-labor jobs that ensured decent pay, stability, and mobility, such jobs are increasingly difficult to find as the gap between bad and good jobs widens. Although affirmative action helps a few, the choice for many U.S.-born Mexican Americans may be restricted to jobs that are not much better than those of their immigrant parents. Our study found attenuated gains for third- and fourth-generation

Mexican Americans who completed high school at least two decades ago, but more recent evidence shows that this pattern continues.[39]

Public schools are the single greatest institutional culprit for the persistent low status of U.S.-born Mexican Americans. High school dropout rates continue for Mexican Americans, making it the group with the lowest levels of education in the country. The public schools that serve Mexican American communities, which are largely in the central cities and remote rural areas, are increasingly segregated and have been among this country's worst.[40] For those in integrated schools, education is often better but Mexican-origin students are disproportionately tracked into lower-level curricula and made to feel unwanted or uncomfortable in school.

Since the late 1970s, schooling has become an ever more important predictor of success in the United States as a restructured economy has led to increased demand for those with college educations and decreased demand for those with high school educations or less. With the loss of high-paid manual jobs from the decline of heavy industry in the United States and the increasing income returns to college education, there has been a growing hourglass shape to the economy. The middle-rung jobs, which allowed earlier immigrants and their descendants to gradually work their way up, are now disappearing. Increasingly, even fully employed workers are living in poverty, while living standards for college graduates have improved. Mexican Americans, with their low educations, are concentrated in the lower rungs of this widening class divide. At the same time, public education has worsened, especially in California, where a voter-led initiative in 1979 undermined its primary funding source.

For the children of our newest immigrants to become successful, we need, above all, a Marshall Plan that invests heavily in public school education. We need to emphasize educational opportunities rather than adoption of American values, which, by the way, Mexican Americans already have. Sociologist Mary Waters of Harvard University, who studied the incorporation experiences of the old classic wave of European immigrants and their descendants, found that the Americanization programs were not nearly as important as the enormous economic payoff to immigration that the descendants of European immigration enjoyed.[41] For Mexican Americans, the payoff can only come by giving them the same quality and quantity of education as whites receive. The problem is not the unwillingness of Mexican Americans and other immigrants or their descendants to adopt American values and culture but the failure of societal institutions, particularly public schools, to successfully incorporate these individuals, as they did for the descendants of European immigrants.

NOTES

1. You *Can* Take It with You
Jared Bernstein

1. Bhashkar Mazumder, "Fortunate Sons: New Estimates of Intergenerational Mobility in the United States Using Social Security Earnings Data," *Review of Economics and Statistics* 87, no. 2 (2005): 235–55.

2. C. Lee and Gary Solon, "Trends in Intergenerational Income Mobility," National Bureau of Economic Research WP 12007, Washington, DC, 2006, available at http://www.nber.org/papers/w12007.

3. Gary Solon, unpublished data provided to author.

4. Jared Bernstein, *All Together Now: Common Sense for a Fair Economy* (San Francisco: Berrett-Koehler, 2006).

5. D. Aaronson and B. Mazumder, "Intergenerational Economic Mobility in the U.S., 1940 to 2000," Federal Reserve Bank of Chicago WP 2005–12, Chicago, 2005, available at www.chicagofed.org/publications/workingpa pers/wp2005_12.pdf.

6. Gary Solon, "Cross-Country Differences in Intergenerational Earnings Mobility," *Journal of Economic Perspectives* 16, no. 3 (2002): 59–66.

7. K.K. Charles and E. Hurst, "The Correlation of Wealth Across Generations," *Journal of Political Economy* 111, no. 6 (December 2003): 1155–82.

8. Jo Blanden, "International Evidence on Education and Intergenerational Mobility," paper presented at the Intergenerational Mobility in Education Conference, Centre for the Economics of Education, London School of Economics, October 9, 2004, available at http://cee.lse.ac.uk.conference_ papers/15_10_2004/jo_blanden.pdf.

9. M.A. Fox, B.A. Connolly, and T.D. Snyder, *Youth Indicators 2005: Trends in the Well-Being of American Youth*, U.S. Department of Education, National Center for Education Statistics, 2005, Table 21, available at http://nces.ed .gov/pubs2005/2005050.pdf.

10. Markus Jäntti et al., *American Exceptionalism in a New Light: A Comparison of Intergenerational Earnings Mobility in the Nordic Countries, the United Kingdom and the United States*, Discussion Paper No. 1938 (Bonn, Germany: Institute for the Study of Labor, 2006).

11. Mary Corcoran and Jordan Matsudaira, "Is It Getting Harder to Get Ahead? Economic Attainment in Early Adulthood for Two Cohorts," in Richard A. Settersten Jr., Frank F. Furstenberg, and Rueben G. Rumbaut, eds., *On the Frontier of Adulthood: Theory, Research, and Public Policy* (Chicago: University of Chicago Press, 2005).

12. Katherine Bradbury and Jane Katz, "Women's Labor Market Involvement and Family Income Mobility When Marriages End," *New England Economic Review* Q4 (2002): 41–74.

13. Tom Hertz, "Rags, Riches and Race: The Intergenerational Economic Mobility of Black and White Families in the United States," in Samuel Bowles, Herbert Gintis, and Melissa Osborne, eds., *Unequal Chances: Family Background and Economic Success* (New York and Princeton: Russell Sage and Princeton University Press, 2005).

2. Educational Quality and Equality
Linda Darling-Hammond

1. Educational Testing Service, *The State of Inequality* (Princeton, NJ: Educational Testing Service, 1991); Jonathan Kozol, *Savage Inequalities: Children in America's Schools* (New York: Crown, 1991); Jonathan Kozol, *The Shame of the Nation: The Restoration of Apartheid Schooling in America* (New York: Crown, 2005).

2. David Tyack, *The One Best System: A History of American Urban Education* (Cambridge, MA: Harvard University Press, 1974); Richard Kluger, *Simple Justice: The History of* Brown v. Board of Education *and Black America's Struggle for Equality* (New York: Alfred A. Knopf, 1976); Kenneth Meier, Joseph Stuart Jr., and Robert England, *Race, Class and Education: The Politics of Second-Generation Discrimination* (Madison: University of Wisconsin Press, 1989).

3. Kozol, *Savage Inequalities.*

4. Kozol, *The Shame of the Nation*, 321–24.

5. *Williams et al. v. State of California*, Superior Court of the State of California, Complaint, filed June 2000, Case No. 312236, 22–23.

6. Jeannie Oakes, "Investigating the Claims in *Williams v. State of California:* An Unconstitutional Denial of Education's Basic Tools?" *Teachers College Record* 106, no. 10 (2004): 1889–906.

7. Gary Orfield, *Schools More Separate: Consequences of a Decade of Resegregation* (Cambridge, MA: Civil Rights Project, Harvard University, 2001).

8. Jennifer Sable and Lee Hoffman, *Characteristics of the 100 Largest Public Elementary and Secondary School Districts in the United States: 2002–03*, U.S. Department of Education, NCES 2005312 (Washington, DC: Government Printing Office, 2005).

9. Educational Testing Service, *The State of Inequality.*

10. William Taylor and Diane Piche, *A Report on Shortchanging Children: The Impact of Fiscal Inequity on the Education of Students at Risk*, prepared for the Committee on Education and Labor, U.S. House of Representatives (Washington, DC: Government Printing Office, 1991), xi–xii.

11. National Center for Education Statistics, *NAEP Trends Online* (U.S. Department of Education, National Assessment of Educational Progress, 2005), available at http://nces.ed.gov/nationsreportcard/.

12. U.S. Bureau of the Census, *Statistical Abstract of the United States* (Washington, DC: U.S. Department of Commerce, 2004), Table A-5a.

13. National Center for Education Statistics, *The Condition of Education, 1998* (Washington, DC: U.S. Department of Education, 1998), 100.

14. Ibid.

15. Jerome G. Miller, "African American Males in the Criminal Justice System," *Phi Delta Kappan* 78 (June 1997): K1–K12; U.S. Bureau of the Census, *Statistical Abstract of the United States: 1996* (Washington, DC: U.S. Department of Commerce, 1996), 219.

16. National Center for Education Statistics, *Digest of Education Statistics, 1994* (Washington, DC: U.S. Department of Education, 1994).

17. Justice Policy Institute, "Cellblocks or Classrooms?" August 28, 2002, available at http://www.justicepolicy.org/reports/coc.pdf.

18. See, for example, Miller, "African American Males in the Criminal Justice System."

19. Paul E. Barton and Richard J. Coley, *Captive Students: Education and Training in America's Prisons* (Princeton, NJ: Educational Testing Service, 1996); Robert J. Gemignani, "Juvenile Correctional Education: A Time for Change. Update on Research. Juvenile Justice Bulletin," U.S. Department of Justice, Office of Juvenile Justice and Delinquency Prevention, October 1994.

20. Robert Dreeben, "Closing the Divide: What Teachers and Administrators Can Do to Help Black Students Reach Their Reading Potential," *American Educator* 11, no. 4 (Winter 1987): 34.

21. Julie E. Kaufman and James E. Rosenbaum, "Education and Employment of Low-Income Black Youth in White Suburbs," *Educational Evaluation and Policy Analysis* 14, no. 3 (1992): 229–40.

22. See, for example, Rebecca Barr and Robert Dreeben, *How Schools Work* (Chicago: University of Chicago Press, 1983); Robert Dreeben and Adam Gamoran, "Race, Instruction, and Learning," *American Sociological Review* 51, no. 5 (1986): 660–69; Robert Dreeben and Rebecca Barr, "Class Composition and the Design of Instruction," paper presented at the annual meeting of the American Education Research Association, Washington, DC, 1987; Linda Darling-Hammond, *Equality and Excellence: The Educational Status of Black Americans* (New York: College Board Publications, 1985); Jeannie Oakes et al., *Multiplying Inequalities: The Effects of Race, Social Class, and Tracking on Opportunities to Learn Mathematics and Science* (Santa Monica, CA: Rand Corporation, 1990).

23. *Rodriguez et al. v. Los Angeles Unified School District*, Superior Court of the County of Los Angeles no. C611358., consent decree filed August 12, 1992.

24. Patrick M. Shields, Daniel C. Humphrey, Marjorie E. Wechsler, Lori

M. Riel, Juliet Tiffany-Morales, Katrina Woodworth, Viki M. Young, and Tiffany Price, *The Status of the Teaching Profession* (Santa Cruz, CA: Center for the Future of Teaching and Learning, 2001).

25. National Center for Education Statistics, *America's Teachers: Profile of a Profession, 1993–94* (Washington, DC: U.S. Department of Education, 1997); Hamilton Lankford, Susanna Loeb, and James Wyckoff, "Teacher Sorting and the Plight of Urban Schools: A Descriptive Analysis," *Education Evaluation and Policy Analysis* 24, no. 1 (2002): 37–62.

26. Oakes et al., *Multiplying Inequalities*, x–xi.

27. Ronald F. Ferguson, "Paying for Public Education: New Evidence on How and Why Money Matters," *Harvard Journal on Legislation* 28, no. 2 (Summer 1991): 465–98.

28. Ibid.

29. Paterson Institute, *The African American Data Book* (Reston, VA: Paterson Institute, 1996); NCES, *America's Teachers*, A-119.

30. Ferguson, "Paying for Public Education."

31. See, for example, Donald Boyd, Pamela Grossman, H. Lankford, Susanna Loeb, and James Wyckoff, "How Changes in Entry Requirements Alter the Teacher Workforce and Affect Student Achievement," *Education Finance and Policy* 1, no. 2 (2006): 176–216; Linda Darling-Hammond, Deborah Holtzman, SuJin Gatlin, and Julian Vasquez Heilig, "Does Teacher Preparation Matter? Evidence About Teacher Certification, Teach for America, and Teacher Effectiveness," *Education Policy Analysis Archives* 13, no. 42 (2005), available at http://epaa.asu.edu/epaa/v13n42/; Parmalee Hawk, Charles R. Coble, and Melvin Swanson, "Certification: It Does Matter," *Journal of Teacher Education* 36, no. 3 (1985): 13–15; Dan D. Goldhaber and Dominic J. Brewer, "Does Teacher Certification Matter? High School Certification Status and Student Achievement," *Educational Evaluation and Policy Analysis* 22 (2000): 129–45; David H. Monk, "Subject Matter Preparation of Secondary Mathematics and Science Teachers and Student Achievement," *Economics of Education Review* 13, no. 2 (1994): 125–45.

32. Julian R. Betts, Kim S. Rueben, and Anne Danenberg, *Equal Resources, Equal Outcomes? The Distribution of School Resources and Student Achievement in California* (San Francisco: Public Policy Institute of California, 2000); Mark Fetler, "High School Staff Characteristics and Mathematics Test Results," *Education Policy Analysis Archives* 7, no. 9 (1999), available at http://epaa.asu.edu/epaa/v7n9.html; Edward J. Fuller, *Do Properly Certified Teachers Matter? A Comparison of Elementary School Performance on the TAAS in 1997 Between Schools with High and Low Percentages of Properly Certified Regular Education Teachers* (Austin, TX: Charles A. Dana Center, University of Texas at Austin, 1998); Edward J. Fuller, "Do Properly Certified Teachers Matter? Properly Certified Algebra Teachers and Algebra I Achievement in Texas," paper presented at the annual meeting of the American Educational Research Association, New Orleans, LA, April 2000; Laura Goe, "Legislating Equity: The Distribution of Emergency Permit Teachers in California," *Education Policy Analysis Archives* 10, no. 42 (2002), available at http://epaa.asu.edu/epaa/v10n42/.

33. Robert P. Strauss and Elizabeth A. Sawyer, "Some New Evidence on Teacher and Student Competencies," *Economics of Education Review* 5, no. 1 (1986): 47.

34. Ferguson, "Paying for Public Education."

35. Robin R. Henke, Xianglei Chen, Sonya Geis, and Paula Knepper, *Progress Through the Teacher Pipeline: 1992–93 College Graduates and Elementary/Secondary School Teaching as of 1997*, NCES 2000–152 (Washington, DC: National Center for Education Statistics, 2000).

36. Linda Darling-Hammond, *Doing What Matters Most: Investing in Quality Teaching* (New York: National Commission on Teaching and America's Future, 1997).

37. Sol H. Pelavin and Michael Kane, *Changing the Odds: Factors Increasing Access to College* (New York: College Entrance Examination Board, 1990).

38. L.V. Jones, "White-Black Achievement Differences: The Narrowing Gap," *American Psychologist* 39 (1984): 1207–13; Lyle V. Jones, Nancy W. Burton, and Ernest C. Davenport, "Monitoring the Achievement of Black Students," *Journal for Research in Mathematics Education* 15 (1984): 154–64; Elsie Moore and A. Wade Smith, "Mathematics Aptitude: Effects of Coursework, Household Language, and Ethnic Differences," *Urban Education* 20 (1985): 273–94.

39. Karl L. Alexander and Edward L. McDill, "Selection and Allocation Within Schools: Some Causes and Consequences of Curriculum Placement," *American Sociological Review* 41 (1976): 963–80; Jeannie Oakes, *Keeping Track: How Schools Structure Inequality* (New Haven: Yale University Press, 1985); Adam Gamoran and Mark Berends, "The Effects of Stratification in Secondary Schools: Synthesis of Survey and Ethnographic Research," *Review of Educational Research* 57 (1987): 415–36; Adam Gamoran and Eileen C. Hannigan, "Algebra for Everyone? Benefits of College-Preparatory Mathematics for Students with Diverse Abilities in Early Secondary School," *Educational Evaluation and Policy Analysis* 22 (2000): 241–54; P. Peterson, "Remediation Is No Remedy," *Educational Leadership* 46, no. 60 (1989): 24–25.

40. Oakes et al., *Multiplying Inequalities*.

41. Valerie White Plisko and Joyce D. Stern, eds., *The Condition of Education: A Statistical Report* (Washington, DC: Government Printing Office, 1985); Oakes, "Investigating the Claims in *Williams v. State of California*"; Donald A. Rock et al., *A Study of Excellence in High School Education: Educational Policies, School Quality, and Student Outcomes* (Washington, DC: National Center for Education Statistics, 1985).

42. Oakes et al., *Multiplying Inequalities*.

43. Oakes, *Keeping Track*; Jeannie Oakes, "Tracking in Secondary Schools: A Contextual Perspective," *Educational Psychologist* 22 (1986): 129–54; Thomas B. Hoffer, "Middle School Ability Grouping and Student Achievement in Science and Mathematics," *Educational Evaluation and Policy Analysis* 14, no. 3 (1992): 205–27; Chen-Lin C. Kulik and James A. Kulik, "Effects of Ability Grouping on Secondary School Students: A Meta-Analysis of Evaluation Findings," *American Education Research Journal* 19 (1982):

415–28; Robert E. Slavin, "Achievement Effects of Ability Grouping in Secondary Schools: A Best Evidence Synthesis," *Review of Educational Research* 60, no. 3 (1990): 471–500.

44. Oakes, "Tracking in Secondary Schools"; D.G. Davis, "A Pilot Study to Assess Equity in Selected Curricular Offerings Across Three Diverse Schools in a Large Urban School District," paper presented at the annual meeting of the American Educational Research Association, San Francisco, 1986; Merrilee K. Finley, "Teachers and Tracking in a Comprehensive High School," *Sociology of Education* 57 (1984): 233–43; James Rosenbaum, *Making Inequality: The Hidden Curriculum of High School Tracking* (New York: Wiley, 1976); Joan E. Talbert, *Teacher Tracking: Exacerbating Inequalities in the High School* (Stanford, CA: Center for Research on the Context of Secondary Teaching, Stanford University, 1990); National Commission on Teaching and America's Future (NCTAF), *What Matters Most: Teaching for America's Future* (New York: NCTAF, 1996).

45. Adam Gamoran, "Access to Excellence: Assignment to Honors English Classes in the Transition from Middle to High School," *Educational Evaluation and Policy Analysis* 14, no. 3 (1992): 185–204; Jeannie Oakes, "Can Tracking Research Inform Practice? Technical, Normative, and Political Considerations," *Educational Researcher* 21, no. 4 (1992): 12–21; E.L. Useem, "You're Good, But You're Not Good Enough: Tracking Students out of Advanced Mathematics," *American Educator* 14, no. 3 (Fall 1990): 24–27, 43–46.

46. Jeannie Oakes, *Ability Grouping, Tracking, and Within-School Segregation in the San Jose Unified School District* (Los Angeles: UCLA, 1993).

47. Curtis C. Mcknight et al., *The Underachieving Curriculum: Assessing U.S. School Mathematics from an International Perspective* (Champaign, IL: Stipes Publishing, 1987); Zalman Usiskin, "Why Elementary Algebra Can, Should, and Must Be an Eighth-Grade Course for Average Students," *Mathematics Teacher* 80 (1987): 428–38; Useem, "You're Good"; Anne Wheelock, *Crossing the Tracks: How "Untracking" Can Save America's Schools* (New York: The New Press, 1992).

48. Adam Gamoran and Robert D. Mare, "Secondary School Tracking and Educational Inequality: Compensation, Reinforcement or Neutrality?" *American Journal of Sociology* 94 (1989): 1146–83; Oakes, *Keeping Track*; Oakes et al., *Multiplying Inequalities*; Adam Gamoran, "The Consequences of Track-Related Instructional Differences for Student Achievement," paper presented at the annual meeting of the American Educational Research Association, Boston, 1990.

49. Thomas L. Good and Jere Brophy, *Looking in Classrooms* (New York: Harper and Row, 1987).

50. Ruth Eckstrom and Ana Maria Villegas, "Ability Grouping in Middle-Grade Mathematics: Process and Consequences," *Research in Middle Level Education* 15, no. 1 (1991): 1–20; Oakes, *Keeping Track*.

51. Oakes, *Keeping Track*; E. Cooper and J. Sherk, "Addressing Urban School Reform: Issues and Alliances," *Journal of Negro Education* 58, no. 3 (1989): 315–31; Davis, "A Pilot Study."

52. Lauren B. Resnick, *Education and Learning to Think* (Washington,

DC: National Academies Press, 1987); Barbara Bowman, "Early Childhood Education," in Linda Darling-Hammond, ed., *Review of Research in Education*, vol. 19 (Washington, DC: American Educational Research Association, 1993), 101–34; J. Braddock and J.M. Mcpartland, "Education of Early Adolescents," in Darling-Hammond, ed., *Review*, 135–70; Eugene Garcia, "Language, Culture, and Education," in Darling-Hammond, ed., *Review*, 51–98; Harold Wenglinsky, *How Teaching Matters: Bringing the Classroom Back into Discussions of Teacher Quality* (Princeton, NJ: Educational Testing Service, 2000).

53. David S. Bernstein, "Achievement Gap: This Is Improvement?" *Boston Phoenix*, June 11, 2004, available at http://72.166.46.24//boston/news_features/this_just_in/documents/03902591.asp.

54. Anne Wheelock, *School Awards Programs and Accountability in Massachusetts: Misusing MCAS Scores to Assess School Quality*, 2003, available at http://www.fairtest.org/arn/Alert%20June02/Alert%20Full%20Report .html.

55. Gary Orfield and Carole Ashkinaze, *The Closing Door: Conservative Policy and Black Opportunity* (Chicago: University of Chicago Press, 1991), 139; Walter Haney, "The Myth of the Texas Miracle in Education," *Educational Policy Analysis Archives* 8, no. 41 (2000), available at http://epaa.asu .edu/epaa/v8n41/; Julian Vasquez Heilig, "Progress and Learning of Urban Minority Students in an Environment of Accountability," PhD diss., Stanford University, 2006; Brian A. Jacob, "The Impact of High-Stakes Testing on Student Achievement: Evidence from Chicago," working paper, Harvard University, 2002.

56. Richard Allington and Anne McGill-Franzen, "Unintended Effects of Educational Reform in New York," *Educational Policy* 6, no. 4 (1992): 397–414; David N. Figlio and Lawrence S. Getzler, *Accountability, Ability, and Disability: Gaming the System?* (Cambridge, MA: National Bureau of Economic Research, 2002).

57. Jacob, "The Impact of High-Stakes Testing"; Haney, "The Myth of the Texas Miracle"; Julian Vasquez Heilig, "Progress and Learning of Urban Minority Students in an Environment of Accountability," PhD diss., Stanford University, 2006.

58. Linda Darling-Hammond, "The Implications of Testing Policy for Quality and Equality," *Phi Delta Kappan* 73, no. 19 (1991): 220–25; Frank Smith et al., *High School Admission and the Improvement of Schooling* (New York: New York City Board of Education, 1986).

59. Haney, "The Myth of the Texas Miracle"; Heilig, "Progress and Learning"; Orfield and Ashkinaze, *The Closing Door*, 139.

60. Suzanne Wilson, Linda Darling-Hammond, and Barnett Berry, *Teaching Policy: Connecticut's Long-Term Efforts to Improve Teaching and Learning* (Seattle: Center for the Study of Teaching and Policy, University of Washington, 2001).

61. Commission on Chapter 1, *High Performance Schools: No Exceptions, No Excuses* (Washington, DC: Commission, 1992), 4.

62. National Council on Education Standards and Testing, 1992, E12–E13.

63. Ibid., F17–F18.

64. Linda Darling-Hammond, "Creating Standards of Practice and Delivery in Learner-Centered Schools," *Stanford Law and Policy Review* 4 (Winter 1992–93): 37–52.

65. David Cohen et al., "Case Studies of Curriculum Implementation," *Educational Evaluation and Policy Analysis* 12, no. 3 (1990); Linda Darling-Hammond, "Instructional Policy into Practice: The Power of the Bottom over the Top," *Educational Evaluation and Policy Analysis* 12, no. 3 (1990): 233–42.

66. Suzanne Wilson, "A Conflict of Interests: Constraints That Affect Teaching and Change," *Educational Evaluation and Policy Analysis* 12, no. 3 (1990): 318.

67. Linda Darling-Hammond and Elle Rustique-Forrester, "The Consequences of Student Testing for Teaching and Teacher Quality," in Joan Herman and Edward Haertel, eds., *Uses and Misuses of Data in Accountability Testing. Yearbook of the National Society for the Study of Education* (Malden, MA: Blackwell Publishing, 2005), 289–319.

68. Bernard C. Watson, *Testing: Its Origins, Use and Misuse* (Philadelphia: Urban League of Philadelphia, 1996).

69. Linda Darling-Hammond, *The Right to Learn: A Blueprint for Creating Schools That Work* (San Francisco: Jossey-Bass, 1997).

70. Linda Darling-Hammond, "Teacher Quality and Student Achievement: A Review of State Policy Evidence," *Educational Policy Analysis Archives* 8, no. 1 (January 2000), available at http://epaa.asu.edu/epaa/v8n1.

71. Slavin, "Achievement Effects of Ability Grouping."

72. Linda Darling-Hammond and James Bransford, *Preparing Teachers for a Changing World: What Teachers Should Learn and Be Able to Do* (San Francisco: Jossey-Bass, 2005).

73. See, for example, Darling-Hammond, *The Right to Learn.*

74. Barnett Berry, *Keeping Talented Teachers: Lessons Learned from the North Carolina Teaching Fellows* (Raleigh, NC: North Carolina Teaching Fellows and Public School Forum, 1995).

75. For a more complete discussion of the federal role in addressing teacher shortages, see Linda Darling-Hammond and Gary Sykes, "Wanted: A National Teacher Supply Policy for Education: The Right Way to Meet the 'Highly Qualified Teacher' Challenge," *Educational Policy Analysis Archives* 11, no. 33 (September 2003), available at http://epaa.asu.edu/epaa/v11n33/.

76. Carl A. Grant, "Urban Teachers: Their New Colleagues and Curriculum," *Phi Delta Kappan* 70, no. 10 (1989): 764–70.

3. Connecting Families to Opportunity
Philip Tegeler

1. Margery Austin Turner and Dolores Acevedo-Garcia, "The Benefits of Housing Mobility: A Review of the Research Evidence," in Philip Tegeler, Mary Cunningham, and Margery Austin Turner, eds., *Keeping the Promise: Preserving and Enhancing Housing Mobility in the Section 8 Housing Choice Voucher Program* (Washington, DC: PRRAC, 2005).

2. Barbara Sard, "Summary Table: Housing Voucher Program Policies That Influence Housing Voucher Mobility," in Tegeler et al., *Keeping the Promise*; Philip Tegeler, Michael Hanley, and Judith Liben, "Transforming Section 8: Using Federal Housing Subsidies to Promote Individual Housing Choice and Desegregation," *Harvard Civil Rights–Civil Liberties Law Review* 30, no. 2 (1995): 451.

3. See Jill Khadduri, "Comment on Victoria Basolo and Mai Thi Nguyen's 'Does Mobility Matter? The Neighborhood Conditions of Housing Voucher Holders by Race and Ethnicity,' " *Housing Policy Debate* 16 (2005): 325.

4. Tegeler et al., *Keeping the Promise*.

5. Gail Christopher, "Public Health and Housing Mobility," in Tegeler et al., *Keeping the Promise*.

6. Xavier de Souza Briggs and Margery Austin Turner, "Assisted Housing Mobility and the Success of Low-Income Minority Families: Lessons for Policy, Practice and Future Research" *Journal of Law and Social Policy* 1 (2006): 25, available at www.law.northwestern.edu/journals/njlsp.

7. The Baltimore housing mobility program is funded by HUD and administered by the Housing Authority of Baltimore County, under contract to Quadel, Inc. (which runs the "tenant-based" mobility program for former public housing residents searching for housing in the five suburban counties), and the Innovative Housing Institute (which runs the "project-based" mobility program, recruiting specific landlords in the suburban counties to set aside units for voucher families). The program is monitored by a panel that includes plaintiffs' attorneys from the Maryland ACLU. The enhanced-mobility work described here is being done in coordination with the Baltimore Regional Housing Campaign with grant support for various elements of the work from the Annie E. Casey Foundation, the Morton and Jane K. Blaustein Foundation, the Abell Foundation, the Baltimore Community Foundation, the Goldseker Foundation, the Ford Foundation, and the Open Society Institute. PRRAC's work on housing mobility and health has also been supported by the Taconic Foundation and the W.K. Kellogg Foundation.

8. See Elizabeth Julian, "Promoting Successful Moves in Dallas" in Tegeler et al., *Keeping the Promise*.

9. Michael Stoll, *Job Sprawl and the Spatial Mismatch Between Blacks and Jobs* (Washington, DC: Brookings Institution Survey Series, 2005), available at http://www.brookings.edu/metro/pubs/20050214_jobsprawl.htm.

10. Margery Austin Turner and Lynette A. Rawlings, *Overcoming Concentrated Poverty and Isolation: Lessons from Three HUD Demonstration Initiatives* (Washington, DC: Urban Institute, 2005).

11. Ibid.

12. Abt Associates, *Effects of Housing Vouchers on Welfare Families* (Washington, DC: U.S. Department of Housing and Urban Development, Office of Policy Development and Research, 2006).

13. Joanna M. Reed, Jennifer Pashup, and Emily K. Snell, "Voucher Use, Labor Force Participation, and Life Priorities: Findings from the Gautreaux Two Housing Mobility Study," *Cityscape* 8 (2005): 2.

14. Ibid.

15. Greg J. Duncan and Anita Zuberi, "Mobility Lessons from Gautreaux and Moving to Opportunity," *Journal of Law and Social Policy* 1 (2006): 110, available at www.law.northwestern.edu/journals/njlsp.

16. See generally Margy Waller, *Transitional Jobs: A Next Step in Welfare to Work Policy* (Washington, DC: Brookings Institution, Center on Urban and Metropolitan Policy, 2002).

17. Margy Waller, "Opportunity and the Automobile," *Poverty and Race*, January/February 2006; Evelyn Blumenberg and Michael Manville, "Beyond the Spatial Mismatch: Welfare Recipients and Transportation Policy," *Journal of Planning Literature* 19 (2004): 182–205.

18. Institute on Race and Poverty, *Determining Equity in Access to Recent Dramatic Job Growth in the Atlanta Region* (Minneapolis: University of Minnesota, March 2006).

19. Qing Shen and Thomas W. Sanchez, "Residential Relocation, Transportation, and Welfare-to-Work in the United States: A Case Study of Milwaukee," *Housing Policy Debate* 16, no. 3–4 (2005).

20. Waller, "Opportunity and the Automobile."

21. Ibid.

22. Emily J. Martin, "Housing Mobility as a Women's Rights Issue," in Tegeler et al., *Keeping the Promise.*

23. Reed et al., "Voucher Use."

24. Turner and Rawlings, *Overcoming Concentrated Poverty.*

25. Turner and Acevedo-Garcia, "The Benefits of Housing Mobility"; Dolores Acevedo-Garcia and Theresa Osypuk, "Racial Disparities in Housing and Health," *Poverty and Race*, July/August 2004.

26. Briggs and Turner, "Assisted Housing Mobility."

27. Christopher, "Housing Mobility and Public Health."

28. Rachel D. Godsil, "Environmental Justice and the Integration Ideal," 49 *The New York Law School Law Review* 1109 (2004–5).

29. For recent research on sexual harassment of girls in concentrated poverty neighborhoods, see Susan J. Popkin, Tama Leventhal, and Gretchen Weismann, "Girls in the 'Hood: Evidence on the Impact of Safety," *Poverty and Race*, September/October 2006.

30. Jennifer Pashup, Kathryn Edin, and Greg Duncan and Karen Burke, "Participation in a Residential Mobility Program from the Client's Perspective: Findings from Gautreaux Two," *Housing Policy Debate* 16, no. 3 and 4 (2005).

31. For a recent summary of the research on school integration, see Harvard Civil Rights Project, "Statement of American Social Scientists of Research on School Desegregation," filed in *Parents Involved in Community Schools v. Seattle School District No. 1, et al., Crystal D. Meredith v. Jefferson County Board of Education, et al.* (pending, U.S. Supreme Court, Nos. 05–908 and 05–915) (2006).

32. Chester Hartman and Todd Michael Frank, eds., "Student Mobility: How Some Children Get Left Behind," *Journal of Negro Education* 72, no. 1 (Winter 2003); see also Poverty and Race Research Action Council, *Fragmented: Improving Education for Mobile Students* (2003).

33. Thus, the positive school outcomes found for suburban vs. city movers in the Gautreaux housing mobility program—see, for example, Julie Kaufman and James Rosenbaum, "The Education and Employment of Low-Income Black Youth in White Suburbs," *Education Evaluation and Policy Analysis* 14, no. 229 (Fall 1992)—were not found in the interim MTO results, likely because most MTO movers did not leave the city.

34. The Dallas mobility program is mapping potential neighborhoods based on the Texas Education Agency's ranking system in which schools are identified as Exemplary, Recognized, Acceptable, and Low-Performing.

35. Briggs and Turner, "Assisted Housing Mobility"; Susan Clampet-Lundquist, Kathryn Edin, Jeffrey R. Kling, and Greg Duncan, "Moving At-Risk Teenagers out of High-Risk Neighborhoods: Why Girls Fare Better Than Boys," Working Paper 509, Industrial Relations Section, Princeton University, March 2006.

36. Briggs and Turner, "Assisted Housing Mobility."

37. Clampet-Lundquist et al., "Moving At-Risk Teenagers."

38. Briggs and Turner, "Assisted Housing Mobility."

39. Clampet-Lundquist et al, "Moving At-Risk Teenagers."

40. Briggs and Turner, "Assisted Housing Mobility."

41. Clampet-Lundquist, "Moving At-Risk Teenagers."

42. Popkin et al., "Girls in the 'Hood"; Martin, "Housing Mobility."

4. Reducing Incarceration to Expand Opportunity
Marc Mauer

1. Shannan M. Catalano, *Criminal Victimization, 2005* (Rockville, MD: U.S. Department of Justice, Bureau of Justice Statistics, September 2006).

2. Bureau of Justice Statistics, *Sourcebook of Criminal Justice Statistics, 2002, 2003*; Paige M. Harrison and Allen J. Beck, *Prisoners in 2005* (Rockville, MD: U.S. Department of Justice, Bureau of Justice Statistics, November 2006). Unless otherwise noted, all further data on prison and jail populations are taken from various reports of the Bureau of Justice Statistics.

3. International rates of incarceration from International Centre for Prison Studies, available at http://www.prisonstudies.org.

4. Teresa A. Miller, "The Impact of Mass Incarceration on Immigration Policy," in Marc Mauer and Meda Chesney-Lind, eds., *Invisible Punishment: The Collateral Consequences of Mass Imprisonment* (New York: The New Press, 2002), 214–15.

5. Elliott Currie, *Confronting Crime* (New York: Pantheon Books, 1985), 110–11.

6. Robert Martinson, "What Works: Questions and Answers About Prison Reform," *The Public Interest* 35 (Spring 1974): 22–54.

7. Ibid., 25.

8. Alfred Blumstein and Allen J. Beck, "Reentry as a Transient State Between Liberty and Recommitment," in Jeremy Travis and Christy Visher, eds., *Prisoner Reentry and Crime in America* (New York: Cambridge University Press, 2005).

9. Ryan S. King and Marc Mauer, *Distorted Priorities: Drug Offenders in State Prisons* (Washington, DC: The Sentencing Project, 2002).

10. David A. Harris, " 'Driving While Black' and All Other Traffic Offenses: The Supreme Court and Pretextual Traffic Stops," *Journal of Criminal Law and Criminology* 87 (Winter 1997): 544–82.

11. "Justice Denied in Virginia," editorial, *Washington Post*, February 10, 2004.

12. John Hagan and Ruth D. Peterson, "Criminal Inequality in America: Patterns and Consequences," in John Hagan and Ruth D. Peterson, *Crime and Inequality* (Stanford, CA: Stanford University Press, 1995), 28.

13. Cassia C. Spohn, "Thirty Years of Sentencing Reform: The Quest for a Racially Neutral Sentencing Process," *Criminal Justice* 3 (July 2000): 453.

14. Eileen Poe-Yamagata and Michael Jones, *And Justice for Some* (San Francisco: National Council on Crime and Delinquency, 2000), 1, available at http://www.buildingblocksforyouth.org/justiceforsome/jfs.html.

15. Patrick A. Langan and David J. Levin, *Recidivism of Prisoners Released in 1994* (Rockville, MD: U.S. Department of Justice, Bureau of Justice Statistics, June 2002).

16. James P. Lynch and William J. Sabol, *Prisoner Reentry in Perspective* (Washington, DC: Urban Institute, 2001).

17. The Sentencing Project, *Felony Disenfranchisement Laws in the United States* (Washington, DC: The Sentencing Project, April 2007).

18. Jeff Manza and Christopher Uggen, *Locked Out: Felon Disenfranchisement and American Democracy* (New York: Oxford University Press, 2005).

19. Marisa Demeo and Steven Ochoa, *Diminished Voting Power in the Latino Community: The Impact of Felony Disenfranchisement in Ten Targeted States* (Washington, DC: MALDEF, 2003).

20. Christopher Uggen and Jeff Manza, "Voting and Subsequent Crime and Arrest: Evidence from a Community Sample," *Columbia Human Rights Law Review* 36, no. 1 (2004): 192–215.

21. Christopher J. Mumola, *Incarcerated Parents and Their Children* (Rockville, MD: U.S. Department of Justice, Bureau of Justice Statistics, August 2000).

22. Donald Braman, "Families and Incarceration," in Mauer and Chesney-Lind, eds., *Invisible Punishment.*

23. Sandra D. Lane, Robert A. Rubinstein, Robert H. Keefe, Noah Webster, Donald A. Cibula, Alan Rosenthal, and Jesse Dowdell, "Structural Violence and Racial Disparity in HIV Transmission," *Journal of Health Care for the Poor and Underserved* 15 (2004): 327.

24. Ryan S. King and Marc Mauer, *The Vanishing Black Electorate: Felony Disenfranchisement in Atlanta, Georgia* (Washington, DC: The Sentencing Project, September 2004).

25. Eric Lotke and Peter Wagner, "Prisoners of the Census: Electoral and Financial Consequences of Counting Prisoners Where They Go, Not Where They Come From," *Pace Law Review* 24 (2004): 587–607.

26. Dina Rose and Todd Clear, "Incarceration, Social Capital, and Crime:

Examining the Unintended Consequences of Incarceration," *Criminology* 36, no. 3 (1998): 441–79.

27. Megan C. Kurlychek, Robert Brame, and Shawn D. Bushway, "Scarlet Letters and Recidivism: Does an Old Criminal Record Predict Future Offending?" *Criminology and Public Policy* 5, no. 3 (2006): 483–504.

28. Ryan S. King, *A Decade of Reform: Felony Disenfranchisement Policy in the United States* (Washington, DC: The Sentencing Project, October 2006).

5. Why Health-Care Equity Is Essential to Opportunity—and How to Get There
Brian D. Smedley

1. National Center for Vital and Health Statistics, Center for Disease Control and Prevention, *Health, United States 2004* (Washington, DC: U.S. Department of Health and Human Services, 2006).

2. Ibid.

3. Institute of Medicine, *Promoting Health: Intervention Strategies from Social and Behavioral Research* (Washington, DC: National Academies Press, 2000).

4. Ibid.

5. Ibid.

6. Ibid.

7. M. Marmot et al., "Contribution of Job Control and Other Risk Factors to Social Variations in Coronary Heart Disease Incidence," *The Lancet* 350 (1997): 235–39.

8. D.R. Williams and C. Collins, "Racial Residential Segregation: A Fundamental Cause of Racial Disparities in Health," *Public Health Reports* 116, no. 5 (2001): 404–16.

9. Henry J. Kaiser Family Foundation, *Key Facts: Race, Ethnicity, and Health Care* (Menlo Park, CA: Henry J. Kaiser Family Foundation, 2003).

10. M.M. Doty, N.J. Edwards, and A.L. Holmgren, *Seeing Red: Americans Driven into Debt by Medical Bills* (New York: Commonwealth Fund, 2005).

11. J. Farley, "Spatial Mismatch and Access to Physicians Among African Americans: Initial Findings and Directions for Future Research," *Edwardsville Journal of Sociology* 4 (2004); Council on Graduate Medical Education, *Tenth Report: Physician Distribution and Health Care Challenges in Rural and Inner-City Areas* (Washington, DC: U.S. Department of Health and Human Services, 1998).

12. K. Lasser et al., "Missed Appointment Rates in Primary Care: The Importance of Site of Care," *Journal of Health Care for the Poor and Underserved* 16, no. 3 (August 2005): 475–86.

13. Families USA, *One in Three: Non-Elderly Americans Without Health Insurance, 2002–2003* (Washington, DC: Families USA, 2004).

14. Institute of Medicine, *Hidden Costs, Value Lost: Uninsurance in America* (Washington, DC: National Academies Press, 2003).

15. Ibid.

16. Ibid.

17. Families USA, *Paying a Premium: The Added Cost of Care for the Uninsured* (Washington, DC: Families USA, 2005).

18. U.S. Department of Health and Human Services, *National Healthcare Disparities Report*, January 2006, available at http://www.ahrq.gov/qual/nhdr05/nhdr05.htm.

19. Robert Wood Johnson Foundation, *Going Without: America's Uninsured Children*, August 2005, available at http://www.rwjf.org/files/news room/ckfresearchreportfinal.pdf.

20. Urban Institute, "Fast Facts on Welfare Policy: Two-Thirds of Uninsured Children in Fair or Poor Health Are Hispanic," April 28, 2004, available at http://www.urban.org/url.cfm?ID=900702.

21. The uninsurance rate among immigrants increased dramatically in the late 1990s, following passage of the Personal Responsibility and Work Opportunity Reconciliation Act of 1996, which imposed a five-year limit on most new immigrants' ability to participate in public health insurance programs. Prior to and shortly following passage of the act (between 1994 and 1998), immigrants accounted for about one-third of the increase in the number of uninsured individuals.

22. Employee Benefit Research Institute, "The Impact of Immigration on Health Insurance Coverage in the United States," *Employee Benefit Research Institute Notes* 26, no. 6 (2005): 1–15.

23. U.S. Census Bureau, *Income, Poverty, and Health Insurance Coverage in the United States, 2004* (Washington, DC: Government Printing Office, 2005).

24. Kaiser Family Foundation, *Key Facts: Race, Ethnicity, and Health Care*.

25. Ibid.

26. Ibid.

27. Ibid.

28. Ibid.

29. U.S. Census Bureau, "Table 1a. United States. Ability to Speak English by Language Spoken at Home for the Population 5 Years and Over: 2000," October 29, 2004, available at http://www.census.gov/population/cen2000/phc-t37/tab01a.pdf.

30. Institute of Medicine, *Unequal Treatment: Confronting Racial and Ethnic Disparities in Health Care* (Washington, DC: National Academies Press, 2003).

31. Pew Hispanic Center and the Henry J. Kaiser Family Foundation, "Survey Brief About the 2002 National Survey of Latinos," March 2004, available at http://www.kff.org/kaiserpolls/upload/Health-Care-Experiences-2002-National-Survey-of-Latinos-Survey-Brief.pdf.

32. Ibid.

33. D. Nichols, "Racial Differences in the Decision Choice Models of the Hospital Assignment Process," working paper, June 20, 2005, available at http://dnichols.wustl.edu/research/Patiet%20Assignment%20Mechanism %20062005.pdf.

34. Henry J. Kaiser Family Foundation and the American College of Car-

diology, *Racial/Ethnic Differences in Cardiac Care: The Weight of the Evidence*, October 2002, available at http://www.kff.org/whythedifference/6040fullreport.pdf.

35. A.C. Klassen et al., "Relationship Between Patients' Perceptions of Disadvantage and Discrimination and Listing for Kidney Transplantation," *American Journal of Public Health* 92, no. 5 (May 2002): 811–17.

36. Institute of Medicine, *Unequal Treatment*.

37. Kaiser Family Foundation, *Racial/Ethnic Differences in Cardiac Care*.

38. Institute of Medicine, *Unequal Treatment*.

39. Ibid.

40. Institute of Medicine, *Hidden Costs, Value Lost*.

41. Henry J. Kaiser Family Foundation, Kaiser Commission on Medicaid and the Uninsured, *Key Facts: Uninsured Workers in America*, July 2004, available at http://www.kff.org/uninsured/upload/Uninsured-Workers-in-America.pdf.

42. Henry J. Kaiser Family Foundation, *Trends and Indicators in the Changing Health Care Marketplace*, April 29, 2004, available at http://www.kff.org/insurance/7031/index.cfm.

43. Henry J. Kaiser Family Foundation and Health Research and Educational Trust, *Employer Health Benefits: 2004 Summary of Findings*, 2004, available at http://www.kff.org/insurance/7148/upload/2004-Employer-Health-Benefits-Survey-Summary-of-Findings.pdf.

44. Institute of Medicine, *Unequal Treatment*.

45. M. Lillie-Blanton, R.M. Martinez, and A. Salganicoff, "Site of Medical Care: Do Racial and Ethnic Differences Persist?" *Yale Journal of Health Policy, Law, and Ethics* 1, no. 1 (2001): 1–17.

46. Henry J. Kaiser Family Foundation, *Racial and Ethnic Disparities in Women's Health Coverage and Access to Care: Findings from the 2001 Kaiser Women's Health Survey*, March 2004, available at http://www.kff.org/womenshealth/upload/Racial-and-Ethnic-Disparities-in-Women-s-Health-Coverage-and-Access-to-Care.pdf.

47. Bronx Health Reach, *Separate and Unequal: Medical Apartheid in New York City*, October 2005, available at http://www.institute2000.org/policy/medical_apartheid.pdf.

48. P.B. Bach et al., "Primary Care Physicians Who Treat Blacks and Whites," *New England Journal of Medicine* 351, no. 6 (2004): 575–84.

49. R.S. Morrison et al., " 'We Don't Carry That'—Failure of Pharmacies in Predominantly Nonwhite Neighborhoods to Stock Opioid Analgesics," *New England Journal of Medicine* 342, no. 14 (2000): 1023–26.

50. D.B. Smith, *Eliminating Disparities in Treatment and the Struggle to End Segregation* (New York: Commonwealth Fund, 2005).

51. Institute of Medicine, *Unequal Treatment*.

52. Ibid.

53. H. Boushey, J. Wright, and M.M. Diaz, *Health Insurance Data Briefs #1: Improving Access to Health Insurance* (Washington, DC: Center on Budget and Policy Priorities, April 2004).

54. Certificate of Need standards and policies have been considerably

weakened over the last twenty-five years as a result of pressures to deregulate the health-care industry. Their strength as a policy tool has therefore been considerably diminished. Some have suggested that this policy tool be reconstituted, perhaps under a different name, with the goal of ensuring that health-care resources—which are often publicly subsidized—are distributed in a manner that meets community need. See Smith, *Eliminating Disparities*, 2005.

55. Institute of Medicine, *In the Nation's Compelling Interest: Enhancing Diversity in the Health Professions* (Washington, DC: National Academies Press, 2004).

6. Measuring the Extent and Forms of Discrimination in the Marketplace
Margery Austin Turner and Carla Herbig

1. See, for example, Dinesh D'Souza, *What's So Great About America?* (Washington, DC: Regenery Publishing, 2002); and Steven and Abigail Thernstrom, *America in Black and White: One Nation, Indivisible* (New York: Touchstone, 1999).

2. See C. Edley, "Implications of Empirical Studies on Race Discrimination," in M. Fix and R. Struyk, eds., *Clear and Convincing Evidence: Testing for Discrimination in America* (Washington, DC: Urban Institute Press, 1993).

3. M. Fix and R.J. Struyk, "An Overview of Auditing for Discrimination," in *Clear and Convincing Evidence*.

4. Testing studies discussed in this section include those designed primarily for research (rather than advocacy or enforcement), including representative samples of housing providers or employers, consistent testing protocols, and statistical analysis of test results.

5. R. Wienk et al., *Housing Market Practices Survey* (Washington, DC: U.S. Department of Housing and Urban Development, 1979).

6. M.A. Turner, R.J. Struyk, and J. Yinger, *Housing Discrimination Study Synthesis* (Washington, DC: U.S. Department of Housing and Urban Development, 1991).

7. In 2002, a methodological workshop convened by the National Research Council confirmed the potential of rigorous paired-testing research, reviewed issues of statistical significance and generalizability, and identified ways in which paired-testing studies could be strengthened. See National Research Council, *Measuring Housing Discrimination in a National Study: Report of a Workshop* (Washington, DC: National Academies Press, 2002).

8. The discrimination estimates reported here are based on the share of tests in which the white tester was consistently favored over his or her minority partner. For a detailed discussion of how measures of discrimination are constructed and how their statistical significance is determined, see M.A. Turner, F. Freiberg, G. Godfrey, D. Levy, and R. Smith, *Other Things Being Equal: Testing for Discrimination in Mortgage Lending* (Washington, DC: U.S. Department of Housing and Urban Development, 2002).

9. Thomas Purnell, William Idsardi, and John Baugh, "Perceptual and

Phonetic Experiments on American English Dialect Identification," *Journal of Language and Social Psychology* 18, no. 1 (1999): 10–30. One of the major concerns about telephone testing is the uncertainty about whether recipients of the calls accurately identify the race or ethnicity of the testers. Not all minority testers necessarily use "typical" accents and speech patterns; so telephone testing has to be carefully designed and monitored to ensure that testers' identities are clearly recognizable.

10. Douglas S. Massey and Garvey Lundy, "Use of Black English and Racial Discrimination in Urban Housing Markets: New Methods and Findings," *Urban Affairs and Review* 36, no. 4 (2001): 452–69.

11. Note that this study did not implement conventional, paired-testing protocols, but rather compared the experiences of men and women with differing speech patterns across a large number of standardized telephone inquiries.

12. Douglas Wissoker, Wendy Zimmermann, and George Galster, *Testing for Discrimination in Home Insurance* (Washington, DC: Urban Institute, 1998).

13. It is important to note that all of these scenarios focused on the pre-application phase of the mortgage lending process; none called upon testers to submit formal applications for a mortgage loan, because federal law makes it illegal to file false credit information.

14. Turner et al., *Other Things Being Equal.*

15. M.A. Turner, M. Fix, and R.J. Struyk, *Opportunities Denied, Opportunities Diminished: Discrimination in Hiring* (Washington, DC: Urban Institute Press, 1991).

16. H. Cross, G. Kenney, J. Mell, and W. Zimmermann, *Employer Hiring Practices: Differential Treatment of Hispanic and Anglo Job Seekers* (Washington, DC: Urban Institute Press, 1990).

17. Turner et al., *Opportunities Denied.*

18. Ronald B. Mincy, "The Urban Institute Audit Studies: Their Research and Policy Context," in Fix and Struyk, eds., *Clear and Convincing Evidence.*

19. D. Pager, "The Mark of a Criminal Record," CDE Working Paper 2002–5, Center for Demography and Ecology, University of Wisconsin at Madison, 2002.

20. Devah Pager and Bruce Western, "Discrimination in Low-Wage Labor Markets: Evidence from an Experimental Audit Study in New York City," submission to the Population Association of America annual meeting, 2005.

21. Marianne Bertrand and Sendhil Mullainathan, "Are Emily and Brendan More Employable than Lakihsha and Jamal? A Field Experiment on Labor Market Discrimination," NBER Working Paper 9873, July 2002.

22. Sandi Cain, "What's in a Name?" *Arab American Business*, April/May 2005, 16–19.

23. See Camille Zubrinsky Charles, "Can We Live Together? Racial Preferences and Neighborhood Outcomes," in Xavier de Souza Briggs, ed., *The Geography of Opportunity: Race and Housing Choice in Metropolitan America* (Washington, DC: Brookings Institution Press, 2005).

24. "Senior Citizen Voice Triggers Housing Discrimination," *Senior Journal*, October 25, 2005, available at http://www.seniorjournal.com/NEWS/Features/5–10–25SeniorVoice.htm.

25. Debbie Wilgoren. "Landlords Accused of Rejecting Vouchers," *Washington Post*, April 11, 2005, Metro section.

26. Ana P. Nunes and Brad Seligman, "A Study of the Treatment of Female and Male Applicants by San Francisco Bay Area Auto Service Shops," Impact Fund, 2002, available at http://www.impactfund.org/press/release_20000613_study.html.

27. The Fair Housing Act of 1968 provides protections for the classes of race, national origin (ethnicity), color, gender, and religion. Misinterpretation of the act—specifically regarding who is protected under it—continues to be promulgated by lawyers, academics, and even fair housing advocates. Under the act, everyone is protected regardless of which racial, ethnic, color, gender, or religious group he or she belongs to. The amendments of 1988 added the protected classes of familial status and disability, but unlike the other protected classes these provide standing only to those persons who are affected; that is, only persons who have children or who are disabled (or who have associations with such persons) have standing.

28. Office of Fair Housing and Equal Opportunity, *2005 State of Fair Housing Report*, available at http://www.hud.gov/utilities/intercept.cfm?/offices/fheo/enforcement/fhmreport05.pdf.

29. ACLU of Northern California, *Language Rights*, available at http://www.aclunc.org.

30. Fair Housing of Marin, "Latinos Turned Away from Rentals by Voice Identification," press release, November 14, 2005, available at http://www.fairhousingmarin.com/news/FinalLatinoauditpressrel.htm.

31. We would caution, however, that paired testing conducted solely by telephone may raise legal concerns. For example, housing providers who have been accused of discrimination based on telephone tests may simply argue that they did not know the race or ethnicity of the caller and, therefore, could not have discriminated.

32. Office of Fair Housing and Equal Opportunity, *2005 State of Fair Housing Report*.

33. National Fair Housing Alliance, *2004 Fair Housing Trends Report*, April 2004.

34. M.A. Turner et al., *Discrimination Against Persons with Disabilities: Barriers at Every Step* (Washington, DC: U.S. Department of Housing and Urban Development, 2005).

35. National Fair Housing Alliance, *2005 Fair Housing Trends Report*, April 2005.

36. Stephen M. Eisendorfer, "Can Municipal Exclusion of School Children Survive Judicial Scrutiny," NJ Land Use Law, available at http://www.nj-laanduselaw.com.

37. Less than 40 percent of respondents know that it is illegal to give different treatment to families with children. M.D. Abravanel and M.K. Cun-

ningham, *How Much Do We Know? Public Awareness of the Nation's Fair Housing Laws* (Washington, DC: U.S. Department of Housing and Urban Development, 2000).

38. Discrimination based on source of income is separate from this discussion and is presented in a later section.

39. "Senior Citizen Voice Triggers Housing Discrimination," *Senior Journal*, October 25, 2005, available at http://www.seniorjournal.com/NEWS/ Features/5–10–25SeniorVoice.htm.

40. S. Cahill, "The Glass Nearly Half Full: 47% of the US Population Lives in Jurisdiction with Sexual Orientation Non-Discrimination Law," National Gay and Lesbian Task Force Policy Institute, January 25, 2005, available at http://www.thetaskforce.org/downloads/GlassHalfFull.pdf.

41. E.K. Yamamoto, S.N.K. Garcia, C.A. Shirota, and K.C. Iwamoto, "Gays in Hawai'i Still Denied Equal Housing," *Honolulu Advertiser*, June 13, 2004, available at http://the.honoluluadvertiser.com/article/2004/ Jun/13/op/ op05a.html.

42. R. Colvin, *The Extent of Sexual Orientation Discrimination in Topeka, KS* (New York: National Gay and Lesbian Task Force Policy Institute, Equal Justice Coalition, 2004).

43. "Race and Ethnicity in Rural America: The Demography and Geography of Rural Minorities," Economic Research Service, briefing room document, available at http://www.ers.usda.gov/Briefing/RaceAndEthnicity/ geography.htm.

44. L.A. Whitener, "Housing Poverty in Rural Areas Greater for Racial and Ethnic Minorities," *Rural America* 15, no. 2 (May 2000): 2–8.

45. Interview with Jeff Moseley, Rural LISC, September 12, 2005.

46. C. Climaco, M. Finkel, S. Nolden, and M. Vandawalker, *Updating the Low Income Housing Tax Credit (LIHTC) Database: Project Place in Service Through 2003* (Washington, DC: U.S. Department of Housing and Urban Development, 2006).

47. Poverty and Race Research Action Council, *Civil Rights Mandates in the Low Income Housing Tax Credit (LIHTC) Program* (Washington, DC: PRRAC, December 12, 2004).

48. Ibid.

49. "Memorandum of Understanding Among the Department of the Treasury, the Department of Housing and Urban Development, and the Department of Justice," signed August 9 by Lawrence H. Summers, August 11 by Andrew Cuomo and Janet Reno, available at http://hud.gov/offices/ fheo/lihtcmou.cfm.

50. B. Maney and S. Crowley, *Scarcity and Success: Perspectives on Assisted Housing. Meeting America's Housing Needs (MAHN): A Habitat II Follow-up Project*, April 1999, available at http://www.hlihc.org/mahn/sec8part5.htm.

51. L. Orr, J.D. Feins, R. Jacob, E. Beecroft, L. Sanbonmatsu, L.F. Katz, J.B. Liebman, and J.R. Kling, *Moving to Opportunity for Fair Housing Demonstration Program: Interim Impacts Evaluation* (Washington, DC: U.S. Department of Housing and Urban Development, September 2003).

52. *Green v. Sunpointe Assocs., Ltd.*, No. C96–1542C (W.D. Wash. May 12,

1997): "Landlord's No-Section 8 Policy Has Disparate Impact, in Violation of the Fair Housing Act, on African Americans, Women, and Children."

53. S. Young, "Proxy for Discrimination: Vouchers in the Section 8 Housing Program," *Chicago Policy Review* 2, no. 2 (Spring 1998).

54. Debbie Wilgoren, "Landlords Accused of Rejecting Vouchers," *Washington Post*, April 11, 2005, Metro section.

55. L. Robinson and A. Grant-Thomas, *Race, Place, and Home: A Civil Rights and Metropolitan Opportunity Agenda* (Cambridge, MA: Civil Rights Project, Harvard University, September 2004).

56. U.S. Equal Employment Opportunity Commission, "EEOC Announces Pilot Projects to Test for Employment Discrimination," press release, December 5, 1997.

57. Nunes and Seligman, "A Study of the Treatment of Female and Male Applicants."

58. See, for example, Agency for Healthcare Research and Quality, *National Healthcare Disparities Report* (Rockville, MD: U.S. Department of Health and Human Services, 2003); R.M. Mayberry, F. Mili, and E. Ofili, "Racial and Ethnic Differences in Access to Medical Care," *Medical Care Research and Review* 57, Supp. 1 (2000): 108–45; J.A. Long, V.W. Chang, S.A. Ibrahim, and D.A. Asch, "Update on the Health Disparities Literature," *Annals of Internal Medicine* 141, no. 10 (2004): 805–12.

59. Institute of Medicine, *Unequal Treatment: Confronting Racial and Ethnic Disparities in Healthcare* (Washington, DC: National Academies Press, 2003).

60. Consumer credit is covered under the Equal Credit Opportunity Act, as well as state laws. Public accommodation discrimination is covered under Title II of the Civil Rights Act.

61. M.A. Cohen, *Report on the Racial Impact of AHFC's Finance Charge Markup Policy*, June 30, 2004, available at www.consumerfed.org/pdfs/hondasummary.pdf.

62. Diane B. Henriques, "Extra Costs on Car Loans Draw New Legal Attacks," *New York Times*, October 27, 2000, Business section.

63. Goldstein, Demchak, Baller, Borgen, and Dardarian, "Minority Car Buyers Sue Major Auto Loan Co.s for Racial Discrimination in Loan Finance Charges," press release, April 10, 2003.

64. Consumer Federation of America, "Report Finds Discrimination in Honda Auto Loan Markups," press release, July 27, 2004.

65. Title II of the Civil Rights Act of 1964 provides protection in all non-private entities and covers lodging, eating establishments, sports and entertainment facilities, and any areas located within the premises of these places. In addition, persons with disabilities are afforded protection under the Americans with Disabilities Act.

66. U.S. Department of Housing and Urban Development, *Case Summaries*, available at http://usdoj.gov/crt/housing/documents/casesummary.htm.

67. Ibid.

68. U.S. Department of Justice, "Justice Department Files Lawsuit Against Adam's Mark Hotel Chain," press release, December 16, 1999.

7. Finding America
Edward E. Telles and Vilma Ortiz

1. James P. Smith and Barry Edmonston, *The Immigration Debate: Studies on the Economic, Demographic and Fiscal Effects of Immigration* (Washington, DC: National Academies Press, 1998).

2. Ruben Rumbaut, "The Making of a People," in Marta Tienda and Faith Mitchell, eds., *Hispanics and the Future of America* (Washington, DC: National Academies Press, 2006).

3. Douglas S. Massey, Jorge Durand, and Nolan J. Malone, *Beyond Smoke and Mirrors: Mexican Immigration in an Era of Economic Integration* (New York: Russell Sage Foundation, 2002).

4. Ibid.

5. Rumbaut, "The Making of a People."

6. Frank Bean, Jennifer Lee, Jeanne Batalova, and Mark Leach, *Immigration and Fading Color Lines in America* (New York: Russell Sage Foundation and Population Reference Bureau, 2004).

7. Jeffrey Passel, *Estimates of the Size and Characteristics of the Undocumented Population* (Washington, DC: Pew Hispanic Center Report, 2005).

8. José J. Escarce and Kanika Kapur, "Access to and Quality of Health Care," in Tienda and Mitchell, eds., *Hispanics and the Future of America*.

9. Passel, "Estimates."

10. Brian Duncan, Joseph V. Hotz, and Stephen J. Trejo, "Hispanics in the U.S. Labor Market," in Tienda and Mitchell, eds., *Hispanics and the Future of America*, 228–90; Barbara L. Schneider, Silvia Martinez, and Ann Owens, "Barriers to Educational Opportunities for Hispanics in the United States," in Tienda and Mitchell, eds., *Hispanics and the Future of America*, 179–227.

11. Gary Orfield, *The Growth of Segregation in American Schools: Changing Patterns of Separation and Poverty since 1968* (Alexandria, VA: National School Boards Association, 1993).

12. Jonathan Kozol, *The Shame of the Nation: The Restoration of Apartheid Schooling in America* (New York: Crown, 2005).

13. Gary Orfield and John T. Yun, *Resegregation in American Schools* (Cambridge, MA: Civil Rights Project, Harvard University, 1999); Schneider, Martinez, and Owens, "Barriers."

14. Duncan, Hotz, and Trejo, "Hispanics"; David Reimers, *Still the Golden Door: The Third World Comes to America* (New York: Columbia University Press, 1985); Stephen J. Trejo, "Why Do Mexican-Americans Earn Low Wages?" *Journal of Political Economy* 105, no. 6 (December 1997): 1235–68.

15. George J. Borjas, "Long-Run Convergence of Ethnic Skill Differentials: The Children and Grandchildren of the Great Migration," *Industrial and Labor Relations Review* 47 (1994): 553–73; Robert M. Hauser, Solon J. Simmons, and Devah I. Pager, "High School Dropout, Race/Ethnicity, and

Social Background from the 1970s to the 1990s," in Gary Orfield, ed., *Dropouts in America: Confronting the Graduation Rate Crisis* (Cambridge, MA: Harvard Education Publishing Group, 2004); Lisa J. Neidert and Reynolds Farley, "Assimilation in the United States: An Analysis of Ethnic and Generation Differences in Status Attainment," *American Sociological Review* 50 (1985): 840–50; Trejo, "Why Do Mexican-Americans Earn Low Wages?"

16. Duncan, Hotz, and Trejo, "Hispanics"; David L. Featherman and Robert M. Hauser, *Opportunity and Change* (New York: Academic Press, 1978).

17. Louis De Sipio, "Latino Civic and Political Participation," in Tienda and Mitchell, eds., *Hispanics and the Future of America*, 447–80.

18. Richard Alba and Victor Nee, *Remaking the American Mainstream: Assimilation and Contemporary Immigration* (Cambridge, MA: Harvard University Press, 2003); Borjas, "Long-Run Convergence"; James P. Smith, "Assimilation Across the Latino Generations," *American Economic Review* 93 (2003): 315–19.

19. Alba and Nee, *Remaking the American Mainstream*.

20. Frank Bean, George Chapa, Ruth R. Berg, and Kathryn A. Sowards, "Educational and Sociodemographic Incorporation Among Hispanic Immigrants to the United States," in Barry Edmonston and Jeffrey Passel, eds., *Immigration and Ethnicity: The Integration of America's Newest Arrivals* (Washington, DC: Urban Institute Press, 1994), 73–100; Borjas, "Long-Run Convergence"; Duncan, Hotz, and Trejo, "Hispanics"; Featherman and Hauser, *Opportunity and Change*; Trejo, "Why Do Mexican-Americans Earn Low Wages?"; Roger A. Wojtkiewicz and Katherine M. Donato, "Hispanic Educational Attainment: The Effects of Family Background and Nativity," *Social Forces* 74 (1995): 559–74.

21. Richard Alba, Dalia Abdel-Hady, Tariqul Islam, and Karen Marotz, "Downward Assimilation and Mexican Americans: An Examination of Intergenerational Advance and Stagnation in Educational Attainment," unpublished paper, Radcliffe Institute for Advanced Study, 2004.

22. Grace Kao and Marta Tienda, "Optimism and Achievement: The Educational Performance of Immigrant Youth," *Social Science Quarterly* 76 (1995): 1–19.

23. Margaret Gibson, *Accommodation Without Assimilation: Sikh Immigrants in an American High School* (Ithaca: Cornell University Press, 1988); Min Zhou and Carl L. Bankston III, *Growing Up American: How Vietnamese Children Adapt to Life in the United States* (New York: Russell Sage Foundation, 1998).

24. Walter R. Allen and Daniel G. Solórzano, "Affirmative Action, Educational Equity, and Campus Racial Climate: A Case Study of the University of Michigan Law School," *Berkeley La Raza Law Journal* 12, no. 2 (2001): 237–363.

25. J. Aronson and C.M. Steele, "Stereotypes and the Fragility of Academic Competence, Motivation, and Self-concept," in A.J. Elliot and C.S.

Dweck, eds., *Handbook of Competence and Motivation* (New York: Guilford Publications, 2005), 436–56.

26. Claude M. Steele and J. Aronson, "Stereotype Threat and the Intellectual Test Performance of African-Americans," *Journal of Personality and Social Psychology* 69 (1995): 797–811.

27. Schneider, Martinez, and Owens, "Barriers."

28. Niel Foley, *White Scourge: Mexicans, Blacks and Poor Whites in Texas Cotton Culture* (Berkeley: University of California Press, 1997); George A. Martinez, "The Legal Construction of Race: Mexican-Americans and Whiteness," *Harvard Latino Law Review* 2 (1997): 321; Marta Menchaca, "Chicano Indianism: A Historical Account of Racial Repression in the United States," *American Ethnologist* 20 (1993): 583–603.

29. Richard R. Valencia, ed., *Chicano School Failure and Success: Past, Present and Future* (New York: Routledge, 2002); Guadalupe San Miguel and Richard R. Valencia, "From the Treaty of Guadalupe Hidalgo to Hopwood: The Educational Plight and Struggle of Mexican Americans in the Southwest," *Harvard Education Review* 68 (1988): 353–412.

30. Massey, Durand, and Malone, *Beyond Smoke and Mirrors*; Orfield, *The Growth of Segregation in American Schools*; Richard R. Valencia, "The Plight of Chicano Students: An Overview of Schooling Conditions and Outcomes," in Valencia, ed., *Chicano School Failure and Success*, 3–51.

31. Valencia, "The Plight of Chicano Students."

32. S.A. Alva and R. de los Reyes, "Psychosocial Stress, Internalized Symptoms and the Academic Achievement of Hispanic Students," *Journal of Adolescent Research* 14 (1999): 343–58; Massey, Durand, and Malone, *Beyond Smoke and Mirrors*; Valencia, "The Plight of Chicano Students."

33. John Ogbu, ed., *Minority Education and Caste: The American System in Cross-Cultural Perspective* (New York: Academic Press, 1978).

34. Roberto Fernandez, "Dropping Out Among Hispanic Youth," *Social Science Research* 18 (1989): 21–52; Maria Eugenia Matute-Bianchi, "Ethnic Identities and Patterns of School Success and Failure Among Mexican Descent and Japanese-American Students in a California High School: An Ethnographic Analysis," *American Journal of Education* 95 (1986): 233–55.

35. Alejandro Portes and Ruben Rumbaut, *Legacies: The Story of the Immigrant Second Generation* (Berkeley: University of California Press, 2001).

36. Kozol, *The Shame of the Nation*.

37. Philip Kasinitz, *Caribbean New York: Black Immigrants and the Politics of Race* (Ithaca, NY: Cornell University Press, 1992); Mary C. Waters, *Black Identities: West Indian Immigrant Dreams and American Realities* (New York: Russell Sage Foundation, 1999).

38. Anna Gorman and Jennifer Delson, "Policies on Illegal Immigrants at Odds," *Los Angeles Times*, November 27, 2005.

39. Duncan, Hotz, and Trejo, "Hispanics"; Portes and Rumbaut, *Legacies*.

40. Orfield, ed., *Dropouts in America*.

41. Mary Waters, *Ethnic Options: Choosing Identities in America* (Berkeley: University of California Press, 1960).

ABOUT THE
CONTRIBUTORS

Jared Bernstein joined the Economic Policy Institute in 1992. He is the author of *All Together Now: Common Sense for a Fair Economy*. His areas of research include income inequality and mobility, trends in employment and earnings, low-wage labor markets and poverty, international comparisons, and the analysis of federal and state economic policies. Between 1995 and 1996, he held the post of deputy chief economist at the U.S. Department of Labor. He is the co-author of eight editions of *The State of Working America* and has published extensively in popular and academic venues, including the *New York Times*, the *Washington Post*, the *American Prospect*, and *Research in Economics and Statistics*. Dr. Bernstein holds a Ph.D. in social welfare from Columbia University.

Linda Darling-Hammond is Charles E. Ducommun Professor of Education at Stanford University School of Education, where she serves as principal investigator for the School Redesign Network and the Stanford Educational Leadership Institute. Her research, teaching, and policy work focus on educational policy, teaching and teacher education, school restructuring, and educational equity. She was the founding executive director of the National Commission on Teaching and America's Future, which produced the widely cited 1996 blueprint for education reform, *What Matters Most: Teaching for America's Future*. Among her more than two hundred publications is *The Right to Learn*, recipient of the 1998

Outstanding Book Award from the American Educational Research Association, and *Teaching as the Learning Profession*, awarded the National Staff Development Council's Outstanding Book Award in 2000. She began her career as a public school teacher and has co-founded several schools, including a charter high school in East Palo Alto, California.

Carla Herbig, formerly a research associate with the Urban Institute, served on the research design, field management, and analysis teams for several HUD-funded testing projects, including the Housing Discrimination Study, the Homeownership Testing Project, and the Disability Discrimination Study. She has trained hundreds of testers and test coordinators around the country to conduct fair-housing testing and has developed testing methodology in other areas, including employment, home insurance, and health care. Her work at the Urban Institute also includes evaluations of programs that assist the homeless and initiatives that promote the desegregation of public housing. Prior to joining the Urban Institute, Herbig was associate program director for the Center for Integrated Living, a program of the Metropolitan Milwaukee Fair Housing Council that assisted families to make pro-integrative moves. She is currently an equal opportunity specialist for the Fair Housing Testing Program at the Department of Justice.

Alan Jenkins is executive director and a co-founder of the Opportunity Agenda, a communications, research, and policy organization dedicated to building the national will to expand opportunity. Before joining the Opportunity Agenda, Jenkins was director of human rights at the Ford Foundation. Previously, he served as assistant to the solicitor general at the U.S. Department of Justice, where he represented the U.S. government in constitutional and other litigation before the U.S. Supreme Court. Prior to that, he was associate counsel to the NAACP Legal Defense and Educational Fund, where he defended the rights of low-income communities suffering from exploitation and discrimination. His other positions have included assistant adjunct professor of law at Brooklyn Law School, law clerk to Supreme Court Justice Harry A. Blackmun, law clerk to U.S. District Court Judge Robert L. Carter, and coordinator of the Access to Justice Project of the American Civil Liberties Union. Jenkins serves on the board of governors of the New School and the board of trustees of the Center for Community Change and the Legal Action Center, and is a co-chair of the American Constitution Society's Project on the Constitution in the Twenty-first Century. He holds a law degree from Harvard Law School, a master's degree in media studies from the New School, and a bachelor's degree in psychology and social relations from Harvard College.

Bill Lann Lee, a distinguished civil rights lawyer, serves as senior counsel and board chair to the Opportunity Agenda. Lee is a partner with the law firm Lewis, Feinberg, Lee, Renaker & Jackson, P.C., in Oakland, California. Lee has extensive experience in the litigation of employment discrimination, police misconduct, housing discrimination, transportation equity, environmental justice, and other civil rights cases. He co-chairs the firm's Employment Practice Group and chairs the Human Rights Practice Group. Lee was an attorney for seventeen years with the NAACP Legal Defense and Educational Fund. He headed the Legal Defense Fund's western regional office in Los Angeles. In December 1997, he was appointed assistant attorney general for civil rights, U.S. Department of Justice, by President Bill Clinton and served until January 2001. Lee is the recipient of numerous honors and awards, including the ABA Spirit of Excellence Award (2004), the Anti-Defamation League Pearlstein Civil Rights Award (2002), the U.S. Department of Justice John Randolph Distinguished Service Award (2001), and the Pioneer Award from the Organization of Chinese Americans (2000).

Marc Mauer is the executive director of the Sentencing Project, a national nonprofit organization engaged in research and advocacy on criminal justice policy. Mauer has written extensively and testified before Congress and other legislative bodies. His critically acclaimed book, *Race to Incarcerate*, was named a semifinalist for the Robert F. Kennedy Book Award, and he is the co-editor of *Invisible Punishment*, a collection of essays that examine the social costs of incarceration. Mauer frequently lectures before a broad range of national and international audiences and appears regularly on television and radio networks. He is also the recipient of the Donald Cressey Award for contributions to criminal justice research and the Alfred Lindesmith Award for drug policy scholarship.

Vilma Ortiz is associate professor of sociology at the University of California, Los Angeles. Her research addresses broad theoretical issues on racial/ethnic stratification and social inequality. For more than twenty years, she has studied the socioeconomic experiences of Latinos in the United States, focusing on both specific Latino groups as well as comparative studies with other racial/ethnic groups. Currently she and Edward Telles are completing a manuscript on a thirty-five-year-long longitudinal and intergenerational study examining socioeconomic mobility and ethnicity among Mexican Americans in Los Angeles and San Antonio.

Brian D. Smedley is research director and a co-founder of the Opportunity Agenda. Formerly, he was a senior program officer in the Division of Health Sciences Policy of the Institute of Medicine (IOM), where he served as study director for the IOM reports *In the Nation's Compelling Interest: Ensuring Diversity in the Health Care Workforce* and *Unequal Treatment: Confronting Racial and Ethnic Disparities in Health Care*, among other reports on health disparities, social and behavioral influences on health, diversity in the health professions, and minority health research policy. Smedley came to the IOM from the American Psychological Association, where he worked on a wide range of social, health, and education policy topics in his capacity as director for public interest policy. Prior to working at the APA, Smedley served as a Congressional Science Fellow in the office of Rep. Robert C. Scott (D-VA), sponsored by the American Association for the Advancement of Science. Among his awards and distinctions, Smedley was honored by the Rainbow/PUSH coalition as a Health Trailblazer award winner in 2004; he was awarded the Congressional Black Caucus "Healthcare Hero" award in 2002; and he was given the Early Career Award for Distinguished Contributions to Psychology in the Public Interest by the APA in August 2002.

Philip Tegeler is the executive director of the Poverty and Race Research Action Council (PRRAC), a civil rights policy organization based in Washington, D.C. PRRAC's primary mission is to help connect advocates with social scientists working on race and poverty issues, and to promote a research-based advocacy strategy to address problems of structural inequality. PRRAC's current work focuses on the continuing legacy of government-sponsored racial and economic segregation in the United States and its consequences for low-income families in the areas of health, education, employment, and incarceration. Prior to coming to PRRAC, Tegeler was legal director of the Connecticut ACLU, where he litigated major civil rights cases in housing, education, criminal justice, gay rights, and prison reform. His recent writings on federal housing policy include "The Persistence of Segregation in Government Housing Programs," in Xavier de Souza Briggs, ed., *The Geography of Opportunity: Race and Housing Choice in Metropolitan America* (Brookings Institution Press, 2005). Philip Tegeler is a graduate of Columbia Law School.

Edward E. Telles is professor of sociology at the University of California, Los Angeles, where he has been since 1990. He is the 2006 recipient of the Distinguished Scholarly Publication Award from the American Sociological Association (ASA) for his book *Race in Another America: The Significance of Skin Color in Brazil.* For the same book, he also received the Oliver Cromwell Cox Award from the Racial and Ethnic Minorities Section in 2006 and the Otis Dudley Duncan Award from the Population Section in 2005 from the ASA. He was also awarded the best book prize from the Brazil section of the Latin American Studies Association and the Hubert Herring Award from the Pacific Council of Latin American Studies. His forthcoming book with Vilma Ortiz, *Generations of Exclusion: Mexican Americans' Assimilation of Race,* is an analysis of intergenerational change in ethnic identity, language use, education, and other issues among Mexican Americans, based on random sample surveys of Los Angeles and San Antonio in 1965 and 2000. In 2004–5, he was a visiting scholar at the Russell Sage Foundation and, from 2002–5, he was a member of the National Academy of

Sciences panel on the status of Hispanics. He has published widely in the area of immigration, race and ethnic relations, social demography, and urban sociology. He has also received major grant awards from the National Institute of Child and Human Development, the National Science Foundation, and the Fulbright Commission. He received a BA in anthropology from Stanford University in 1978 and a Ph.D. in sociology from the University of Texas at Austin in 1988.

Margery Austin Turner directs the Urban Institute's Metropolitan Housing and Communities Policy Center. A nationally recognized expert on urban policy and neighborhood issues, Turner analyzes issues of residential location, racial and ethnic discrimination and its contribution to neighborhood segregation and inequality, and the role of housing policies in promoting residential mobility and location choice. Much of her current work focuses on the Washington metropolitan area, investigating conditions and trends in neighborhoods across the region. Turner served as deputy assistant secretary for research at the Department of Housing and Urban Development (HUD) from 1993 through 1996, focusing HUD's research agenda on the problems of racial discrimination, concentrated poverty, and economic opportunity in U.S. metropolitan areas. Prior to joining the Clinton administration at HUD, Turner directed the housing research program at the Urban Institute. She has co-authored two national housing discrimination studies, which use paired testing to determine the incidence of discrimination against minority home seekers. She has also extended the paired-testing methodology to measure discrimination in employment and to mortgage lending. Turner has directed research on racial and ethnic steering, neighborhood outcomes for families who receive federal housing assistance, and emerging patterns of neighborhood diversity in city and suburban neighborhoods.